Developing Social Skills

A Learning Resource Manual for Trainers and Educators Working in Non-traditional Learning Environments

Gillian Squirrell

Russell House Publishing

Developing Social Skills

Russell House Publishing Limited

First published in 1999 by:
Russell House Publishing Limited
4 St. George's House
The Business Park
Uplyme Road
Lyme Regis
Dorset DT7 3LS

British Library Cataloguing-in-Publication Data:
A catalogue record for this manual is available from the British Library.

ISBN: 1-898924-28-7

Design and layout by: Jeremy Spencer, London

Printed by Bookcraft, Midsomer Norton

Contents

Note: Details of how to organise and play the numerous games mentioned in the text can be found from page 243 onward.

About the author

Gillian Squirrell works as a manager in CLACC (Centre for Learning in Alternative and Community Contexts) and as a trainer and researcher specialising in working with trainers and learners in non-traditional learning situations. She also works with managers in public and voluntary organisations to improve management effectiveness.

CLACC is a not-for-profit learning organisation which offers a range of training and management development programmes. CLACC can be contacted at:

    P O Box 1269
    Bristol BS99 2YD

Acknowledgements

Work in preparing and writing this manual has been helped through the input of ideas, proof reading and word processing from Jackie Hearn, Debbie Nash and Vivienne Nelson.

A number of colleagues have also contributed various ideas, field tested and helped revise the modules.

What are social skills?

Social skills help people to better manage themselves and their interactions with others. Social skills enable people to be more aware of others' feelings, the cues offered by others and to be more responsive to the range of social, work, living and other situations to which they are daily exposed.

Developing social skills, being more adept at managing interactions, becoming more aware of ourselves and others are skills and awareness which can never be considered as tasks completed or skills fully learnt. Everyone can usefully take stock of the ways in which they manage encounters with others or with people in certain types of social role. For example, have certain habits of poor or even miscommunications crept into the management of your close relationships as you opt not to face difficult discussions? Have working relationships become frictionful after changes in your employment? Have you thought about why this may be so? Social skills can fall into disrepair as circumstances change or as they rest unpractised.

The learners towards whom these resources are directed may have missed opportunities for developing their social skills or may not have experienced using their social skills in a range of situations. There can be a host of reasons for limited development of social skills or a lack of awareness of the importance of developing and refining how interactions with others are managed. Some learners may lack the awareness that they can play a part in shaping interactions and so the outcomes of contacts with others.

The development of social skills are key stones in successfully making life changes. Social skills can be learnt, can be developed, and do need to be practised.

Social skills are largely about:

1. developing good communication skills: listening well, thinking about what is said, being aware of non-verbal cues, knowing how best to respond and anticipating the possible consequences of words and actions

2. being aware of others' feelings, vulnerabilities, concerns, preoccupations and wants and knowing how best to respond to these

3. being aware of one's own feelings, wants, preoccupations, ways of interpreting and shaping the world and the ways in which these impact on others and interactions with others

4. knowing how groups work, knowing why people are different on their own, with friends or in situations where they are dealing with authority

5. developing the skills to understand, to channel and to manage personal feelings and emotions

6. knowing how to manage interactions with others: to not be bullied or give in; to stop conflicts from developing; to make people less anxious or tense, to feel less threatened or concerned, to show power, status, rage or dominance

7. being able to leave a social encounter knowing that you have done your best to express your feelings, ideas, needs, to have had them acknowledged and understood and not to have undermined anyone else in the process

Social skills are:

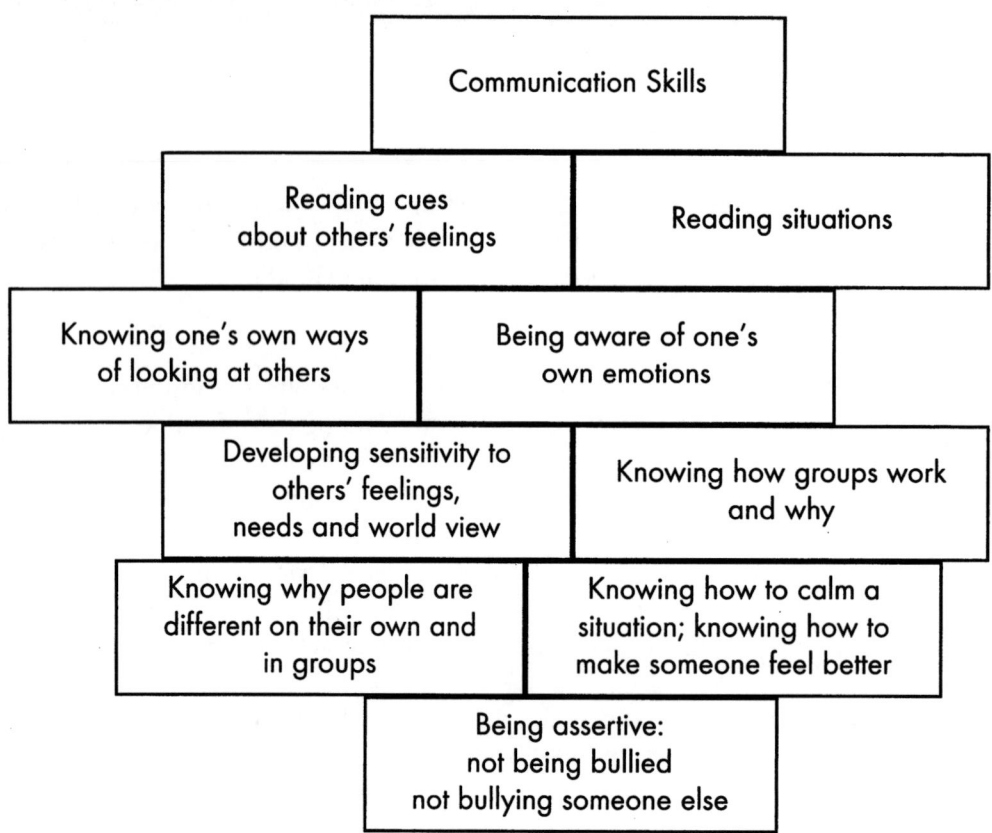

Why work on social skills?

As a trainer you will need an answer to this question. It will help you to think through carefully what you are offering and trying to achieve in facilitating the learning activities. It will help you to be clear and convincing in your explanations to the learners about the immediate term and longer-term value of working on social skills. A simple way to answer the question is to ask yourself and your learners *What are the consequences of not developing your social skills?*

Answers might include:

- not getting what I want
- being pushed about
- feeling bad about myself – giving in or forcing myself on others
- not knowing what other people think/feel
- being alone or isolated
- never feeling I belong
- being thought a bore or a bully
- getting into trouble – temper getting out of control, getting into fights
- not keeping a job for long
- not presenting myself to others as the person I know I am
- not having intimate relationships
- not having relationships which last for long
- always getting into arguments with people
- feeling I let myself and others down

Poor social skills can be a starting point for a host of difficulties which the learners may face: problems with employment; money; housing; family; experiencing social isolation; desperation; a sense of not belonging or fitting into society; poor or dysfunctional intimate or sexual relationships; pursuing harmful or damaging lifestyles; not understanding emotions nor managing them; not being able to communicate effectively with others and not reading social contexts or others' cues. Failures to communicate may lead to involvement in conflict situations and to escalating conflict. Poor social skills can lead to problems with authority, with bureaucracy and to not getting appropriate support. People can become labelled: as a troublemaker, as quick-tempered, as surly and uncommunicative, as not worth helping and so on. Carrying such labels will be barriers to effective communication.

Developing social skills is of immediate term benefit. It is a route to better self-image, improved self-esteem, improved social acceptability, less friction and fewer confrontations. Working to develop social skills will lead to better management of personal problems and relationships, to greater social acceptability and integration within various communities.

Not having the currency for social acceptability and not knowing how best to use it can lead to great social isolation, experiences of anger, frustration, conflict, depression, loneliness and to increasingly damaged self-esteem.

This manual has been written to help you to work with your learners to:

- understand the 'bricks' of social skills, to be aware of their importance, how they are used and fit together

- practise activities which encourage the development of social skills

- think about the value and importance of developing meaningful and non-confrontational relationships with others

Poor social behaviours can be unlearned, sensitivity to reading others' cues and the external environment can be learned. Learners can develop greater awareness of how better to manage themselves and their emotions.

Support and development in your work as a trainer

Whatever your level of experience, devising programmes of structured and planned activities for learners in non-traditional contexts can pose challenges for both new and experienced trainers. Support in this work can be obtained from the companion volume *Becoming an Effective Trainer* which:

- provides information on developing and managing effective learning opportunities

- encourages you to think about your training style

- encourages you to develop as a reflective practitioner, and become someone who thinks seriously about how to execute your role as a trainer, and how to develop your role in the future

- gives you greater confidence about your management of learning situations

- enables you to feel more competent in working towards the realisation of appropriately determined learning goals

- offers guidance on undertaking the evaluation and marketing of learning activities

- offers guidance on working with other trainers.

To develop the training that you can provide by using *Developing Social Skills* there are three companion volumes which draw on the practices promoted in *Becoming an Effective Trainer*. They describe and resource learning activities in key areas of *Developing Life Skills*, *Addressing Anti-social Behaviour* and *Confronting Offending Behaviour*. These learning resource manuals each carry trainer's notes to support the activities and can therefore be used as stand alone items;

however, they are most effective when you have developed an understanding of how learning takes place and how best to promote and manage learning. This is described in *Becoming an Effective Trainer*.

In planning the learning and development routes for individual learners, therefore, trainers may wish to select appropriate modules from several of the manuals. Each manual emphasises the importance of the learner engaging with their own situation and taking responsibility for making changes. All the manuals are available from Russell House Publishing.

The role of the trainer

The role for the trainer is nowhere more vital than in working with learners on developing their social skills. The role is one of assisting in awareness-raising, of helping to create opportunities to experience effective social skills and to explore the consequences of poor social skills. However in working on developing social skills the trainer has to ensure that the sessions are conducted in such a way that they support and demonstrate effective social skills. There is little point in the learner attending a session on developing their social skills and feeling the trainer does not listen, only asks closed questions or that the trainer allows a session to continue even though all the non-verbal language expressed by the learners communicates discomfort or distress. The social skills sessions should be opportunities for the learners to practice aspects of social skills and interactions through role plays and through hot-seating. They should also offer the learners the opportunities to experience successful interactions, to feel socially competent, to gain skills and understandings about managing social interactions and social skills.

The trainer has therefore to consider carefully his or her own communication skills, awareness of others and to consider carefully the ways in which the learner may experience the sessions. Some notes on evaluation and self-assessment are included in Section Four and there is further discussion in *Becoming an Effective Trainer*.

Using this manual

This manual has been designed as a:

- resource manual of learning activities addressing various areas of social skills
- structured programme which can be undertaken with learners who have various starting levels of social skills competence to encourage them to engage with their own personal development and devise their own plans for improvement
- trainer's aid and guide in developing social skills. To support the trainer each module is prefaced with explanatory material and many of the learning activities are prefaced with guidance notes and instructions.

To ensure that this manual is as comprehensive as possible, all the practical 'tools' that you will need have been included (handouts, checklists, questionnaires, action plans and OHTs. In order to provide these valuable resources in a volume that is not too bulky and at a sensible price, we have reduced these 'tools' from A4 to A5 size. To restore them to their original size you will need to photocopy them using the standard 'enlarge' feature (normally 141%).

To gain the greatest benefit the learners should be exposed to a thorough investigation of a social skills area and encouraged to consider how the information and approaches may meet their learning needs and be implemented within their own circumstances. It is not recommended that the trainer dip into learning activities at random and offer what would be in effect a brief and random exposure to a range of social skill areas. This would not enable learning to be consolidated. There are a number of check-lists and aids to personal reflection which the learners are asked to complete. These activities do encourage the learners to focus on the issues and the ways in which they may best be applied to their own situations. There are a number of action planning activities within each module to encourage the learners to think about how they may best develop in that area. The trainer should be aware that the learners need to set well defined, bounded and realisable goals.

There are some guidance notes in the module to guide the trainer, to alert him or her to particular areas which may be difficult to manage or to the ways that particular exercises need to be conducted. The trainer is advised to read the Trainer's Notes before embarking on the activities, to read the activities through thoroughly and to review the information for trainers in Section Four before starting on activities with the learners.

The learning activities are also of varying lengths. Breaks between the activities are usually not indicated; the trainer will need to plan where breaks best suits their groups and timetables.

The trainer needs to be:
- familiar with the material before attempting a training session
- aware of the resources which may be needed
- familiar with the appropriate agencies and organisations to which learners may wish to be referred. There are some national addresses included in the manual.
- able to explain what is wanted or the concepts behind an activity in various ways appropriate to the learner
- familiar with the learning techniques used
- able to help the learners to see how the learning points can be implemented within their own lives
- comfortable with one-to-one reviews of learning and discussions of learning goals as well as comfortable with whole group activities
- able to create a safe and secure learning environment in which the learners understand the parameters and expectations of the learning sessions but then have the freedom to explore the issues and to test out skills development
- aware of learners' needs, concerns and possible areas of vulnerability
- able to supplement an activity with additional resources where this is indicated e.g. providing magazines or newspapers.

The trainer should:
- have prepared the learning activities and materials in advance of the session
- work with the group to create group groundrules and not be afraid to challenge behaviours which contravene these
- provide clear explanations about activities and feedback to the learners. Learners need to understand why they are doing something and how they are performing, they also need to be given every opportunity to undertake the activities well, and clear explanations will help them to do this.
- assist, guide and keep the group on task. Small group activities are not an occasion to leave the learners alone and to do something else
- check on learners' understanding of the task, should make use of effective questioning to encourage deeper analysis of an issue or to encourage the learner to address it from another perspective
- not relinquish responsibility for the group to a dominant learner or learners. There is however no reason why in promoting the learning a group member should not run a brainstorm session or other activity
- be fully cognisant of the processes of active learning and the learning cycle and action planning
- be able to encourage the learners to reflect on what they have experienced. The sessions should be run as opportunities for the learners to explore their understandings, extend their awareness and knowledge and to develop their skills. The sessions are not opportunities for the trainer to dominate or tell the learners what to do.

- be consciously improving on his or her communication skills
- make use of learners' evaluations to inform later planning or session delivery
- cultivate the skills of reflection and self-assessment

Above all the trainer should believe in the possibility that people are able to make possible changes in their lives and to the ways in which they live them. It is important to believe that the skills and strategies for so doing can be learned and that all individuals have the right and capacity for such learning and therefore for making changes.

The trainer should encourage the learners to take some responsibility for what they are learning and how they implement what has been learned. The modules are structured in such a way as to promote this.

An overview of the manual and the learning activities

Following this introductory section is Section Two, which offers exercises to explore social skills with the learner to begin to identify learning needs and to establish the ways in which the group will operate and manage itself.

The largest section in the manual, Section Three, is that containing the eleven social skills modules.

The final section, Section Four, carries some notes on evaluation and self-assessment; some notes on valuing what the learner has done and some discussion of tools for use in the training session.

The modules

Each module is subdivided. An introduction raises learners' awareness and encourages a review of some of the issues. The mid sections rehearse various themes and issues, encouraging further awareness raising, exploration of information, techniques and skills which the learners can develop and integrate into their lives.

Each module closes by asking learners to draw together the main ideas and skills of the module and often requires production of a final learning plan or summary plan.

Much of the learning will take place during the learning activity sessions. However, and this will depend on the environments in which this manual is used, there are suggestions that the learners undertake some activities out of session. These consolidate the learning and encourage implementation within their everyday lives.

There are also occasions when it is suggested that the learner works on an individual basis with the trainer to devise and review an action plan. The importance of one-to-one surgeries should not be underestimated. They encourage a close working relationship, make the learner feel more valued and so encourage him or her to work on the plan because it is being taken seriously. One-to-one planning or review meetings help develop understanding, help the trainer to know more about the learner and help identify any particular learning needs. Such sessions consolidate the learning activities and can help the learner take better control over the ways in which they think about and work to shape and implement their personal development.

At the outset of each module there is a list of other modules with which there is a close relationship or complementarity. In constructing a social skills learning programme the trainer should note the importance of working through several complementary modules and reminding the learners of the ways in which learning in one social skills area will support the learning in another.

For example, Developing Assertiveness Skills links with work on:
- developing self-esteem

- making good use of time and defining one's own goals
- developing communication skills
- learning about others' reactions to your behaviour
- compromise and determining own expectations
- negotiation skills
- developing and maintaining functional relationships with other people
- learning what makes someone feel good about themselves and ensuring that this happens

It is important that the learners understand the links between various social skills and are motivated to see that improvements in one area will also meet learning needs within another.

A note about literacy

The trainer needs to be aware and sensitive to any problems learners have with literacy. Learners may: be struggling with written instructions and completion of worksheets; be slow to put pen to paper; may try to cover their worksheets; try to copy others; become obstructive or exhibit other blocking behaviours when a worksheet or reading task is presented. These can be signs of difficulties.

The trainer should, for clarity of instruction-giving and helping with any literacy problems, go through each worksheet activity explaining what is required, checking understanding and, as appropriate, working an example on the flipchart.

Learners who experience problems in completing worksheets should not be penalised or stigmatised. They can work with the trainer or with a partner. The importance of discussion and exploring concepts are opportunities which should not be closed to a learner just because he or she currently experiences problems in recording answers. If possible, the learners should use a tape-recorder to make notes on key learning points or action plans and the tape could become an important part of the learners' portfolio.

Referrals to help learners improve upon literacy must be made and the trainer needs to know how to do this.

The learners' role

Each learner in the group has a number of responsibilities to him or herself as an individual learner and as a group member. This should be made explicit to the learners:
- in the creation of the group contract or groundrules
- in the creation of group and individual learning plans
- through the whole process of working together in an active and experiential way
- through the heavy investment of time in self-assessment check-lists, considering past experiences and aspirations and dwelling on the power of the individual to take control over personal development and make life changes.

The learning activities require a seriousness on the part of the learners to take what they can from the activities and to share insights, skills and interests with others, through discussion, role-play, listening or questioning.

The learners should be encouraged to:
- take themselves seriously as learners
- support others in their learning activities
- develop their learning skills and willingness to try a range of learning activities

- apply learning from the training sessions to their lives
- be self-analytical
- be self-critical
- try out learning activities and plans and accept that they do not always work and that this is itself part of the learning process
- accept and give feedback
- consider their performance, skills, qualities and interests. Develop the skills to discuss and to describe them.
- understand the importance of working with others and treating fellow learners with tolerance and respect
- understand such issues as the health and safety of the learning environment
- understand and work within the group's own rules
- understand the ways in which they and others learn

The learning process

The social skills modules are written to:
- explore the learners' current understandings, practices and values
- encourage the learners to engage in broad-based exploratory thinking
- receive new information
- test out and challenge ideas through such media as role-play, practical applications or discussion
- consider how to incorporate changes and undertake planning processes.

The learning activities:
- work from and build on from the learners' own starting points
- encourage an active handling, testing and manipulation of ideas
- encourage reflection of learning activities
- encourage planning about how to make use of the learning
- where possible, encourage evaluation of learning after it has taken place.

The activities acknowledge the importance of experiential, contributory and active learning. There are few occasions of information giving. Where possible learning should be reinforced by practical activity and subsequent reflection.

Becoming an Effective Trainer explores the conditions in which adult and young adult learners learn most effectively. The trainer is referred to this to review the material on the nature of learning and the learning process.

It is suggested that each learner has a Learning File and that the materials from sessions: the handouts; the worksheets; the evaluations; action plans and the self-assessment checklists are stored in the File. The learners will need to retain self-assessment materials and action plans. They will be a source of reference about starting points and so a means to measure progression, and a reference about aspirations and their achievement.

The File will also contain material which learners may use in completing personal statements, application letters and a CV.

Throughout the modules it is important to emphasise that learning is a process of small changes, of exploration, of mistakes, as well as successes and larger changes.

Section Two: Introducing social skills to the learner

 The Introductory module is divided into three parts:

1. Opening activities (1 hour 50 min)

2. What am I like?: Taking stock (3 hours 20 min)

3. Planning and individual work (approximately 2 hours)

The module could last for 7 hours 10 minutes but this will depend on the amount of time given to 1:1 planning sessions.

There is much material on the significance of the first session and guidance on running it in *Becoming An Effective Trainer*.

The first session will have to be scheduled to meet the time available, but it should include:

- ice-breaking activities
- review of practical/domestic matters
- brainstorming social skills
- initial activities on social skills designed to:
  - engage participants' interest
  - raise awareness
  - encourage a sense of having begun the course
  - help identify learning needs
- finding out the learners' hopes, expectations and concerns about the course
- an evaluation of the first session

 The first session makes use of the training and learning techniques of:

- lecturette
- self assessment
- brainstorming
- discussion – small and whole group
- one-to-one planning and review
- learner evaluations
- planning and goal setting

🍎 Trainer's notes

This introductory module to the social skills programme has several functions. It is:

- a chance for the trainer to get to know something about the group
- a chance for trainer and learners to identify areas which individuals and the group would like, or indeed, need to know more about
- an opportunity to encourage all group members to explore any prejudices they have about social skills and about working in a group
- an opportunity to explore the practical matters of running the programme, for example:
  - attendance times
  - any out of course work
  - roles and procedures for goal setting and review
- opportunities for individual meetings between learner-trainer
- the chance for individuals to record early on any particular expectations, hopes or concerns about the course
- a chance to engage the learners early on in different types of learning activities

Opening activities

The early sessions may be ones of apprehension or tension, as trainer and learners find out about each other, why they are there and how the power is distributed in the group. The early sessions will be occasions for setting parameters and expectations for behaviour and for participation. Instructions need to be given clearly and the activities need to be well managed. All learners need to understand clearly what is asked of them. The learners will be focused on establishing themselves within the group as well as looking at what is being offered. It is important that all are encouraged and helped to participate and to succeed in these sessions.

Introduction and welcome (40 min)

- Introduce yourself
- Ask the learners in turn to give their names and one or two things about themselves. It does not have to be very personal or revealing
- Other name games may be useful, especially ones which encourage the learners to move about or to undertake some activity e.g. Throwing the Ball, Liar
- Introduce any domestic/practical matters, e.g. fire exits, health and safety matters, break times, start and finish times
- Check that the learners have received information about the course and why they are attending

Outline a few points to introduce the programme as a whole and the purpose of the first session. Put these points on an OHT e.g.

The programme looks at:
- ways people communicate
- how to help people communicate better
- how people get on with others
- the importance of communication skills in developing good relationships
- relationships and why they may go wrong
- why we have feelings and how better to manage them

Today we will:
- begin to know each other
- find out about the programme
- find out what areas of social skills the group wants to look at
- find out what you want from the programme
- try out some practical activities

Any questions to ask me?

- Ask the learners to work in small groups to generate questions about anything they are still unsure about. Leave up the Introductory OHT.
- Bring the group back together and ask for any questions.

Change the tempo of the session by playing Fruitbowl to get people moving or a game to consolidate learning names.

Exploring social skills (30 min)

Brainstorm:

> ### 1. What are social skills?
>
> ### 2. What happens if people have poor social skills?

Explain the purpose and role of brainstorming and groundrules for the activity. That it is about the quantity of different ideas and the flow of ideas. No-one should be criticised for their contribution. All ideas can be considered at a later date for their feasibility. The group many offer suggestions such as:

1. What are social skills?

- getting on with others
- being polite and considerate of others' feelings
- knowing how to speak to others
- knowing what to wear or do in different situations
- being confident with others
- communicating well

2. What happens if people have poor social skills?

- get frustrated and angry
- get into conflict with others
- arguments and fights
- loss of jobs, relationships
- fall out with people at home – houseshare, in digs or in the family
- don't feel confident
- don't feel able to cope very well with others
- feel lonely
- can't express feelings or ideas
- always seem to say the wrong thing
- feel bad about oneself
- bully other people
- not liked by others
- having nothing to say to other people

Keep the brainstorms moving, prompt the learner to think about other areas. Try to encourage a range of ideas.

At the close of the second brainstorm ask the group to cluster the ideas and try to decide what social skills help the learners to avoid certain situations. Natural clusters may be:

- communication skills: listening, asking or questioning/checking what others mean
- being assertive and not aggressive
- knowing what you feel
- knowing how to express feelings
- being aware of others' feelings and needs
- not being insensitive
- not bullying others

Explain that the programme will look at a number of these areas, help in developing skills in these areas and to practice them.

Working alone (10 min)

Ask the learners to look at the social skill areas on the flipchart in order to help them to decide what areas they would like to develop. Ask them to complete activity sheet (SSINT1). Explain how this should be done.

Group feedback (10 min)

List out the areas the group has prioritised so far. This will be useful for you and interesting for the group to see if there are any patterns in what they have decided is personally important.

Keep this list and return to it at the close of this first session.

Hopes, fears and expectations (20 min)

Close this first set of activities by asking each learner to complete a Hopes, Fears and Expectations sheet (SSINT2).

Ask the learners to take five minutes to think alone and then in pairs or threes to share ideas.

Finally have a group feedback session for ten minutes. Check that everyone understands the sorts of areas to be covered; list people's goals and list any fears. Tackle the latter immediately if possible. Keep the list and ensure that all fears have been discussed by the close of the first module.

What am I like?

Trainer's notes

The purposes of these activities are to encourage the learners to think about their own social skills and to think what and how they might like to develop their own skills. The first activity looks at two situations to get the learners thinking about some communication skills. Subsequent activities ask the learners to use check-lists to self-assess and this information is then used in group and individual learning plans.

Communication skills and situations (50 min)

Introduce the session by explaining that the activities are to encourage the learners to think about the importance of communication skills and their own communication skills.

Explain that the first activity is a role play. Outline what is required of the learners in a role play. Emphasis that it is not about acting but about seeing what it is like to be in someone else's skin and exploring what the world looks like from their point of view. Ask the learners to work in twos or threes. Each small group should be given either Situation One or Situation Two (SSINT3a or SSINT3b)

Each group should read through their situation and check with the trainer that they understand what it is about and what the problems are.

The groups should then take roles and work out solutions and explorations of the problems.

Guidance on running role-play activities is included in the End Notes.

After twenty minutes ask the small groups to perform the role-plays. After each one ask the players and those watching to consider such questions as follow, and record their answers on the flipchart.

- Why did the situations have the outcomes they did?
- What communication activities took place, e.g. verbal, non-verbal?
- What assumptions did the people make in the role-plays, e.g. no-one likes me: backing down and being bullied: adding to confrontation
- What went wrong and why?
- What could have made the situations have different outcomes? e.g. challenging aggression but not with aggression: not just giving up.

Be sure to thank those who have taken role play parts.

For a final 10 minutes ask the group what they have discovered about social skills, about getting on with others; managing interactions; communication skills and reading other people's behaviour from having looked at these situations.

Individual assessment activities

Having explored some aspects of communication skills and social skills in the role-play/discussion work the learners are now asked to work alone and think about their communication and social skills and how they appear to other people. There are two blocks of exercises:

i) Looking at Social Styles (1 hour 20 min)

ii) Looking at Skills

The first, an examination of social styles is demanding and requires the trainer to work through it with the learners.

Looking at social styles: how I seem to others (1 hour 20 min)

1. Explain the purpose of the exercise
2. Read through the four boxes of statements and ask each person to decide what they are like (SSINT4)
3. Completing the grid. Ask the learners to decide how like type 1, 2,3 and 4 they are. The more like a type they are then they should mark closer to the end of the line. (SSINT5)
4. Making sense of the findings. Help the learners to interpret their own grid – to decide how like a certain type of person they are and what this may mean about others' behaviour towards them. Take one or two examples and discuss these as a group (SSINT6)

Pairwork (15 min)
Ask the learners to work in pairs to decide how people may respond to the type of person they are (use SSINT7). Check how each pair is coping

Feedback (10 min)
Bring the group back together to discuss what they have found.

- Are there any particular things people may now consider changing?
- How useful was the activity?

Working alone (20 min)
Ask the learners to look at SSINT8 and to think whether they are always the same type of person in all situations. Explain that people sometimes have different social styles with different types of people – those they know well or those they know less well. Ask for some examples before the learners start working alone.

Feedback (10 min)

Bring the group back together and ask for volunteers to say what they have found out about themselves.

Thinking about themselves (10 min)

Ask the learners to use these discussions and activities to complete SSINT9.

Break and game (20 min)

The group will have spent a long time on this exercise and should do something quite different to recharge its batteries. Break and then set up a game.

Looking at social and communication skills (20 min)

Ask the learners to work alone on the various check-lists SSINT10 and 11 which asks them to consider their social and communication skills. Read through the check-lists and make sure the learners know what to do.

Feedback (10 min)

Ask what the learners have found out about themselves.

Planning (10 min)

Ask the learners to work alone on their own summary of areas to address.

Group groundrules (30 min)

The final part of this session focuses the group on developing its own groundrules to manage its behaviour and functioning as a group. Introduce the idea to the group that it needs to think about how it can make sure it is successful as a group and to encourage all the members to have the opportunity to learn and feel comfortable in the group.

Ask for some examples of rules the group may like for itself. Run this as a brainstorm. Encouraging good communication is a useful starting point so:

- everyone has a right to be listened to
- everyone should be encouraged to and have the opportunity to speak

There will need to be rules to encourage everyone to participate, to try activities and not to personally criticise others. There may be matters pertaining to Health and Safety or Equal Opportunities policies of your institution which need to be included.

A draft could be produced at this early stage and then after a couple of sessions checked by the group to see if it works or is in need of revision. The group should then have it in final printed form, each group member sign it and have it as part of their learning file.

Discussions and examples of groundrules can be found in the book *Becoming An Effective Trainer*.

Programme and individual planning

 Trainer's notes

The learners will have completed a number of exercises and engaged in a number of communication skills. This final session should be shared between group concerns and goals and discussion with individual learners.

Group discussion (20 min)

Open the session by asking what the learners have discovered and if there is anything they would like to add to the group list of goals, expectations or fears.

Explain what areas can be covered during the course of the sessions explaining what each area will better enable them to do or how it will improve understanding. Work out with the group what they would prioritise. SSINT11 may help with this.

Deal with any outstanding concerns about the sessions – type of work, what may be required of the learners etc. Offer evaluation form SSINT12 to be completed and explain it will help with the next sessions and with the next introduction to the programme.

Thank the learners as a group.

Individual reviews (10-15 min per learner)

The remaining time should be used for one-to-one work, 10-15 minutes with each learner. Discuss how the learner has found the sessions, what they have discovered about themselves and ask what aspirations they have. Review the check-lists completed to date.

Then complete an individual plan with the learner (SSINT13). This can be modified and reviewed during the course but will offer a personal starting point for the learner.

Thank each learner individually for work they have done so far. These individual sessions can also be used to tease out any problems which have arisen within the group.

SSINT2: Hopes, concerns and expectations

1. My feelings about doing this course are …

2. My greatest concerns about this course are …

3. My greatest hope is that this course will give me a chance to …

4. By the close of the course I would expect to have gained …

Name: _____   Date: _____

SSINT1

Complete each of the circles with a social skill you would like to develop – add reasons for why you would like to develop these skills

SOCIAL SKILLS TO HELP ME GET ON BETTER WITH OTHERS

SSINT3b: Situation Two – The phone call

You are making a phone call to find out about an allowance to which you think you are entitled. You have been on the phone for ten minutes and keep getting passed from one person to another. You are spending a lot of money and getting nowhere.

You are in a phone box and there's a queue outside. One bloke is getting fed up with you.

What happens?

How do you deal with the person outside?

How do you find out about the allowance you think you should have?

What do you want to happen?

What do you think does happen and why?

What might you do differently next time?

SSINT3a: Situation One – At work

You have been employed in a new job for three weeks and have been trying your hardest to get on well with your team mates to do a good job and to make a good impression on your boss. You need this job and the chance to show others and yourself that you can make good.

Since you've been in the job one person is determined to have a go at you. He/she puts you down, is critical of what you do and makes personal comments about you.

You've decided you've had enough and have to do something when he/she says about a suggestion you've made:

"That's a really stupid idea – it would have to be you who came up with it."

What happens next?

What do you do?

What do you want to happen?

What does happen and why?

Taking stock – Activity One: What is my social style?

Most people have particular ways of behaving with other people. Knowing what your ways are will help you think about the type of person you are.

Once you have decided this, you can think about your strong and less strong points when you are with other people – at home, at work and socially. Knowing your strengths and areas to improve on will help you to:

- make changes to help you get on better with other people

- knowing why people behave towards you as they do.

SSINT4

Read the statements below and circle those applying to you

Type 1 Person

Quite cautious
Careful about showing my feelings
Don't give much of myself away
Don't want to get involved with other people's personal lives
People think I am cold
Don't feel comfortable making social talk with people
Prefer to know the facts rather than people's feelings about a situation

Are you like this?   Circle either Yes   or   No

Type 2 Person

Like others and show it
Smile at other people a lot
People think I'm easy to talk to
I listen to people and let them make a point in their own time
I don't mind talking about myself
I enjoy being with other people
I get involved in what other people are saying

Are you like this?   Circle either Yes   or   No

Type 3 Person

Not very pushy about getting my way
Tend to sit back and let others take the lead
Often ask questions rather than make statements
Don't push my point of view in an argument
Don't take up a lot of physical space when others are around
Tend to give way

Are you like this?   Circle either Yes   or   No

Type 4 Person

Keen to make my views known
Keen to make decisions
Like people to notice me
Not worried about talking to strangers
Don't mind telling others what to do
Like having my own way

Are you like this?   Circle either Yes   or   No

SSINT5

On the vertical line mark where you come as a Type 1 or 2 person. Then, mark where you come as a Type 3 or 4 person.

Type 1 Person

Type 3 Person

Type 4 Person

Type 2 Person

SSINT6

On the vertical line mark where you come as a Type 1 or 2 person. Then, mark where you come as a Type 3 or 4 person.

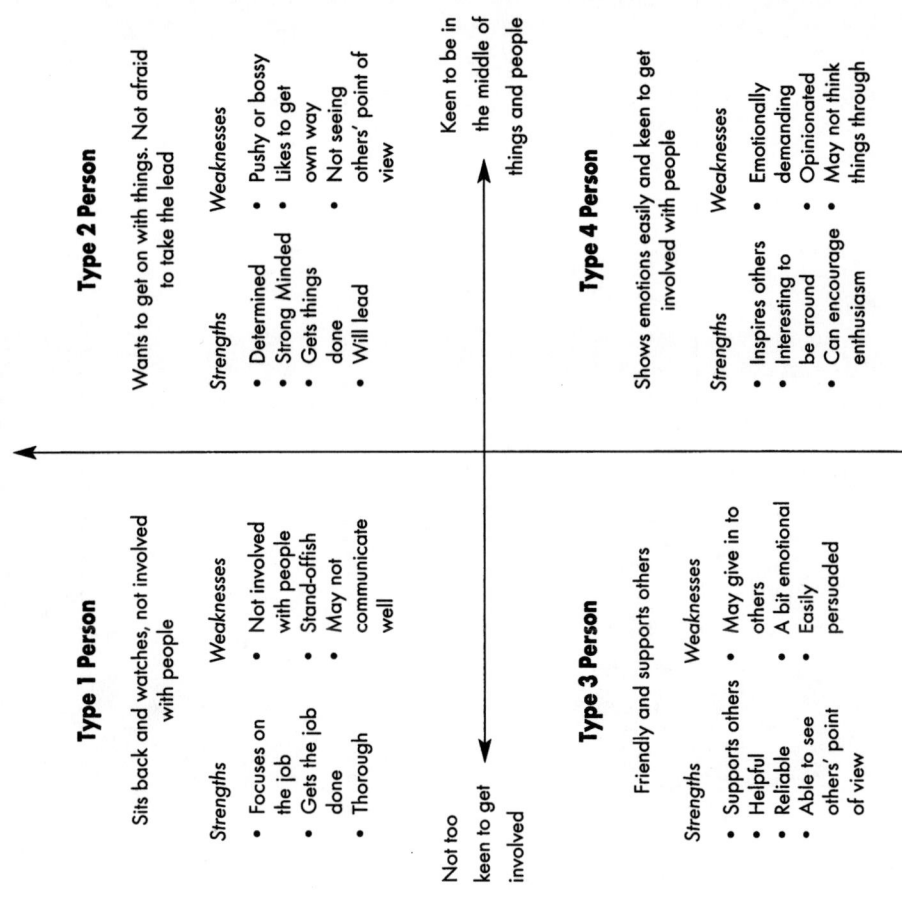

Not very quick to be interested in others

Most interested in other people

Keen to be in the middle of things and people

Not too keen to get involved

Type 1 Person

Sits back and watches, not involved with people

Strengths
- Focuses on the job
- Gets the job done
- Thorough

Weaknesses
- Not involved with people
- Stand-offish
- May not communicate well

Type 2 Person

Wants to get on with things. Not afraid to take the lead

Strengths
- Determined
- Strong Minded
- Gets things done
- Will lead

Weaknesses
- Pushy or bossy
- Likes to get own way
- Not seeing others' point of view

Type 3 Person

Friendly and supports others

Strengths
- Supports others
- Helpful
- Reliable
- Able to see others' point of view

Weaknesses
- May give in to others
- A bit emotional
- Easily persuaded

Type 4 Person

Shows emotions easily and keen to get involved with people

Strengths
- Inspires others
- Interesting to be around
- Can encourage enthusiasm

Weaknesses
- Emotionally demanding
- Opinionated
- May not think things through

SSINT8: Think about the type of person you are

At home I am more like:

With friends I am more like:

At work or in formal situations I am more like:

With people in authority I am more like:

SSINT7

I am like:

I behave like:

List the things people may not like about your type of person:

List the types of things people may like about your type of person:

Do you have different social styles in different situations? Give two examples

SSINT10: Thinking about myself

Read through the following and decide how you rate yourself at certain things.

	Agree	Disagree
I am good on the phone with my friends		
I can manage official telephone calls		
I don't get tongue-tied with strangers		
I don't often let my feelings get out of hand		
I don't often get into conflict		
I am good at managing difficult situations		
I am not good at keeping my temper under control		
I often let myself be put down		
I find it hard to express what I want		
I often don't get what I should have – benefits, consumer rights – because I let myself be talked out of it		
I am persistent with getting others to see my point of view		
Sometimes I buy things I don't really want		
I like to find out what other people think		

SSINT9: Thinking ahead

Things I know about myself from this activity are:

Things I might want to change about myself now:

What might I need to do to make these changes?

SSINT11

Look through these areas of getting on with others. Tick the ones you really need to look at, then put down in order of importance to you.

Social Skill	I really do need to look at this	Don't need to look at this	My order of importance
Talking to people in authority			
Talking on the phone			
Making complaints			
Understanding why things go wrong with others			
Not getting into conflict with others			
Standing up for myself			
Knowing what to do with strangers			
Making a better impression at work			
Not putting people's backs up			
Feeling I listen properly to others			
Managing my feelings better			
Knowing what I want and saying so			
Not taking people for granted			
Feeling more confident with other people			
Making and keeping friendships			
Making my relationship with partner/family better			
Thinking about others' feelings			

SSINT12: Evaluation of first session

Could you please help me get the programme off to a good start by answering these five questions

1. What have you enjoyed about this first session and why?

2. What have you not enjoyed and why?

3. Is there anything which concerns you or that you feel you still need to know?

   I am concerned about...

   I want to know about...

4. What has been the most useful part of the session?

5. What are you particularly keen to find out about now you are doing this programme?

Thank you for completing this

Name: .... Date: ....

SSINT13: Learning plan

Name:

Priority Areas for Developing Social Skills	Reason	Date of Sessions

Agreed Between: ....

On: .... Date for Review: ....

Section Three: The social skills modules

Developing communication skills

 This module is divided into five sessions. These are:

1. Why communicate? (2 hours 30 min)
2. Communication skills (10 hours 30 min)
3. Getting communication right (6 hours and 25 min)
4. The written word (45 min)
5. Summary and planning (1 hour 15 min)

The module may take 21 hours and 25 minutes to complete. Additional time will be needed for the one-to-one planning sessions which should then support the rest of the learners' work on developing their social skills.

 This module links with all others in this manual. Some of the areas covered are further explored and extended in other modules. The sessions in this module serve to introduce such important ideas, skills and strategies as:

- assertiveness
- making no-blame statements
- saying what is felt rather than thought
- taking charge of communication episodes

 This module uses:

- brainstorm
- small and large group discussion
- role-play
- hot seating
- self-assessment
- some games and practical exercises

🍎 Trainer's notes

This module offers learners the chance:

- to explore and to practice some key communication skills
- to consider the appropriate ways of communication with different types of people
- to consider a range of methods of communication – oral, written, non-verbal
- to focus their attention on their own ways of communicating
- to think carefully about their own strengths as communicators and the areas which they would like to improve
- to think about the ways in which others receive their communications
- to consider how they can improve or can destroy encounters with others through good or bad communication

- to experience how others may view them more positively through better communication
- to consider the vast range of situations in which they practice communication and so the importance of taking themselves most seriously as communicators

Effective communication skills are essential to the conduct of all relationships; to supporting a person's sense of self-esteem and self-value and to an individual being able to function well in society. Learners may have failed to develop good communication skills because they have had limited opportunity to practice a range of communication skills or they may have had a limited number of types of relationships. Some may not have been effectively taught and so have literacy problems, some learners may have mental health and other problems which could affect clarity of speech, their concentration or listening skills. The list of possible reasons for poor communication skills are endless.

However it is certain that without addressing communication skills many other aspects of improved social functioning will not be possible. Work on developing pro-social behaviours, impulse control and behaviour modification will not be successful without improved basic communication skills.

Session One: Why communicate?

 Trainer's notes

This first session focuses learners' attention on communication as an important part of their daily lives and as something which should not be taken for granted.

Ranking exercise (15 min)

Ask the learners to rank themselves along an imaginary line. They should decide where to stand in relation to, at one end, 'communication is very important to me' at the other 'communication is not important to me'.

Ask why the learners have placed themselves where they have, especially ask people at the two extremes and in the middle. Record their places on paper. Allow the learners to move if after hearing each others' ideas they feel they want to. Ask for reasons for change. Record changes in their places. Save this for later in the module. Thank the learners for sharing their thoughts.

Opening brainstorms (30 min)

Run three brainstorms to encourage the learners to think about communication. Encourage the flow of ideas and encourage everyone in the group to contribute something. From the outset it is important that everyone is helped to feel comfortable in the training activities and able to offer their ideas, to develop their listening and questioning skills and to develop their confidence as an effective communicator. In sum while it is important to talk about communication and getting it right, it is just as important to offer opportunities to practice and to improve on communication skills.

1.

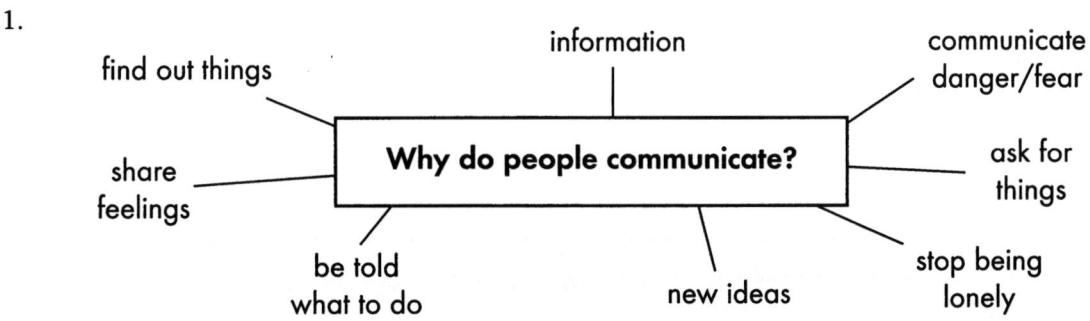

find out things • information • communicate danger/fear • share feelings • **Why do people communicate?** • ask for things • be told what to do • new ideas • stop being lonely

2.

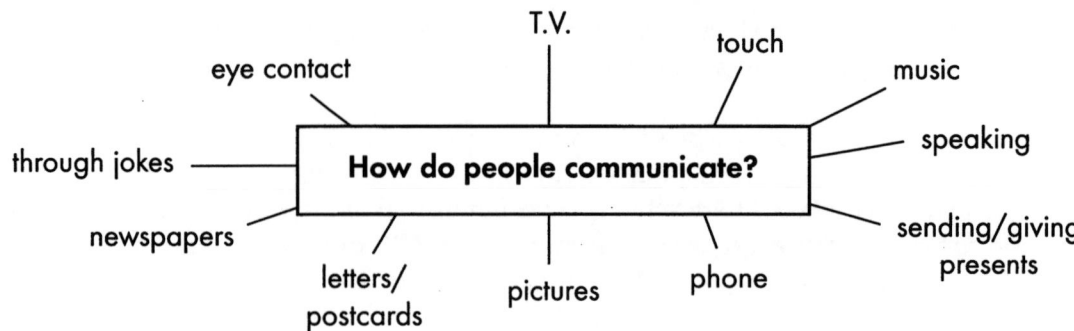

3.

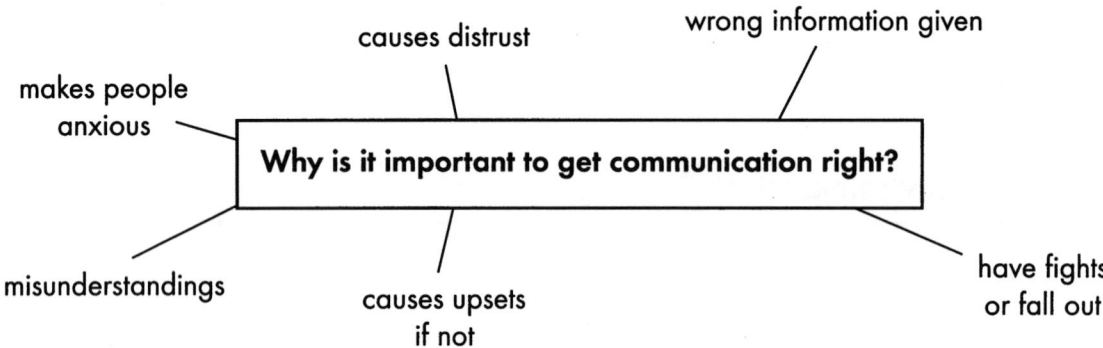

Review (5 min)

Explore some of the reasons for the importance of good communication and the range of ways in which communication can take place. Check whether learners are surprised at the range of ways communication can take place.

Brainstorms (20 min)

Run small group brainstorms on:

> **What happens if you don't communicate with other people?**

The learners should offer suggestions covering:

- misunderstandings
- communications at home, in the workplace and in social lives
- feelings, their's and others'
- communications in close relationships, children and partners

Review (30 min)

Ask for the small groups to feed ideas into a whole group brainstorm. Run this as an extended spider diagram, developing the consequences of some of their suggestions. So, for example, focusing on misunderstandings the spider's arms may be developed as:

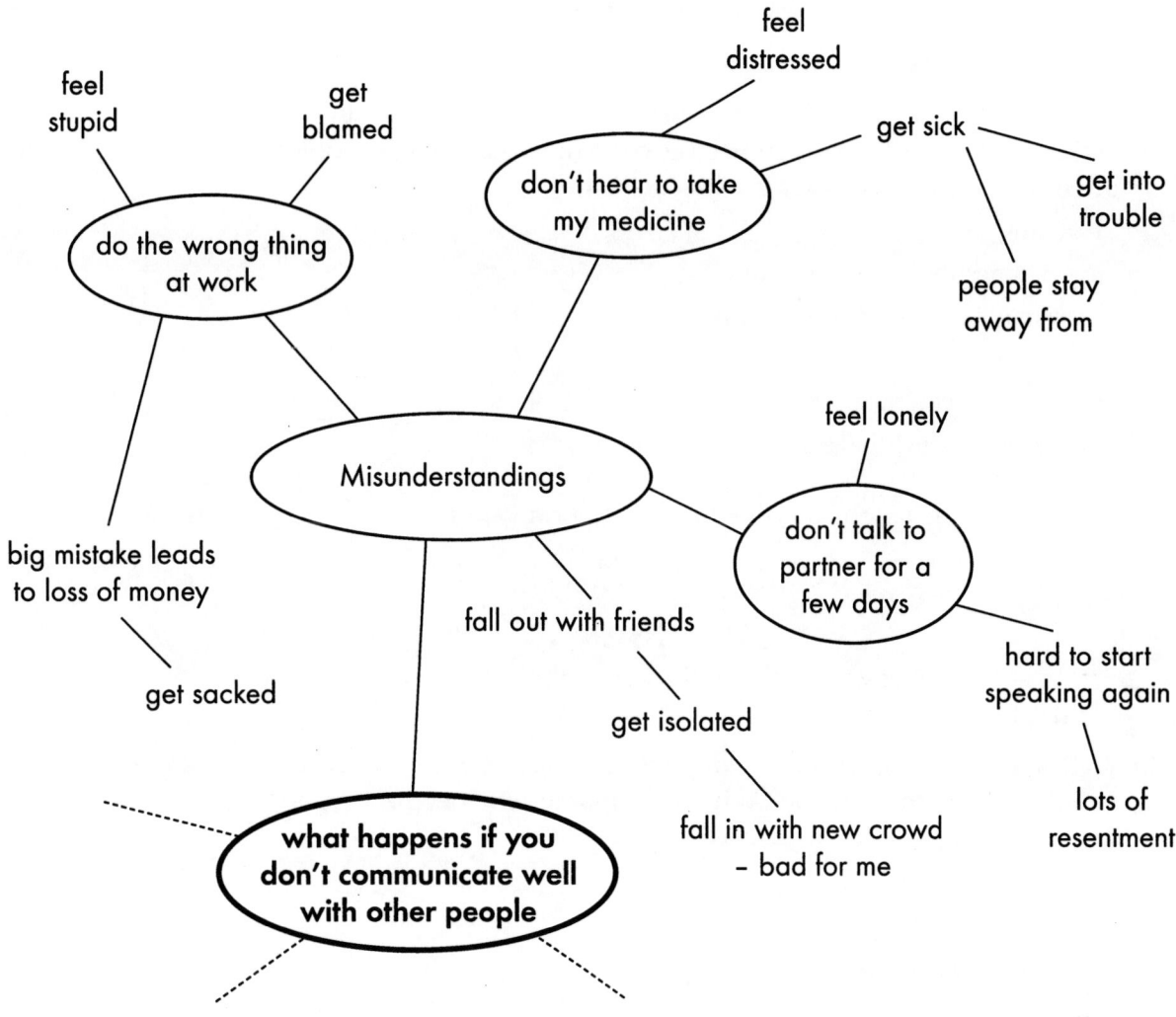

The benefits of communication (15 min)

To balance the dangers of not communicating ask the group to brainstorm the benefits from good communication. Encourage them to think of some of the fun and entertaining aspects of communication as well as the more serious aspects. Suggestions could include:

- sharing ideas
- having friends
- TV, radio etc.
- good relationship with partner
- having a laugh
- starting relationships
- feeling/belonging
- humour and jokes

Self assessment check-lists (15 min)

Ask the learners to complete DC1, a set of cards which look at communication. Then ask them to identify any areas they would like to develop and complete DC2.

Group review (20 min)

What areas have they considered important to develop?

Compile a group list to inform the targeting of the future delivery and to encourage sharing of experiences and perceived needs within the group. Explain the purpose of the module, the importance of communication and some of the areas the module will cover.

Thank the learners, check they have understood the ideas covered so far.

Session Two: Communication skills

 Trainer's notes

This session looks at some skills for successful communication. Throughout the work on developing learners' social skills these basic components of communication skills will need to be reinforced. This session looks at six areas. These are:

- listening
- asking and finding out information
- instructions: giving and receiving
- taking turns
- saying what you mean
- giving and receiving feedback

Each area is fundamental for effective communication.

LISTENING

 Trainer's notes

Although working on listening may not seem exciting it is one of the most vital areas for developing good communication skills. The importance of developing good listening skills will be illustrated through the following activities.

Opening brainstorm (15 min)

Ask the learners to consider:

> **What happens if you don't listen?**

Encourage the learners to think about social, work and home situations and some of the consequences in these situations of poor listening.

After the brainstorm ask the learners to sum up why listening is important.

Ask the learners whether it is easy to pretend to be listening well and to not really be. Ask whether they have ever thought they were listening well but not have been.

Ranking exercise (15 min)

Run a ranking exercise asking the learners to rank themselves as good or bad at listening along an imaginary line. Ask those at either extreme or in the middle to say why they have taken that position.

Mark their places on a diagram. Allow the learners to change places if they want. Record the new positions and ask for reasons for the change.

Listening matters (30 min)

The following activity encourages the learners to think about whether they are good listeners and what it is like to be a poor listener.

Ask the learners to form into pairs. Ask each to take a turn to talk to the other about something of interest for four minutes. Suggest:

- home
- a recent holiday
- a project
- a particular concern
- work
- an interest or hope
- a hobby
- a friend

Then at the close of the time ask each of the listeners to share with the group what the speaker talked about. The original speaker should comment on accuracy of what has been said and how well they felt they were listened to. The listener should comment on what it felt like to listen and how they felt a) they helped the speaker; b) how they could have better helped the speaker.

Swap roles and repeat the exercise. Discuss with the learners if when repeating the exercise they felt they had improved from the first time they tried this activity as a pair.

Small groups (15 min)

1. Ask the groups to think about what makes someone a bad listener. They could work on this by thinking and talking about those people who really annoy them as listeners.

2. The groups should list their ideas about how people show they are not listening well.

Review (15 min)

Ask the learners to share some of their small group's ideas.

Ask for some volunteers to mime or offer a sketch of poor listening skills.

Brainstorm (10 min)

Brainstorm:

> ### What are the effects of bad listening?

Encourage the learners to consider how they and others feel when they are on the receiving end of bad listening.

Ask the learners how it feels to be a bad listener. What do they think about after a conversation in which they had not listened properly or had been preoccupied?

Good listening means (15 min)

As a group explore what does it mean to be a good listener. Make a list and then prioritise the five key attributes of a good listener.

These should include suggestions such as:

- checking on what you have heard. Asking if this is what someone said or repeating back the main ideas
- asking if you are not sure what has been said. Asking for clarification or another example
- checking on facts and key ideas

- showing interest and encouraging people – "um", nod of head, "tell me more"
- asking open questions to encourage the speaker
- not finishing sentences or trying to guess what is to be said
- not interrupting or cutting across someone

Brainstorm (10 min)

Brainstorm:

What are the effects of good listening?

Again what does it feel like to have listened well or to have been listened to. What are the consequences?

Summary (5 min)

Summarise the points about good and bad listeners and the effects which this has on communication.

Ranking exercise (10 min)

Re-run the ranking exercise on being a good or a bad listener. Mark their positions and compare with the first exercise. How many have changed their positions? Ask why? How many have remained the same? Ask why?

A skills plan (10 min)

Ask the learners to complete DC3 a developing skills plan.

ASKING AND FINDING OUT INFORMATION

 Trainer's notes

This session builds on from listening skills. Active listening is a way to draw out information. This session also brings in questioning skills. Finding out information from written texts is addressed briefly.

Opening brainstorm (10 min)

Ask the learners to list all the ways they can think of to get information.

Explain that many examples will involve other people. For example in finding out how to get somewhere, which item to buy, how to manage or to solve a problem, about an illness or how much a repair would cost. All of these are everyday encounters and may depend on good questioning and effective listening.

Asking questions (20 min)

Prepare two of the group to help with this exercise. Each will be given a character. They will be asked questions and the group needs to guess who the person is. The exercise works through the skill of the questioner in drawing out the character. If only closed questions are asked then the character will not be able to say much. e.g. Do you have children? May lead to yes or no responses. If open questions or encouragements are offered to the character then the group will learn more, e.g. How many children do you have? with subsequent questions or prompts, e.g. that's interesting tell us something about them.

Set up the exercise so the group can listen to the two volunteers. They should be ready to say of which character they have a clearer idea and be encouraged to say why this is the case.

Open and closed questions (10 min)

Define open and closed questions. Work through the examples of both types of questions to show the difference in the amount of information the two types of question can draw out.

In pairs (10 min)

Ask the group to work in pairs to try questioning each other. Check on understanding.

Images and Information

 Trainer's notes

The learners will be able to gather information from pictures, from the way people present themselves and from the way they appear to others. Information can be given and can be asked for without language. Work first with images.

Images (30 min)

Form the learners into pairs. Give them a couple of magazine images. The same two to each pair. Ask them to decide what is going on, who is involved and what they can discover from the pictures.

Compare the pair's ideas and create a list of suggestions. How much similarity was there? What did some pairs miss? How did the pairs shape their ideas? What were the clues?

Explore how the learners have gathered clues and framed ideas and collected information from images.

If there is time and the resources available, look at the ways in which images can be presented to distort the truth, e.g. picking on a certain person in a crowd and claiming the crowd was made up of such people. Taking a shot of a small group and pretending it was a large one. Using particular images of people which may well not best represent who they are or how they have changed. An example would be images of Myra Hindley as the public knew her.

Body language (10 min)

This is the subject of the next module. But introduce the idea that much information can be given and can be gained through paying attention to body language. Certain facial expressions and body postures are universally understood. Ask for volunteers to demonstrate sad, happy and angry. Explain that facial features, use of hands and arms, the way the body is held all convey messages to others.

Brainstorm (15 min)

Ask the learners to brainstorm why knowing about non-verbal information may be helpful.

The suggestions may include:

* knowing how someone feels
* knowing how to present a better impression

Mimes (20 min)

Ask the learners to all try to present various emotional states through their body language and expressions. These states may include:

- confident
- nervous
- depressed/miserable
- afraid
- disappointed
- shocked

Review: how it **felt** to portray these states. What gestures or expressions were adopted? Ask how they thought others had captured the emotional states. What was most effective in others' mimes?

Information and texts

 Trainer's notes

An awareness of problems which any learners present with literacy should be noted and discussed with them. Appropriate referrals should be made.

Many people become overwhelmed when trying to seek information from texts. There is often too much written and they don't know where to start. Some documents are prepared in a question and answer format to help the reader.

This exercise helps the learners to think about what he or she needs to know before they start reading.

Discussion (10 min)

Ask the learners how they would approach getting information from a document.

This is somewhat abstract so examples could be used. Such as:

- how would the learners find out about ways to reduce heating bills?
- how would the learners find out about the effects of drinking to much?
- how would the learners find out about stress and how to manage it?

The examples should encourage learners to think about what material they might get and how they may use it.

Activity (20 min)

Ask the learners to look at the extract (DC4). They should work alone and find out what it is about. Then working in pairs the learners should decide on the key points.

Review (10 min)

As a group decide on the main points. How did the learners find these points?

Discuss some strategies for finding information:

- Decide what you want to know – ask yourself the questions you want answers to. List these.
- Read through the material trying to get answers to your questions
- See what else may be useful and make a note

Finding information can be easy. Getting swamped on information is very easy. Finding just the right bits and the right amount needs some planning and some sorting.

Suggest that leaflets or personally owned materials can be underlined, notes made in the margins or bits of paper used to make important points.

Closing exercise (10 min)

Ask the learners to complete the second half of DC3 on information-getting skills.

INSTRUCTIONS: GIVING AND RECEIVING

 ### Trainer's notes

This session looks at instruction giving. Again it highlights the importance of listening skills. But it also requires that the instruction giver carefully considers the listener:

- who is the listener?
- what preconceptions may the listener have?
- what assumptions could be made?
- what assumptions should not be made?

Giving instructions 1 (20 min)

Using DC5 give each learner a sheet of shapes and ask for them to be cut out. Ask the learners to form into pairs and for these pairs to sit back to back. Ask one of the pair to use the shapes to make a pattern and then to tell the other how to make the pattern. The other should follow the instructions.

The learners should have ten minutes to complete the task. During that time the person listening should not ask questions. Neither of the learners should look at or try to guide the others' work.

At the close of the exercise use DC6.

Review (10 min)

Ask the listeners how they found the task. What made the work easier for them? What made it hard?

For those giving instructions ask the same questions.

Ask both listeners and instruction givers how they thought instruction giving could be improved.

Giving Instructions 2 (20 min)

Again working back to back, ask one of the learners to draw what the other learner describes. A selection of simple pictures will need to be available for use.

After ten minutes ask the pairs to work together to decide what worked well and what worked badly.

- What language did the instruction giver use?
- What assumptions were made?
- Were simple or obvious things not mentioned?
- How did it feel to be trying to draw the picture?

Giving Instructions 3 (30 min)

As a final exercise ask the group to work in threes to work out a set of simple instructions for an ordinary task. The group should check that they have been unambiguous in their language, that the steps to completing the task are in the right order and that nothing obvious has been ignored or assumed.

Ask for a volunteer to give the instructions to a volunteer from another group. There should be three or four mimes performed.

As each one is completed, explore what worked well and why, and what may have been forgotten and why. How did the instruction giver feel? How did it feel to be trying to perform the actions – were assumptions made? Were key links between activities missed out? Were things in the wrong order?

Discussion (10 min)

As a group list the key features of good instruction-giving which they should remember both when giving instructions and when receiving instructions.

Remind the learners of what may happen if instruction-giving is not clear. There is:

- wasted time
- frustration
- people feeling silly or doing the wrong thing
- potential for an accident or dangerous incident

When receiving instructions it is important to check understanding and to question what has been said before starting.

TAKING TURNS

 ### Trainer's notes

Basic to all communication is turn taking. Without sharing the opportunities for speaking, responding or commenting communication could not be said to be taking place.

Working alone (10 min)

Ask the learners to think about a recent conversation they have had. Ask them to decide:

- Who did most of the talking? Why?
- Who did least? Why?
- How satisfactory was the conversation?
- Did they get from it what they wanted?
- Did the other person?

Discussion (25 min)

Explore the answers to these questions. Ask:

- What makes an encounter more satisfying?
- What does it feel like if they do not have a chance to express their ideas or to ask for what they want?
- Who takes over conversations with them?
- With whom do they take over conversations?

The answers are likely to yield issues of fairness, and unfairness, not feeling good when they dominate a conversation and when others dominate. They are likely to feel more satisfied when a conversation is balanced. The learners may find that certain situations or certain people make them more likely to dominate and not take turns or may make them more likely to let others dominate.

For example they may be less likely to speak with a boss, in an interview or other difficult situation or with strangers. In a close relationship they may not let someone else speak very much. They may say they "know" what someone else is going to say or may not want to hear what is to be said.

Working alone (10 min)

Ask the learners to work on DC7.

Review (10 min)

Share any thoughts the learners have had and explain there are links between turn taking and assertiveness. Both are based on respecting that all people in the encounter have rights to speak.

Being aware of turn taking is important. An exercise would be artificial so the learners should be encouraged to think and to keep a log of turn taking in the various conversations they have over a period of three to four days.

SAYING WHAT YOU MEAN

 Trainer's notes

This session links to the module on developing assertiveness skills and with all the work on managing interactions. It also ties into work on giving feedback. This session is a very brief review of the importance of assertiveness and making clear statements.

Opening brainstorms (15 min)

Brainstorm:

> **Why is it important to say what you mean?**

The learners may suggest:

- not doing things you don't want
- not getting resentful later
- asking for what you want
- everyone knows where they stand
- not having to make excuses later
- not blaming others for situations to which you agreed

Brainstorm:

> **Why may people not say what they mean?**

Check if it is simply about avoidance or not being assertive or maybe other reasons such as:

- not really knowing what you feel or think
- trying to spare someone's feelings
- not having prepared what to say and getting side-tracked

In pairs (15 min)

Ask the learners to discuss in pairs times when they have not said what they meant and the consequences. DC8 may help them structure their discussion.

Review (10 min)

Ask the learners to share their ideas. Are there common situations, e.g. Close relationships? With people in authority? When emotions are involved?

Role-plays (30 min)

Ask the learners to work in pairs on one of the three situations on DC9. The learners need to work out how to manage the situation and to say what they mean. They should have some time to prepare the role-play.

Ask for one or two to be performed. Question the learners while still in character:

- What situation are you in?
- What are you trying to say?
- What do you want?
- Do you feel listened to? Why/why not?
- What do you think will happen next – are you happy with this?

Discuss with the whole group:

- How do the two characters see the situation?
- Where are their major differences?
- What will happen and what are the consequences?
- What else could happen and how?
- Could this be achieved?

Encourage the groups to think how the dialogue between the characters could be developed. How could each character behave differently.

Ask the characters to follow the suggestions:

- What happens?
- Do the characters find this more satisfactory?
- What are the likely consequences?

If there is time repeat the activity with the second role-play.

Discussion (15 min)

Explore with the learners what may make it hard to say what they mean. What tactics can the learners think of to help them to say what they mean?

The list should include:

- Taking time to prepare something important – writing notes if necessary
- Asking someone for time to talk about something important

- Asking to be listened to, not spoken over, to be able to finish what needs saying
- Acknowledging something may hurt but that it needs to be said
- Deciding what one feels and thinks and then not being persuaded otherwise
- Taking a break if a conversation is difficult
- Asking to return to a discussion if you don't feel you have been taken seriously
- Checking someone has listened by asking them what they think you mean and why

Learning plans (10 min)

Ask the learners to think about their own past behaviours, any aspects they may like to change and the sorts of things they may do. They should complete DC10. Check on progress. Thank the learners for what they have done.

GIVING AND RECEIVING FEEDBACK

 ## Trainer's notes

This links with developing assertiveness skills, saying what you mean and is an important communication activity to keep relationships healthy. Feedback is a vital part of keeping relationships on track and ensuring that proper attention is paid to behaviours. However, giving and receiving feedback can be difficult. People often understand it in terms of criticism or of being critical of each other. This will need to be explored. Feedback may also be positive. Accepting and making positive comments can be hard for some learners.

Self-assessment (15 min)

Ask the learners to read through DC11 and then to think about what this tells them about themselves.

Discussion (30 min)

Take a show of hands:

- who finds it hard to be positive to others?
- who can't take compliments?
- who is often critical of others?
- who keeps quiet because it is easiest?

Work through each of these four areas and find out the consequences of each one and why people may do this. Make notes on the flipchart.

Then decide with the group what can be done to encourage acceptance of compliments or to make saying critical things less destructive.

Brainstorms (20 min)

Explain that feedback is about being honest about how people feel or think about a situation or something which has been done or said.

Brainstorm with the group:

> **What happens if feedback is not given?**

They may suggest:

- don't know where you stand
- can't expect anyone to change
- don't know how things are seen by others

Then brainstorm:

> **What are the advantages of giving/receiving feedback?**

They may suggest:

- know where you stand
- can change what you do

- feel better having told the truth
- can expect people to change

Summarise (10 min)

Feedback has a role in relationships because it helps people to know where they stand and what is liked or not liked.

It may be hard to give feedback because of the fear of hurting people. It may be hard to hear because it seems like a criticism. Feedback should be about respecting and being respected. It is about taking people seriously. It is important not to attack the person but speak about his/her actions or behaviours. It is important to think of alternative ways for him/her to behave or act and not to be simply critical.

Giving and receiving feedback links with assertiveness and with developing equal relationships.

Feedback can be positive as well as negative. It is important to practice giving and receiving positive feedback.

Ask the learners to watch carefully over the next few days for times when they should give or should ask for feedback and to try to do this.

Session Three: Getting communication right

 Trainer's notes

This session addresses several areas where communications can go wrong:

- close relationships
- not knowing your audience
- being shy and avoiding encounters

The session can help raise awareness of some of these issues. Each may need to be dealt with in greater depth, for example by looking at another module in this manual or by referring the learners to specialist sources of help such as RELATE.

Opening brainstorm (15 min)

Ask the learners to brainstorm:

> **What stops communication going well?**

Responses should be varied and cover such as:

- feelings getting the better of you
- being too self-preoccupied
- being shy and avoiding people
- not being aware of others and their concerns
- making fun of someone/thing
- agreeing to something to prevent conflict
- not thinking about what is being said

Ask for some examples of what some of these suggestions mean.

Issues for me (10 min)

Ask the learners to think about situations or issues which bother them, use DC12. List an order of issues which seem most important and need to be dealt with.

Check on progress.

Review (10 min)

Take a show of hands on how many of the learners think that things can go wrong for them in communications episodes. Ask for

- often
- quite often
- sometimes
- not very often

Ask them to volunteer the types of areas where things may go wrong and which they would like to change. Start a group list of issues.

Outline the areas the session covers and check which are most useful to the learners.

CLOSE RELATIONSHIPS

Opening brainstorm (30 min)

Ask the learners to brainstorm:

> **What can go wrong in relationships with people you are close to?**

The range of suggestions could cover such as:

- money worries
- arguing
- loss of interest
- children don't talk to you
- growing apart
- sexual problems

Encourage as many ideas and then ask the group to find all the ones which are to do with communication. It is likely all problems will have communication as a reason for things going wrong.

Take a couple of examples from the brainstorm and work through all the ways in which communication could help or lack of poor communication has made things go badly.

e.g.

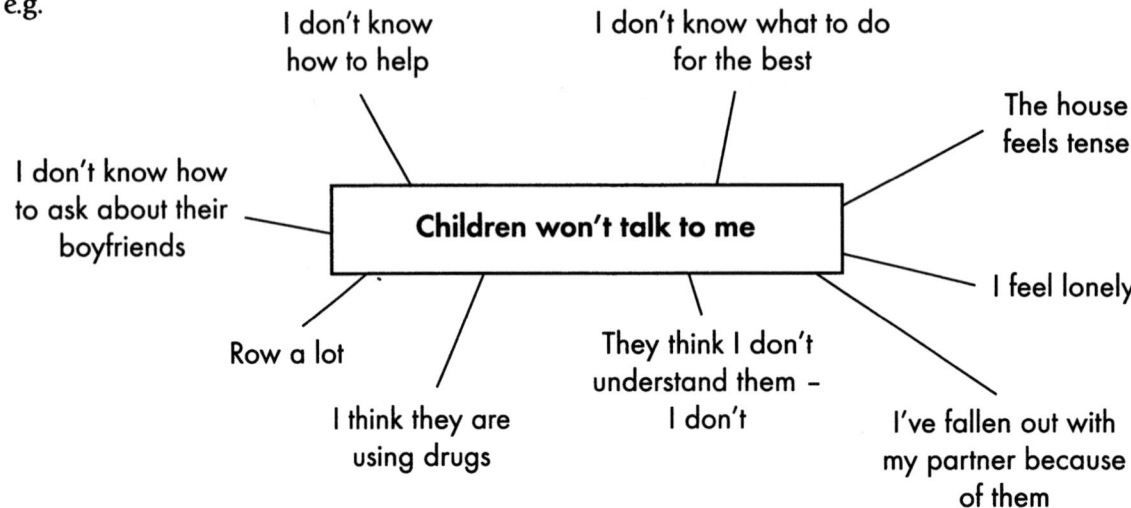

Discuss and list the reasons why there may be problems with communication in close relationships.

From the list ask the learners to work up a role-play based on poor communication.

Role-plays and discussion (40 min)

Ask for two pairs to volunteer to role-play their situations.

Explore with the learners in role:

- how the situation arose
- how the pair had been communicating
- when communication got worse
- whether each feels the other listens or speaks properly to them

Discuss with the group what could be done to improve the situation or what could have prevented it from getting as it has.

Pair work (15 min)

In pairs consider what types of communication, strategies or communication skills are needed to help close relationships to work.

Introduce the importance of making statements which are simply about offering feedback or about saying something which would be a preferred behaviour or action. Emphasise the importance of not blaming the other person.

Review (15 min)

Start a group list of all the ideas the pairs have thought of. As a group, mark with a star those areas with which they may need help. Keep a note for future programme planning.

Planning (10 min)

Ask the learners to use DC13 to record their learning needs.

KNOWING WHO YOU ARE SPEAKING TO

Trainer's notes

An area of communication which needs careful thought is that of who is being communicated with and why. Learners may not recognise the importance and significance of different levels of formality and informality. This session helps raise awareness of this.

Introduction (10 min)

Open the session by introducing the idea of different levels of informality and formality. Explain that when they are speaking or writing to someone it is important to consider who the person is, what they may expect and what it is appropriate to say or to ask and what language it is appropriate to use.

Give some examples, such as: when speaking to a judge in court it would be unhelpful to say things like: "here you"; "oi Judge"; "Guv"; "boss" etc. It would be wise to find out if he should be called Sir, your honour etc. Ask the learners for some examples.

Creating Examples (15 min)

Ask for examples:

Person/Job	Type of language to use	What you might call them
Partner		
Doctor		
Young children		

When all the learners seem happy with this, brainstorm why it is important to use correct address and language. Make a list of the benefits of using proper language.

Brainstorm (10 min)

Brainstorm:

> **What might happen if you use the wrong language/ address someone the wrong way**

Suggestions may include:

- not get taken seriously
- thought rude or ignorant
- not get what you want
- no matter how serious/important the issue may be, it doesn't get heard

Role-plays (30 min)

Ask the learners to work in threes to devise a sketch based on a situation in which one character uses the wrong language, way of speaking or goes about things in an inappropriate way.

Examples:
- an interview
- complaining about a faulty item
- going to ask for a pay rise/promotion
- asking someone out for the first time

The sketches should be entertaining to devise and to watch. Ask for a couple to be played for the group. Explore with the group the reasons for the humour.

Preparation (30 min)

Another way in which people can fall down is in not thinking through what expectations there are of certain situations. So, not behaving properly or not knowing what should be said.

Ask the learners to work in pairs on DC14. Work through one of the situations with them so they know what they should be doing.

Group Review (10 min)

Collect some of the group's ideas on each situation. Add further suggestions as necessary.

Writing (25 min)

Explain that there are conventions in writing to people in the layout and type of language used. Trying to follow conventions means that letters are taken seriously, that what is asked for is more likely to be considered seriously. Sometimes there are instructions to follow on types of information to include.

Ask the learners to work on DC15 in pairs.

Review (10 min)

Collect the pairs' ideas and add any further thoughts.

BEING SHY

 Trainer's notes

This session cannot cure shyness but it may help learners to be aware of what this means for others who experience shyness and may offer some strategies for those who feel shy. Some suggestions for appropriate referrals would be helpful for those who suffer from shyness.

Brainstorm (20 min)

Brainstorm:

> **Being shy means ...**

Cover feelings, actions, occasions and possible causes. Allow the group to cover as much ground as possible. Ask for examples, instances and illustrations. Create an extended spider diagram.

Swapping stories (20 min)

In pairs ask the learners to continue with some of the brainstormed ideas by exploring occasions when they have themselves been shy or been with others who are. The learners should try to gather ideas on:

- what may cause shyness
- what it feels like to be shy
- what it feels like to be with people who are shy
- what do you do when shy
- how can you help those who are shy

Review (15 min)

Share the ideas from the story telling and listing.

Explore:

Are there certain ages when people are more likely to be shy?

Are there certain occasions when people are more likely to be shy?

Brainstorm (10 min)

Then ask the learners to brainstorm how shyness may appear to others, e.g.

- as avoidance
- as rudeness
- as quietness

The learners should draw on their own experiences and think of things they have heard other people say about shy people.

Problem page (10 min)

Ask the learners to work on DC16. A problem about a shy person. The pair should try to think of some solutions.

Solutions (15 min)

Review the suggestions to Jim Jones' problem. Conduct a broader brainstorm looking for other solutions to shyness problems. Remind the learners of the various strategies for handling conversations both on the phone and face-to-face. These include:

- writing some notes about what you want to say
- reminding others that you need to complete what you are trying to say
- standing back from a situation so you can feel sure about what needs to be said
- listening carefully and then checking you know what is being said

Shy people are well advised to find ways to be less self-conscious. So developing other interests and meeting people through an activity is one way to tackle a concern about people paying attention to them. A reminder to people that others are often more concerned about *themselves* could also help.

Closing the session: Review (10 min)

Ask the group for a couple of things which each has discovered from working on close relationships, and thinking about your audience shyness. Ask for one idea which they will try to put into practice.

Session Four: Managing the written word

 Trainer's notes

Before embarking on this module, find out where nearby Adult Basic Education centres are, drop in and open learning centres, community provision and college provision. There may be some learners with clear literacy needs in the group and they should not feel exposed by this session.

Feeling confident in handling the written word is important in our society. People who are unable to cope with written English are at a considerable disadvantage. So much so that many people whose command of written English is weak, will go to tremendous lengths to cover this up. On the other hand, many people will almost boast about not being able to handle numbers.

Introductory brainstorms (15 min)

1. Ask the learners to think of occasions when they need to be able to express themselves on paper. They may suggest:
   - filling in forms
   - writing letters of complaint
   - writing to loved ones, especially if they are away for some time
   - writing letters of application
   - writing to housing associations
   - writing letters to arrange appointments

2. Then brainstorm all the occasions in day-to-day life when they need to read the written word.

Self assessments (20 min)

Ask the learners to work alone and to do check-lists DC17 to DC19. These will help the learners think about areas they may want to develop. Check on learners' progress. Check for common areas of problems.

Information-giving (10 min)

Offer suggestions about ways learners may be able to gain help:
- local drop in centres for ABE
- library facilities
- easy adult readers which may be available
- college and community education classes for developing skills in English and reading for pleasure
- ESOL classes and support

Session Five: Summary and planning

Spider diagram summary (25 min)

Brainstorm with the learners all the main areas covered in this module. Check on what content can be remembered. Add in areas they have forgotten. Encourage some prioritising of the areas which the learners have found most useful.

Plans (20 min)

Ask the learners to use the extended spider diagram for their own review and planning activities. Use DC20. They will also need earlier planning sheets for this work.

Check on learners' progress.

Review (20 min)

Ask the learners to highlight the:
- areas they want to work on
- why they want to do this
- what they will do

Spend more time on what they will do and in offering support strategies for so doing.

Games (10 min)

Complete the session with a game. Thank the learners.

I give in to arguments, others always seem to have better ideas	I don't really know how to talk about my feelings	I find filling in forms hard
I prefer talking to people on the phone	I'm only really confident with people I know well	I don't know what I'm going to say until I say it
I leap to conclusions	I'm confident with other people	I often remember all the things I meant to say after it's over
I'm not too good at following instructions	I don't get my ideas across in a group	I just don't really notice what other people are thinking/feeling
I don't think I listen too well to what people are saying	I'm happy talking to strangers	I prefer to be told things than have to read them

DC1

I only like being with people I know well	I think it's soft to talk about how you feel	I'm not good at writing letters
I'm just shy	If I asked more questions I'd find out what I should be doing	I often fly off the handle
I don't like having to read timetables or things with figures	I just agree to things – anything for a quiet life	I do as much as I can to avoid meeting new people
I'm often told I just don't listen	I can't manage phone calls very well	I get carried away with my own ideas and talk over other people
Sometimes I just say the first thing I think of	I don't really know how to behave with people in authority, bosses, the police, social services	I don't do well at interviews

DC2: My communication skills

Areas I think I am good at are:

I think this because:

Areas in which I would like to be better are:

I think this because:

DC3: Developing my communication skills

My Listening Skills

I think I am a good listener when – *write down in particular situations or with particular people*

1.
2.
3.
4.

I think I could become a better listener by – *write down what steps you will take*

1.
2.
3.
4.

Questioning and Getting Information

I think I am not so good at getting information from – *write down the situations/people*

1.
2.
3.
4.

I will improve this by – *write down the steps you will take*

1.
2.
3.
4.

A and B need a sheet of shapes each. Both cut around the shapes.
Follow the instructions offered by the trainer.

DC4

Read the following piece of writing
What is it about?
What would help you to make better sense of it?

Alcohol and other drugs

Many people who drink too much also take other drugs, such as tranquillizers, anti-depressants and sleeping pills, not to mention painkillers, stomach preparations and many more. This is because heavy drinkers suffer a lot of physical and psychological ill health. Many try to treat the symptoms of excessive drinking with other mood-altering drugs. This never works in the long term and can lead to terrible problems.

Why is this? One reason is simply that alcohol and some other drugs can interact to produce an effect which is far greater than the sum of each of the individual effects. Therefore 'safe' amounts of alcohol taken with 'safe' amounts of some other drug can together be lethal. For no drug is this more true than barbiturates, commonly used in the treatment of epilepsy. One or two barbiturate tablets taken with three or four drinks can kill you, yet in the past barbiturates were widely prescribed as sleeping pills!

There is also evidence that alcohol and tranquillizers can show cross-tolerance. That is, if you become tolerant to one, this tolerance can carry over to the other. So, for instance, if you have been on a tranquillizer for several months so that it no longer has the same effect as before, and you then begin to drink, the alcohol may not have much of an effect until you have several drinks. This is obviously dangerous, because it means you will tend to take more of both drugs to achieve the effects they had at first. Thus dependence on one drug can 'spread' to another.

'Stimulant' drugs, such as the caffeine found in coffee and tea, are sometimes taken to try to counteract the effects of alcohol. The 'black coffee cure' is a myth, as we said in the last chapter. Large amounts of stimulant drugs taken with alcohol can place great strain on the cardiovascular system, and amphetamines are the worst offenders here. So beware of 'diet drugs' which contain stimulants: the combination of these with alcohol may put an excessive strain on your heart. Many other drugs may interact with alcohol. Some antidepressants, for instance, seem to exaggerate the depressive effects of alcohol on the central nervous system, much in the way that barbiturates do. Antihistamines can make you drowsy and, taken with alcohol, this effect may be increased. Car driving and the operation of machinery may suffer and you run the risk of injury in an accident. This, of course, applies to many of the drugs which we have mentioned. If taken with alcohol, some painkillers – including aspirin – can result in a worsening of various stomach problems. And alcohol tends to reduce the absorption of antibiotics and hence makes them somewhat less effective.

From Heather and Robertson A Self Help Guide to Sensible Drinking.

DC7: Thinking about conversations with others

People I don't let speak much are	People I share conversations with 50:50 are	People who talk over me are
Situations where I speak too much are	Situations I speak 50:50 are	Situations I don't speak much are

To get things better balanced I will:

DC6: Analysing the exercise

How easy or difficult was it to give instructions – why?

How easy or difficult was it to receive the instructions – why?

How did the speaker assist you to understand the pattern which was formed?

How could the speaker have made it easier for you to visualise the pattern?

Did the listener feel that the speaker was trying to help? Why was this so?

How did your sitting positions help or hinder you in this task?

DC9

Situation One: The Break-up

Della and Steve have been going out for two years. Della is fed up with Steve's drinking, his loud behaviour with his mates and not being taken seriously. He doesn't want to spend time with her on his own. Steven thinks all is well.

Della

Is fed up. She had been upset and tried to talk to Steve about how she felt. She's been feeling hurt for months but knows she needs to do something. A guy at work has asked her out. She is not going to go, but it makes her realise what she is missing. She now doesn't care about the relationship with Steve and just wants out. The problem – Steve's temper.

Steve

Just doesn't want to hear anything is wrong. He thinks to be dumped is to lose face with his mates. He doesn't want to talk seriously but he really does like Della. He's jealous, quick to temper and just now very insecure – he's just lost his job.

Situation Two: Bullying

Jerry's been putting up with Winston and his mates for a long time. He's been picked on, he's had practical jokes played on him. He's fed up. He needs help to sort it out. The new training manger wouldn't listen to him when he tried last week. He's made another appointment.

Jerry

Jerry's fed up with being the butt of these stupid jokes. He thinks he might get hurt one day. He needs this job. He's had too many and has to know he can stick at something. He thinks the new training manager is really just as afraid as he is. He has to make him see sense.

Tom – Personnel Manager

Tom's keen to look good with his new boss. He doesn't want any trouble. Jerry's a bit of a wet. He knows Winston's a bully and he thinks most of his mates are probably not his friends but just going along with it.

Situation Three: The Landlord

Sam has been in his bedsit for three months. The Landlord said he'd sort out the cooker the first month. It hasn't happened. The last ring has gone and now he can't even heat soup; It's cold. He can't afford take-aways. He's fed up.

Sam

He's shy and hates causing trouble. He's always been like it. He often backs down and just suffers. It is cold, he is fed up. The baby belling also put some heat in the room. He thinks the room is damp as well. He can't face moving again, he's only just settled and the people in the house don't pick on him. Mr Harris has got to do something about it.

Mr Harris – The Landlord

The house has given him a good rent but he can't be bothered with sorting it out anymore. He wants to sell and doesn't want to waste money. Things are tight in his clothing business and he can't waste money buying cookers. So what if the bedsits are run down? He hopes to get shot of the building over the next four months.

DC8

Situation	Instead of saying what I meant I...	The consequences were	What I would have preferred to happen was...

Read the statements below and ◯ the one which applies to you

I give compliments:
- never
- often
- sometimes

I say what I think:
- never
- often
- sometimes

If anyone is critical about something I've done I:
- sulk
- get angry
- won't listen
- feel hurt
- think about why they said it

I make critical comments:
- frequently
- all the time
- never
- sometimes

I say positive things:
- even if I don't mean it
- not very often and not even when I should
- when I want to

People think I am:
- too hard on myself
- easy going
- can't be bothered to do things right

When someone is positive about me:
- I think it's a windup
- I hate it
- I like it
- I take no notice

What might this say about me?

Thinking about the past I think that I don't say what I mean when...

To make matters better I need to:

I have decided that I will:

DC12: What can go wrong for me?

Read the statements and ✓ what applies to you

Communication Issue	✓
I don't know what to say to new people	
I often blame my partner for things	
People think I'm rude – I'm just shy	
I never really talk with my kids	
Sometimes I don't listen, I just react	
The boss thinks I'm rude	
I find it hard with new people	
I don't have the words to talk about my feelings	
At interviews I just clam up	
I don't really think before I speak	
When my partner wants to talk about us I can't cope	
I find it hard to say no	
With new people I just can't stop talking	

Look at the statements you have ✓
Are there any particular problems? e.g. not listening well, being shy….

Put a * by the five things you would like to improve

Look at your *, now write down three things you want to get better

Communication Area	Reason
1.	
2.	
3.	

DC13: My close relationships

With people I should be close to things go wrong because:

I could improve the situation by:

1.

2.

3.

4.

5.

Types of formal letter to write	Asking for/Saying what	What sorts of information to include

---

DC14: Situations

1. Going for a job interview to work in an office:
   List what you might wear, how you would behave, what might be expected.

2. Having an interview with the bank manger/building society manager. To review your account and see whether you can apply for a small loan.

3. Phoning about a job advertised in the local paper. The advert warns that some questions will be asked to check suitability of possible applicants.

4. You have been involved in a road accident. You were driving. So far no-one has been blamed. You have an interview with the police.

DC17: Skills checklist

Name:

	OK	Need Help
Read my name and address		
Read local place names		
Read some common words		
Know the initial sounds of words		
Form most of the letters of the alphabet		
Copy my name and address		
Spell my name		
Spell my address		
Spell some of my family/friends' names		
Spell some common words		
Other		

DC16

Dear Agony Aunt,

I am in my twenties and fancy a girl at work. She doesn't seem to know that I exist, and every time I try to talk to her I say something silly, or worse still, dry up completely. She has worked in the shop for three years and knows everyone and always seems to be in the middle of things. I feel such an outsider. What can I do?

Yours

J M Jones

Dear Mr Jones...

DC19: Checklist

How's your reading?	confident	not so confident	need help	no need
reading a newspaper or magazine				
books for yourself				
stories to children				
job adverts				
road signs				
timetables				
maps				
instructions				
cheques				
letters				
forms and leaflets				
invoices				
catalogues				
labels				
packets				
diagrams				
notes in handwriting				
dictionaries				
computer screens				
phone directories				
reference books				
structure words				
social words				
letter names and the alphabet				
word and letter shapes				
letter sounds and patterns				
syllables				
grammar				
punctuation and layout				
predicting (getting meaning from the context)				
reading between the lines				
skimming and scanning				
proofreading				
asking for help				
choosing reading materials				

DC18: Skills checklist

Name:

	OK	Need Help
Read short texts		
Read adverts		
Read letters and messages		
Follow written instructions		
Read signs and labels		
Find my way using a map		
Use a timetable or chart		
Use a TV programme guide		
Follow instructions in picture form		
Read a form		
Fill in a form		
Write cheques		
Write notes and messages		
Write letters		
Write a few lines about my ideas		
Write a few lines about what I've done		

DC20: Communication skills plan

Name: _____

Priority Areas and Reasons	Action to take – include dates

Agreed Between: ....

On: .... Date for Review: ....

Non-verbal communication

 The module is divided into four sessions.

1. What is non-verbal communication? (2 hours 40 min)

2. Being aware of non-verbal communication and using it appropriately (2 hours 25 min)

3. Creating positive impressions (2 hours)

4. How do I appear to others (1 hour 20 min)

The module could take 8 hours and 25 minutes to complete

 The module links with all work on developing effective social relationships. It links with work on:

- developing assertiveness skills
- knowing what is appropriate in the workplace
- knowing how to better read and respond to others
- cultivating a positive self-image and developing self-esteem
- developing more effective communication skills

 The module uses:

- mimes
- movement
- sketches
- small groupwork

- collage
- brainstorm
- discussion

🍎 *Trainer's notes*

Why consider non-verbal communication?

As much as 60% of all communication is said to happen non-verbally, through eye contact or lack of it, postures and gestures adopted, proximity to the other person and facial expression. The way we stand or sit, what we do with our hands and feet, how we look at someone can convey many messages such as happiness, concern, fear or anxiety. In some situations these non-verbal messages will reinforce what we want to say, will encourage others to see us as sincere, as taking an interest in them or the situation. In other circumstances our body language and other non-verbal communications may give away things we would rather keep to ourselves. Non-verbal communications may show our anxiety or fear at an interview, may demonstrate a lack of self-confidence or our lack of genuine concern in someone. Non-verbal communication may undermine our verbal messages or may allow others to see how emotionally driven we are.

An awareness of non-verbal communication is important because we should know how others can 'read' us and what messages we may offer intentionally or unintentionally. To ensure successful interactions we should know how to 'read' others

This module encourages the learners to:

- have greater awareness and understanding of non-verbal communication
- understand how non-verbal communication can support or undermine what they are saying
- understand how their body language and other non-verbal communications can put others at their ease or can make others uncomfortable

- understand how to 'read' others' non-verbal communications and to respond more appropriately
- better manage their non-verbal communication
- find ways to convey positive messages about themselves

Session One: What is non-verbal communication?

Introducing body language (20 min)

Ask the learners to walk about the room carefully and being aware of the other learners. Ask them to stop and to express *without words* e.g. fear. They should then be told to move on, stop and express e.g.

- happiness
- sadness
- anxiety
- panic
- upset

Work through several cycles of walking and stopping to express an emotion. Ask the learners to return to their seats. Ask them to brainstorm how they expressed the emotion and how they recognised it in others.

They should suggest:

- position of eyes
- way the head is held
- use of facial features e.g. smiling
- using physical size e.g. throwing back shoulders
- posture: standing straight, hunched over etc.
- use of room space and proximity to others

Brainstorms (20 min)

Explain that they have been describing non-verbal communication. Extend the discussion to brainstorm two questions:

> **What is non-verbal communication?**

> **What does non-verbal communication tell us about others and they about us?**

Continuum (15 min)

Ask the learners to form a continuum on whether or not knowing about non-verbal communication is important. One end of the continuum represents very important, the other end no importance.

Explore the reasons the learners selected positions towards the centre and at the two extremes. Mark the position of the learners and allow them to change position if they wish. Mark the new positions and check on reasons for making these changes.

What is body language? Explanation (15 min)

Summarise the learning so far.

1. That non-verbal communication is about observing and interpreting non-verbal signals given through:
   - eye contact – or lack of it
   - facial expressions – frowns, smiles etc.
   - posture of the body when standing, sitting or walking
   - use of space between people

2. Explain that much of what is communicated is non-verbal.

3. Explore some of the reasons for the importance of non-verbal communication.
   - to support or undermine a verbal message
   - offering other impressions and insights into how confident, afraid, nervous etc. we may feel
   - as a way of better tuning into what others feel

Gestures (20 min)

Write out the following phrases and ask the learners to work in pairs to think of gestures to express them.

- Hi
- I'm broke
- How do we get out of this?
- Leave me alone!

- Have you any money?
- Which way?
- He's a fool!
- You're for it

Ask for some to volunteer their gestures. What other commonly used phrases are expressed with gestures or have accompanying gestures?

By the close of the exercise the learners should be fairly convinced that gestures are used a lot, at least in this culture. Depending on the mix of cultures within the training group there can be interesting discussions about the ways in which other cultures may use gestures.

Postures (20 min)

Ask the learners to think about the way people sit and stand and convey clear messages and then ask them to all:

- show boredom
- be intimidating
- show keenness
- be telling a lie

- show feeling defensive/attached
- show they feel crushed or defeated
- show they feel fit and healthy
- show feeling confident

Ask for and list the ways in which posture may be changed to show these differing feelings. Ideas might include e.g.:

- use of shoulders
- position of arms and legs
- where hands are placed

- way head is held
- how straight they stand

Facial expressions (20 min)

Facial expressions should match what a person is saying or feeling or be appropriate to the situation. Examples may include:

- it would be wrong to smile at a funeral
- to be looking miserable while congratulating someone would make them think you were not sincere
- to not express any feeling may make you seem cold or aloof
- in an interview to have all your feelings showing through facial expression may undermine the image you want to project of confidence

Ask the learners to work in pairs to consider the arrangements of eyes, eyebrows, use of nose, mouth, chin to convey the following:

- disgust
- sulking
- they're a fool
- fear
- surprise
- lack of confidence – they won't give me the job
- feeling confident
- it smells bad
- sadness
- trust me – I'm reliable
- shock

Ask for some demonstrations.

In pairs (20 min)

Ask the learners to work in pairs to express the following through non-verbal and verbal communication. They should correctly combine non-verbal communication to support the verbal message. They should then try to combine the opposite or wrong non-verbal clues with the verbal message. They should find it hard to combine opposites.

- I don't care about this any more
- I really want to be involved with ...
- I am reliable and won't let you down
- Don't muck me about, I won't put up with it
- I'm confident I'm the right person

Ask for some volunteers to demonstrate and to discuss their experiences.

Review (10 min)

Summarise the key points.

Session Two: Being aware of non-verbal communication and using it appropriately

This session looks at ways people can undermine what they say, make others feel uncomfortable, appear as insincere, nervous or appear overly emotional in the wrong situations.

Brainstorm (15 min)

Brainstorm:

> **How can our non-verbal communication upset others?**

Encourage the learners to consider:

- insincerity
- not caring
- being stressed or fearful
- taking up other people's space etc.

- lying
- being anxious or afraid
- being domineering

Explain that this session will look at a range of ways one can upset others through non-verbal behaviour.

Use of personal space (30 min)

Ask for two volunteers. Tell them you will give them several roles (see below). They should stand as close to or as far away from each other as seems appropriate. They can touch if appropriate.

After each positioning of the two volunteers in the roles ask the others to decide if they agree with the non-verbal messages communicated; if they want to make changes they should say what they would like the learners to do. Once the group is in agreement record the positioning on the board e.g.

Relationship	Closeness/Distance	Type of Touching

The relationships to adopt are:

- friends of same sex
- gang leader/tough guy tries to intimidate another person
- headmaster/pupil
- people in a bus queue
- partners – married or living together for a long time
- people who have rowed
- friends of opposite sex
- boss is telling worker off
- having just been introduced
- new people just going out with each other
- boss congratulates worker

Explore what gives the clues to those watching. Why is it disconcerting if people do the wrong thing in using personal space?

Discussions (15 min)

Use the following questions to explore use of space.

- What is meant by invading personal space?
- How does it feel?

- Why might it be done?
- When is being close with someone not an intrusion?

Use of space can be a powerful way to get messages across, as can use of touch.

Use of touch (15 min)

Explore:

- When is touch used? What for and by whom?
- What parts of the body can be touched or referred to and by whom?
- What happens if people break these 'rules'?

Summarise (10 min)

Use of space and touching can cause upset if not used appropriately. There are ways to convey intimacy, power over someone or intimidation. They can, if thoughtlessly used, create upset.

Eye contact (20 min)

Brainstorm:

> **How do people use their eyes to show what they think/feel**

Cover such areas as:

- averting their eyes, looking down, looking away. Is this a lack of interest or shyness?
- looking a lot. This may be interest, staring may be confrontation

Ask how we are able to tell the difference between e.g. confrontation and interest in someone – both may involve looking a lot.

Activity: The learners should each take a turn to talk about something of personal importance for four minutes. A should talk and B should use eye contact to encourage and show interest. How did it feel? B should then talk and A not be bothered to listen. This should be shown with/without eye contact. How did it feel? Did B stop talking?

Facial expression (20 min)

Reiterate the importance of using facial expressions to show interest, to support what is said and to demonstrate awareness of the situation. Discuss the effects of using the wrong facial expression; having no facial expression, or too much expression.

Activity: In pairs ask the learners to try to use the wrong/right facial expressions to go with saying the following:

- my partner is leaving me
- we're going on holiday tomorrow
- my mother has recently died
- I've won £5,000 on the lottery
- my child is really ill
- I've got a new job
- I've got a really bad headache

Mimes (20 min)

Ask the learners to think of an appropriate and an inappropriate way to use body language in these situations:

- I'm really interested in you and what you are saying
- Just leave me alone!
- I'm sorry you're upset what can I do to help?
- I know you want to be left alone to think about our relationship

Ask for some to volunteer their mimes. Check whether or not the learners agree with the representations.

Session Three: Creating positive impressions

This session looks at the ways in which learners could create positive impressions. It covers non-verbal communication to:

- appear confident
- manage interviews
- manage first meetings and tackle difficult situations

Brainstorm (15 min)

Ask the learners to brainstorm how they know someone is confident. Encourage them to think across a range of situations. The suggestions might include:

- an open smile
- a good handshake
- looking someone in the eye
- standing still and not fidgeting
- clothing worn and the way it is worn
- walking purposively

Being positive (15 min)

1. Ask the learners to walk about the room to project a positive impression.

2. Ask the learners to sit and to project a positive image.

3. Ask the learners to shake hands with the person next to them to appear as a positive person.

Ask them to repeat the three actions but to do so in the manner of someone who is anxious or nervous.

Review (15 min)

Explore and list the differences between the way they and others behaved. Look at the walk, sitting down and handshake as three separate activities. This should help others to find the essence of what it means to appear as a positive person.

Managing difficult situations and appearing positive (20 min)
Brainstorm
Ask the learners to brainstorm in threes how they would tackle the situations (NV1) in terms of ensuring their non-verbal clues were:

a) appropriate

b) positive

Review (15 min)

Collect each small group's ideas as the groups work through the situation. Have they found all the pitfalls? Are they clear about how to appear positive? Add any further ideas as they seem necessary.

These could include:

- preparing what to say
- visualising the situation and running it as if it is going well, e.g. imagine going into the room, be prepared to shake hands, to introduce yourself, to say what your main ideas are etc.
- thinking about what to wear

Clothing and messages (15 min)

People are very influenced by what people wear. Clothes make clear statements. Ask the learners to think about any occasions when they have worn clothes which have made them feel awkward. Ask for any to volunteer their experiences. For example:

Situation	Type of clothing worn	Feeling because of the clothes worn	What was appropriate
Interview – clerical job	Jeans and T shirt, trainers	Awkward – others at the interview knew what to do	Smart suit/ shirt/ jacket/blazer

Summarise the types of clothes needed for certain situations. Like using appropriate expression or posture, clothing reinforces the image people wish to project.

Images (20 min)

In pairs ask the learners to work through some magazines and find images of people. They should select images and say what the people are doing, what others think of them or they think others should think about them. They should take clothing, posture, facial expression, how close they stand to other people etc. into account.

Review (15 min)

Allow ten minutes for the learners to review the collages and to comment on the range of images.

Close the session by checking that there are no areas of confusion or unanswered questions.

Session Four: How do I appear to others?

This session needs careful handling. It is not an opportunity to attack other learners. The purpose of the activities is to encourage greater self-awareness on the part of individual learners about the ways they use non-verbal communication.

Copycat (20 min)

Divide the group into two. Group A should move about the room, to sit down, stand up or look at things on the wall. Each member of Group B should pick a person in Group A to copy and then move round the room in the manner of that person.

At "stop" the Bs should mirror the As they are copying. Can the As tell who is copying them? How? How did the Bs feel trying to copy the body language, gestures and expressions of someone else? Repeat and reverse the roles with the As picking a B to copy. Repeat the questions.

This will have made people feel self-conscious. Has attention been drawn to anything e.g. a particular way of moving, a frequently used gesture etc.?

Sharing stories (20 min)

This exercise of close observation can be repeated by putting the learners in threes. Having one as an observer and two sharing stories.

The observer should look for e.g. any particular gestures, the ways in which each may encourage the other's speech, may show boredom or interest. The observer may note how alike in posture the pair may become or how distant they become when they are sharing stories. Why might the two share similar postures? Why might they differ?

The observers should report back to the group.

The talking pairs should state what they observed of each others' non-verbal communication and the effect this had.

They should comment on how they felt they were behaving e.g. trying to encourage talk, being bored etc. They should say how accurate they thought the observer was.

Self assessment (15 min)

Ask the learners to look at NV2 and consider their own non-verbal behaviour.

Summary (25 min)

Ask the group for the ideas from the four sessions which have been interesting or useful. Record these.

Rerun the original continuum to see who may have shifted their opinion on non-verbal communication. Explore the reasons for change or for not changing.

Close the session and thank the learners.

NV2: Checklist

On a scale of 1–10 I would rate myself as being aware of non-verbal communication.
1 = low, 10 = high

1   2   3   4   5   6   7   8   9   10

I give myself this mark because I think I am aware of my non-verbal communication because:

I give myself this mark because I think I am aware of others' non-verbal communication because:

The areas which I think I could improve on are:

I could do this by:

NV1: Situations

Read through the following situations.
How should the person respond? What aspects of non-verbal communication
do they need to manage to make it right and to seem confident?

1. Bob is going for a job interview. He is fairly sure he can do the work but he gets scared by interviews.

2. Jo has decide she's finishing with her boyfriend. She's had enough and doesn't want to try again. She doesn't want to hurt him and doesn't want an ugly scene. She's bothered about both.

3. Sam and a friend are applying for a small business loan. They are clear about their ideas and think they could be successful. They've never run a business or applied for a loan before.

4. Kev's made several mistakes over the past three months. He's had to start with his counsellor again. He knows he is going to have to prove that he really means to make changes to his lifestyle and get some direction in this life. He has applied for two jobs this week. It's a start. How will he appear at his case review this afternoon?

Communities and relationships

 This module is divided into six sections.

1. Introducing communities (1 hour 50 min)

2. Life without communities (1 hour 40 min)

3. Making communities work (2 hours)

4. Conflict in communities (2 hours)

5. Communities and our needs (50 min)

6. Concluding the session (35 min)

 Trainer's notes

This module aims to help learners:

• to improve their knowledge about what it means to belong to a community

• to be in a position to make informed judgements about the benefits, or otherwise, of belonging to communities

• to be more aware of the varieties of communities that exist around them

• to improve their critical reasoning

• to increase their ability to negotiate

• to raise their awareness about the number of ways difficulties can be resolved, as well as learning experientially what may/may not work.

Focusing on communities is important, especially for those who may have been leading isolated or restricted lives, either because they have withdrawn from communities or have had limited opportunities to participate in community life.

The benefits of belonging to communities may include:

• a sense of belonging

• increased self-esteem

• a sense of shared purpose

• sharing ideas and experiences

• having a range of learning and other experiences

• friendship

• a role, or roles, to be fulfilled within the community

• a network of relationships

• a sense of identity

• the feeling of strength that belonging to a group/community gives

• support in times of difficulty

• offering support to others

This module looks at the responsibilities as well as the benefits of being a community member.

Session One: Introducing communities

Opening brainstorm (15 min)
Brainstorm the word community. Encourage learners to consider a range of communities: those related to home, work or training, to social or sports events and to local and national communities, political or pressure groups, religious and ethnic communities.

The diversity of communities the learners suggest should raise awareness of communities as being held together by interest, birth or belief and that communities may form around particular events, have a limited life or be lifelong.

Ranking (20 min)
Ask the learners to rate themselves on an imaginary line on two issues.

1. How important is community in your life?
   One end very important, the other not very important

   Ask learners at random along the line why they have selected that spot. As the learners hear each other speak they may want to change position. Give the opportunity for this. Then note each learner's position on a piece of paper.

2. How many communities do you belong to?
   One end many, the other end of the continuum very few

   Again, ask why learners have placed themselves in this way. Allow learners to re-arrange themselves along the continuum if they find they participate in more communities than they thought, or less.

Small groups (15 min)
Ask the learners to consider in small groups the benefits of belonging to communities. The groups should be prepared to feedback their ideas in a group review. They may want to prioritise any ideas which are particularly important.

Group review/discussion (30 min)
Benefits may include:
- sense of common purpose
- sense of belonging
- community offers structures for living
- morality or rules to live by
- identity
- a role within the community
- doing something for others

Test whether different communities offer different things or whether there are common gains from being in a community. Use suggestions from the first brainstorm, e.g. a football club, campaign group about a local pedestrian crossing, a church group etc.

This discussion may shade into a consideration of transferable skills and support networks, *Developing Life Skills* will be useful for these areas.

Group definition (10 min)

Ask the group to reform and to brainstorm a definition of community. A dictionary or sociology text may help. Try to reach a consensus.

Any downsides to being in a community? (15 min)

As a group brainstorm are there any disbenefits of being in a community.

Close the session by reviewing the main ideas.

Session Two: Life without communities

The focus of this session is on whether the learners believe they can function without community involvement.

Identifying personal communities (25 min)

Ask the learners to work on a piece of A1 paper, they should put themselves as a circle in the middle and then link their circle to other circles which are the communities they are involved with.

Having established the range of communities, ask the learners to then list the range of things they can gain from these involvements.

Group activity (30 min)

Ask the learners to imagine that they can no longer access communities and any of the benefits, how will they manage daily life?

The learners should work in pairs or threes to consider how life would be where there are no communities. The small groups will need to present to the whole group either a role-play or a spoken account. This is a hard activity and the trainer should check on understanding, progress and have ideas to offer the groups.

Group presentation (30 min)

As each group presents, encourage questions:

- What has been lost?
- What is life like?
- Has anything replaced a community?
- Is even communicating over e-mail and the Internet a community?

Review (15 min)

Ask the learners to summarise what they have discovered from this activity.

Session Three: Making communities work

 Trainer's notes: Introduction to Sessions Three and Four

The purpose of Sessions Three and Four is to encourage learners to see themselves as autonomous moral agents within a community (or communities) with the rights, privileges and obligations that this implies, and with the power to influence decisions and the ability to take some control over what happens to themselves and to others.

It will be necessary to demonstrate clearly through the role plays that a group or a community has a right to insist that certain basic rules are kept. If, as will be the basis of this session, the community is one of several people sharing accommodation, then no-one has a right to eat the food that someone else has bought. If this rule – presumably agreed to by everyone – is broken, some sanctions must be applied. The reason for the sanction should be stressed: the behaviour is unwanted and must not happen again. The whole group should be involved in deciding how to handle the situation without damaging the person who committed the 'crime' while still safeguarding others who behave honourably. The need here is for clear thinking and tremendous interpersonal skills from community/group members. Although the community or group that the learners concentrate on is likely to involve a fairly limited number of people the rules, behaviours, sanctions and so on might well apply to society and whole nations.

Throughout these sessions is stressed the interdependence in communities and the need for co-operation between the individuals and groups that make up a community. Human beings are 'herd animals' and, for most people the only possible life is a life led in communities with others. However, it cannot be denied that when someone transgresses a community's agreed rules, action must be taken.

This session will emphasise the importance of effective communication – being assertive, listening, questioning, finding ways to make a point. The session will emphasise the importance of joint decision-making. The next, the importance of rules.

Small groups (25 min)

Ask the learner to describe to each other experiences they have had sharing accommodation with other people. Towards the close of the time they need to have three lists.

- What is needed in shared accommodation?
- What works well in shared accommodation and why?
- What works badly and why?

Group review (10 min)

Ask the groups to offer some of their ideas. How much overlap was there between ideas and experiences?

The groups may have offered criteria for effective living together such as:

- enough bathrooms
- lockable kitchen cupboards
- clear ways to share bills

Small group rule setting – 15 minutes explanation

Now describe a house which they will share.

- 10 bedrooms most with washbasins
- a garden at front and back
- 1 parking space
- rubbish day on Tuesday
- one communal phone – not a pay phone
- a large kitchen
- a large dining room
- a large sitting room
- a TV area

- a shower room
- a bathroom
- two more WCs

Divide the group into two. Ask each group to imagine they have moved into the house and that they need to agree some rules.

- What problems have or would arise?
- What are the best ways to deal with these issues?
- What rules can they all agree on?

Write these up on the flipchart so the groups know what they are to do. Tell each group that have 20 minutes to reach a solution.

Ask two learners to be observers and give them CR1 to work on.

Ask for each group to elect a spokesperson and for this person to feed back the group's ideas.

Small group exercise (20 min)
Check on learners' progress.

Group review (30 min)
Take the two groups' ideas, write up the main points. Discuss areas of agreement and difference. Ask how each group found the exercise, encourage individuals to offer suggestions.

Then ask the two observers, what they saw and what they felt was going on. Who dominated? Who could not be bothered? Who was the peace-maker? Where was there compromise?

What have the learners gained from the session:

- perhaps the gains were about the substance of the agreed rules and as a group anticipating problems
- perhaps some of the learning was about managing the discussion as a member of a community

Extension discussion (15 min)
1. Ask the learners how they imagine the group in the house to get along. What would be the differences if two of the 10 were a couple? Why?

2. Ask the learners to consider how thinking about getting on as a group in a shared house might have parallels in living in a community. Write up these suggestions.

3. Remind the learners of the earlier brainstorms in which they considered the benefit of community and downsides to community life. How many saw rules and guidelines as a benefit and how many as a downside? How realistic would it be to live without rules?

4. Brainstorm what society would be like without rules.

5. Ask the group to consider how much rules are needed to create communities and to help structure them.

Summary (10 min)
Summarise with the group the learning points from the session and ask for a show of hands from any learners who may have changed their minds about the value of rules and agreeing rules for community life. Find out why.

Session Four: Conflict in communities

 Trainer's notes

This session asks the learners to consider conflict and why it may come about and how it may be resolved. It works by continuing to consider problems in the shared house. It emphasises the importance of developing good personal skills.

Role-plays (Explanation 15 min)

Explore with the group possible things the 'difficult tenant' may do. Suggestions could include:

- not wanting a turn in household tasks
- not entering the amount they spent on phonecalls in the house book
- helping him/herself to others' foodstuffs
- using other people's things
- going into another person's room uninvited
- getting drunk and making a major mess/noise and not being bothered to clear up/apologise

Ask the group to divide into groups of three. Ask two to work together as concerned tenant and the third to be difficult. The pair are not to be abusive to the third. The pair should review the list of group house rules and feel comfortable with having house rules. The pair should consider lots of good reasons for having such house rules. The third role player is not happy with such rules and takes on the role of the difficult tenant. This tenant should decide which 'rule' to break. Once the role-play begins this tenant should make clear to the pair who are in the kitchen or other communal area his/her unhappiness at the house rules.

The pair should decide what to do and how to manage the situation. The aim will be to resolve the issue not to have full-scale conflict.

Ask the group to rehearse their ideas and then call for volunteers.

Role-play and discussions (1 hour)

After each role-play ask the learners to remain in character. Then work through how each saw the situation:

- did anything make them more fixed in their view?
- how did each character feel that the others spoke to him/her?
- what effect did this have?
- could they see someone else's point of view?
- what would have been needed to reach a compromise?
- could a compromise have been agreed?
- why was/wasn't it?

Encourage the characters to continue to talk to each other still in role.

Ask the audience to comment on what they heard, the type of language and how the negotiation was managed. Keep a note of these ideas.

Thank the learners for their contribution.

Managing conflicts (30 min)

As a group review the scenes:

- what it felt like to be in the dispute
- why compromise may not have been reached
- why there may have been conflict
- the language used
- whether or not there was room to save face and to reach agreement

Brainstorm what the group knows about:

> **Reaching compromise**

Focus the group on:

- their feelings about compromise
- strategies for reaching a compromise

Use different colours for each series of thoughts.

Review the brainstorm and as a group select five key features for reaching compromise.

House rules to world rules (15 min)

Ask the group to look again at their list of house sharing rules and agreements. Ask how these could be changed/extended to apply to whole communities, nations or behaviours between nations. It is likely that the group will find the 'simple' house rules they invented will either be laws, civil liberties, moral obligations and rights or reflect the Ten Commandments.

Session Five: Communities and our needs

This session considers why we live together in communities and how this arrangement meets our needs.

Why communities? (10 min)

Ask the learners to brainstorm why people live in communities. Answers may include:

- company
- defence – safety
- support
- to protect the vulnerable
- to trade
- because people can't manage alone

Meeting needs (20 min)

Introduce the learners to Maslow's hierarchy of needs. Some may already be aware of this. Stress that it is only one way of looking at people but it is a widely accepted one.

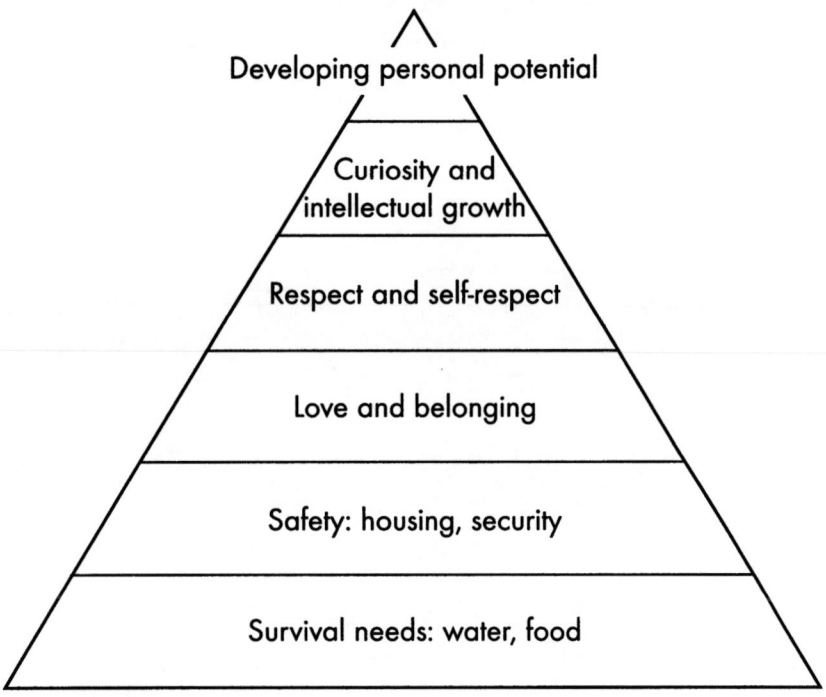

Draw the hierarchy on the flipchart or make an OHT. Ask the learners how far they think that communities meet these needs. Ask for examples of evidence to support these suggestions and write these alongside each layer.

Communities to which I belong (20 min)

Ask the learners to work alone on CR2. This asks the learner to think again of the various communities to which they belong or would like to belong. For those with limited exposure this exercise may be changed to a group review of possible communities to which individuals could belong. This group review is the second half of this 20 minute exercise.

Review the suggestion of groups and communities to which the learners may belong. Record the benefits which learners feel these groups/communities offer and how these communities could be joined.

Session Six: Conclusion

Review (15 min)

Ask the learners to each offer a gain or an interest point from the module. Add some points of your own.

Action plan (10 min)

Ask them to complete CR3, an Action Plan.

Closing Game (10 min)

Closing activity. A game such as Counting to Ten may be used.

CR2

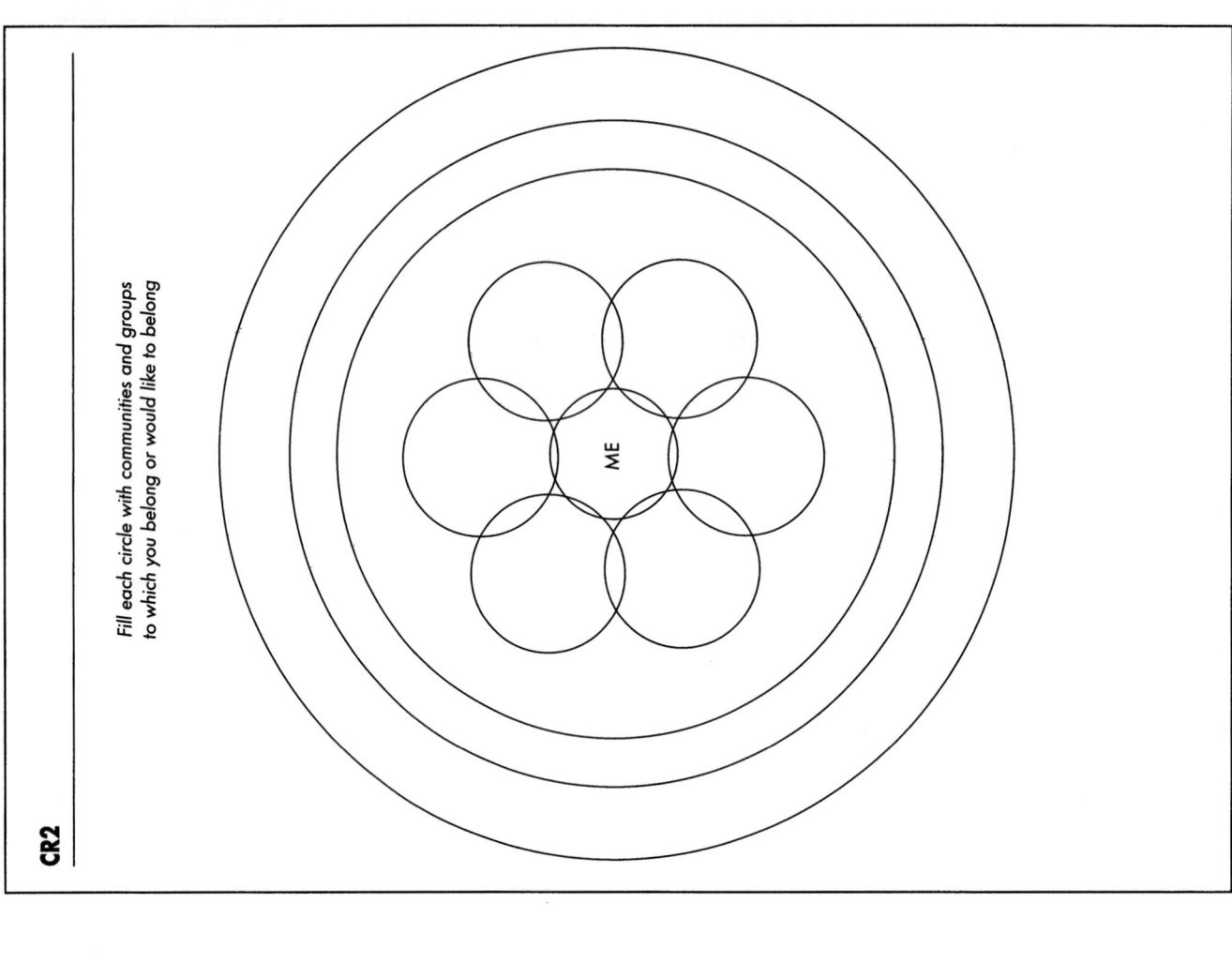

*Fill each circle with communities and groups
to which you belong or would like to belong*

ME

CR1: Observer's checklist

How much time was spent electing the group representative?

Was everyone happy?

Who started the discussion?

Who seemed to do most talking?

Who wanted to get their own way and how was this done? Was this achieved?

Who encouraged compromise?

What ideas or whose ideas were not discussed and why?

Was everyone in agreement?

CR3: my relationship with others

Write down three things community means to you:

To which communities would you like to belong?

Think about what you could gain from being in a community. Write down three benefits.

What might you need to do to make these gains?

What will you do to join these communities?

Understanding and managing emotions and feelings

 The module is divided into four main sessions. These are:

1. Introducing emotions (1 hour 30 min)
2. Emotions and responses (3 hours 45 min)
3. Reviewing and reframing (Introduction 30 min)
   Sessions as needed from:
   1. Managing anger (2 hours)
   2. Managing conflicts (3 hours)
   3. Expressing feelings (3 hours 30 min)
   4. Managing disappointments (3 hours 30 min)
   5. Using humour (2 hours)
   6. Feeling guilty (2 hours 30 min)
   7. Feeling anxious (3 hours 35 min)
4. Review and conclusions (1 hour 10 min)

It will take 6 hours 25 minutes to complete the basic programme. Additional time being needed to meet the identified needs of the group.

 The module links with others in this manual and in Developing Life Skills such as:

- Developing assertiveness skills
- Developing effective communication skills
- Developing positive attitudes
- Better self management
- Managing stress
- Managing change
- Managing time

 The module uses the training and learning styles of:

- brainstorming
- small and large group discussions
- lecturette
- role-play
- hot seating
- self-assessment

Trainer's notes

This module is intended to raise learners' awareness of:

- the role emotion and emotional responses plays in their lives
- the ways in which they can recognise their own emotions and better manage their feelings and responses
- the value which emotions and emotional responses have in other people's lives
- ways to acknowledge and appropriately express emotion
- the consequences of the mismanagement of emotional responses
- the differences between positive and negative emotions

Session One: Introducing emotions

🍎 *Trainer's notes*

This first session raises the following questions:

- What are emotions?
- Why do we have them?
- What are positive emotions?
- What are negative emotions?
- What value do emotions have in our lives?

This session uses a number of brainstorms, discussion and self-analysis exercises to help the learners consider these issues and outlines an information-giving input for the trainer to conduct.

Opening brainstorms (40 min)

1. As a group brainstorm

> **What are emotions?**

Try to cover the range of positive and negative emotions.

2. Extend this brainstorm by:
   Asking the learners to think about the differences between emotions and feelings. List these ideas on a separate sheet.

3. Ask the learners to sort the emotions they have suggested into positive and negative ones. There may be some difficulties in doing this as many emotions are situation dependent and much of what may be positive or negative depends upon how someone uses or manages their emotions. In making the list of positive and negative emotions try to draw these points out and make a note of them on the flipchart.

4. Now brainstorm:

> **Life without emotions would be ...**

If the learners get stuck use an example such as Spock from Star Trek.

Ask the learners to think about what having emotion adds to their lives. Discuss with the group whether they would rather have emotions or not have them and why this is so. List their reasons.

This activity should have sketched out some value in having and expressing emotions and feelings. It may have highlighted areas of difficulty which individuals have. These should be carefully noted. For example: problems with anger; feeling guilty a lot of the time; feeling fearful and not managing these potentially destructive negative emotions. Managing emotions is an important area for better management of social interactions and personal development and is addressed later.

Lecturette (40 min)

Trainer's note

Understanding emotions takes the learner into the world of physiology and psychology. The following notes can be used to help the learners to better understand the physical feelings and changes to their bodies, the feelings they experience and why sometimes they say they cannot control their emotions. The notes do little more than sketch some ideas. Interested trainers and learners may want to read more about the psychology of emotions in a psychology text book.

These notes cover:
- everybody has emotions
- the emotions wheel
- the biological basis of emotions
- recognition

1. Everyone has emotions

Emotions make life richer. They may give energy, they may direct behaviour, they may make a person feel all things are possible. They can also be experienced as negative or stressful, as emotions of despair, of not coping, as a sense of not being able to meet demands, make decisions or manage what needs to be done.

Psychologists, amongst others, have spent much time investigating emotions and trying to decide what causes them and what role they have. It is accepted that certain emotions are experienced by everyone whatever their age or culture and expressed in very much the same way through for example, facial expressions. Universally recognised emotions would be fear, happiness, surprise, sadness, anger and disgust.

Check with the learners whether they think this is true. To demonstrate the point use some newspaper/magazine pictures and find out which emotions the learners think are represented. Most learners should be able to agree on the emotions represented.

Why is it helpful to be able to read people's faces?

Some people are better able to 'hide' their emotions than others and may not show them facially. In some situations it is better to try to hide emotions. Ask the learners for some examples of such situations. These may include:
- at an interview appearing confident not fearful
- a friend tells of an illness/difficult personal situation and looking disgusted won't help them but trying to appear calm might
- being faced with a conflict situation and trying not to let anger/fear show to cool it down

2. Wheel of Emotion

Certain emotions are thought basic to all humans. These can be illustrated by the wheel below. (This could be made into an OHT for the group or a handout.)

Plutchik's Wheel of Emotion

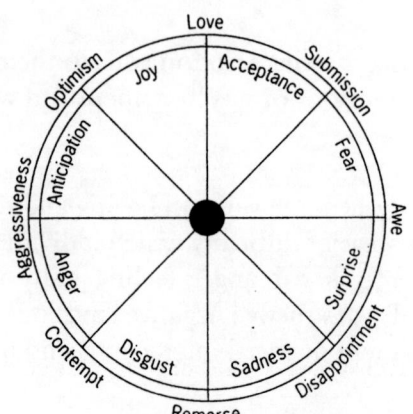

Plutchik thought there were eight basic emotions or four pairs of opposite emotions. The emotions on the outside of the circle are more complex emotions and are combinations of basic emotions.

Check how far the group agrees with Plutchik's ideas. For example

- What emotions do they think are missing?
- Are these missing emotions a combination of more basic ones?
- Does the group agree the pairs of opposites?
- Could the group agree there are eight basic emotions?

The idea of basic emotions comes from the fact that certain emotions were thought fundamental to helping people better manage situations and so helping the species to survive. So for example being able to fight or to run when under threat. Such emotions are experienced physiologically, before we are aware of them. For example the release of adrenaline into the bloodstream means a faster heart rate, dilated pupils, being able to breathe faster, not wasting energy on e.g. production of saliva or digestion. Energy is made ready for fighting or for running away.

How helpful is it to think of emotions in this way?

3. It's biological it can't be controlled

There is agreement that emotions have a physiological basis, but not agreement that all emotions have a different physiological basis. There are two main types of physiological basis to emotions, one for positive emotions and one for more negative ones.

There are changes to people's bodies as part of experiencing emotions but these physical changes are not the whole basis of emotion. People have a physical experience, skeletal or visceral. But people also know why they have certain emotions – and the feelings which goes with an emotion. These feelings may be based on things which have happened in the past and similar experiences and responses. So experiencing emotions is a complex response of body, of feeling and cognition.

A state of arousal can be misunderstood and wrongly attributed if the person does not know what it is which has caused those bodily changes. There is a tendency to think the causes are always negative ones. It is important to know why certain changes are taking place and to know what emotional responses are based on in order to not to make mistakes and so give inappropriate emotional reactions and responses to situations. People who don't care about how they behave or respond to situations, who don't care about why they feel certain feelings are more likely to make mistakes about what causes certain feelings.

Some people think that emotions are not so much out of our control:

- some people think that by assuming a smiling and confident pose and appearing as such to others that these feelings will be more likely to be experienced
- some people think expression of emotion is socially controlled. In some cultures expression of grief over a death is expected to be very noisy, public and open while in others that it should be suffered silently. People are able to behave and express their emotions in these more controlled ways. Other examples of emotional control would be phrases like "big boys don't cry" or "keeping a stiff upper lip".

4. Recognition

If emotions can be controlled, then an individual needs to recognise that a situation may cause e.g. stress, anger, disappointment. The individual needs to be aware of bodily changes, e.g. getting aroused to fight, having a faster heart beat, faster breathing and dry mouth. The individual needs to know how they have behaved in the past and what the consequences were. Having all this information will help the individual decide how best to manage an emotional response.

Check with the learners if they believe they can control their emotions. Check if they think that there are several parts to an emotion or just uncontrolled physical changes. Check what the learners thought about what has been said, what makes sense to them, what is not clear or what has not been understood.

The group may want to discuss what they found interesting or helpful or offer examples from experience which supports a point.

Take a break – try a physical game or take a coffee break after sitting still – **10 minutes**.

Session Two: Emotions and responses

Build on the first session by:

1. emphasising the importance of recognising emotional responses
2. recognising the importance of past ways of behaving

Brainstorm (10 min)

As a group try the following brainstorm:

> **Why might it be important to know how I usually respond to emotions?**

Responses may include:

- knowing I don't manage emotions well
- getting too handy with my fists if I feel angry
- not managing stress and getting drunk/drugged
- let myself get carried away with the feelings of the moment or not looking at the consequences

Small groups and large group discussion (30 min)

Ask the learners to tell each other of some occasion when they did not use or manage their emotions as well as they could or should have.

As a whole group ask for one or two of these stories to be shared. Write up the key points on the flipchart under headings such as:

- situation/event/issue
- emotion felt
- the action/reaction
- the consequences

Then explore with the group:

- alternative emotional responses or modifying the response
- alternative ways of dealing with the situation
- alternative ways of seeing the situation
- the alternative consequences there could have been

Discuss with the individual and group how easy or hard they may have found it to respond differently.

Case and consequences (1 hour)

Individual work

Give out one of the two situations (ME1a/b) and ask them to work through the sheet thinking about what emotion they would feel, how they might respond and what would happen.

In pairs

Ask the learners to discuss the situations and their responses. Ask the pairs to think of as many other ways of managing the situations as possible. Ask the learners to be sure that they understand the consequences of what they have suggested.

Whole group feedback

Ask for a couple of pairs to volunteer to share their cases and suggestions. Find out how far the rest of the group agree or what other suggestions they can make.

Group discussion (30 min)

Ask the learners to think about the characters in the situations and to suggest what sorts of things the characters may have said to themselves to increase their emotional responses or to control them. Make a list e.g.

- I'll show him
- I'm not going to be pushed around
- It's a stitch up and I'm going to get even
- I'll get him
- I'm not going to be messed about like this

Ask the group to add other examples of the ways they 'talk up' or control their emotions.

Ask the group members to rate themselves on a scale of 1 to 10 (10 highest) as to how much they 'talk up' their emotional states. Check how they rate themselves for controlling their emotions.

Are there differences? How valuable do the learners think it may be to better control themselves by talking themselves down or into a state of control.

Find some examples of statements the learners can use. List these. The learners may like to have a copy of such coping statements.

In the manner of (15 minutes)

Give out to each learner a card with an emotion on it (ME2) and ask them to walk about the room 'acting out' that emotion. Stress there should be no physical violence – shoving, punching etc.

At the close of the activity each learner should list against the other learners' names as many of the emotional states they have guessed.

Go round the room asking each learner for a name and an emotional state. Ask:

- which emotions were easy to identify and why?
- which were hard and why?
- how many found it hard to think about others' emotional states because they were preoccupied with their own feelings and performance?
- how much like real life is this situation?

Role-plays (40 min)

Ask the learners to work in pairs to small groups on one of the three situations (ME3). As a group they should consider the emotions – physical responses, feelings and awareness of the situation/past experiences and play out the scene.

Two groups should be prepared to perform their scenes.

While still in role ask the main character such questions as:

- how do you feel now?
- how were you feeling? (check both physical states and feelings)
- what other situations does this remind you of?
- are you pleased with the outcome?
- what could you have done differently?
- what was it that made you react as you did?
- what could the other character have done?

Encourage those watching to ask questions and enter the discussion. Ensure the learners are de-roled by thanking and applauding them for taking part. Ask if they have any comments to make on the character they played.

Take a break or introduce a game to further dissolve any remaining tension.

Session Three: Reviewing and reframing

Trainer's notes and re-cap (10 min)

The previous sessions have introduced emotions, why we have them and what can happen if they are not managed. The sessions have suggested that people are not victims to their emotions and that they can alter their responses or deliberately try to behave in a way opposite to how they feel. For example, smiling and appearing confident even if they feel nervous.

Recap on these points with the learners and then ask them to complete (ME4) a check-list which asks them to reflect on their emotional behaviour and to think about areas of their emotional life which they might usefully focus on.

Completing the checklists (20 min)

While the learners complete the checklists, the trainer should review their progress, ask for evidence or examples.

At the close of the exercise construct a group list of the types of emotional areas it would be useful to look at. A list of possible sessions covering different aspects of emotional life appears below.

Trainer's notes

The following sessions can all be used or a selection may be made. They deal with different aspects of emotions and managing emotions. From the previous exercises it should be clear what will best suit particular individuals and groups.

The short sessions cover:

1. Managing anger (2 hours)
2. Managing conflicts (3 hours)

3. Expressing feelings (3 hours 30 min)

4. Managing disappointments (1 hour 55 min)

5. Using humour (2 hours)

6. Feeling guilty (3 hours 15 min)

7. Feeling anxious (5 hours 25 min)

1. MANAGING ANGER

Working alone (15 min)

Ask the learners to list (use ME5) the things or situations which often make them angry. This may need to be kick-started with a group brainstorm. Examples might include:

- someone not paying back what they borrow
- someone pushing in front in a queue
- a partner breaking a promise
- being put-down
- having too much to do and not knowing where to start
- feeling taken for granted
- not being listened to
- their own behaviour

Check on the learners' progress, then tell them to complete the other two columns.

In pairs/threes (20 min)

Learners should share their lists in pairs or threes, gathering as many suggestions from each other to complete the column of things they can do to avoid getting angry.

Group sharing (15 min)

Ask for some volunteers to share examples of situations or events which make them angry. As a group brainstorm the ways in which the person's anger could be better managed.

Brainstorm (20 min)

What strategies can be taken to better manage angry feelings?

The list might include:

- learning to be more assertive – telling someone how you feel and why you feel like this and not just sitting on feelings and then exploding
- learning about your feelings, why you have them and how best to express feelings
- acknowledging feelings of upset, disappointment, annoyance, anger etc. are all normal ones and learning how to explain them to others
- planning time/money so you don't get into difficulties, get stressed and take it out on others
- taking exercise, taking a break, thinking about other things or other people to get a different perspective

- waiting to speak to someone until you have a cooler head etc.
- knowing that feelings change with time
- learning how to talk things through with others to hear their views and perspectives

Role-play (40 min)

Ask the group to work in pairs/threes. There are no prepared scenarios for this role-play. Each pair/three will need to select a situation which makes one of the group angry. That person who is angered by a certain situation should role-play that situation but try to use some of the strategies generated by the brainstorm. This needs to be handled with care. If the group member feels the task is too difficult then another group member should undertake the main part in the role-play.

One or two groups should be asked to volunteer to play out their scenarios:

- Ask the main character how it felt to behave in this new way
- Ask how it differed from usual behaviour
- Ask how this difference feels
- Ask whether it will be possible to try this in real life – and how this will be done

Thank the role players.

Summing up (10 min)

Ask each learner to complete ME6. Then go round the group asking for one item from each person's sheet.

2. AVOIDING CONFLICTS

Working alone: getting into conflict (10 min)

Ask the learners to work on ME7.

Getting into conflict

Ranking (20 min)

Ask the learners to spread themselves along an imaginary line depending on whether they feel they get into a lot of conflict or very little. Care should be taken to make no comments and not to allow other learners to comment on the positions which others assume. The learners are very exposed in adopting their positions.

Definitions

Ask several learners for some definitions of conflict and reasons for why they have placed themselves on the line at that point. Write up some of their ideas about what is conflict. Ask the learners to re-arrange themselves along the line, should they wish to, having heard the discussions and definitions.

Group discussion (30 min)

Use the headings on ME7 and go through each asking the group to share ideas. Record these on flipchart. As each list is produced try to find common patterns. These could include:

1. Common situations for conflict, e.g. relationships; money; feeling put down. Are there particular triggers?

2. Common groups of people who spark conflict, e.g. always with people in authority; with people they know they will win against. Are there particular groups?

3. Try to draw out any physical signs or particular feelings experienced by the learners prior to them getting into conflict. Are there any signs which may serve as indicators of conflict or warning signs?

4. Explore the ideas of winning and losing and their associated feelings. Does winning always make them feel positive? What emotions do they experience?

5. Explore what effect getting into conflict has on their interactions with others. Is a tendency to get into conflict situations something to work on to prevent future conflicts? Why? Is it something to be proud of? Is it something to ignore? What are the consequences of ignoring it?
   i) Review the common features of conflict. Ask the learners to write down any which apply to them. Explain that it is important for them to know what triggers conflict situations in order for them to manage it better.
   ii) Try to bring the group to a consensus position that conflict is not a good thing and managing it is useful.

Brainstorm (10 min)

Brainstorm the possible gains from better management of conflict. These could include:
- feel better about self
- have more self-control
- better relationships with partner
- able to get on better with workmates
- get on better with people in authority
- better relationships with my family
- able to keep a job for longer
- fewer fights
- not have the reputation of difficult or a fighter
- don't feel so negative
- don't feel so stressed all the time
- not so exhausted from always battling with others
- not always looking for people putting me down, putting my back up etc.

Strategies for diffusing conflict (20 min)

From the positive starting point of wanting to better manage conflict ask the learners to work in pairs/threes and to think of occasions when they or someone else stopped conflict from escalating. As they tell the stories ask them to list the ways conflict was stopped or at least did not escalate.

Encourage the groups to add to their lists and to be ready to share them. They should try to prioritise the five best ideas for 'cooling conflict'.

Feedback and review: cooling conflict (30 min)

Ask for each group's top five strategies. List these – tick or star those most frequently mentioned. Ask for additional ideas.

Suggestions could include:

- taking time out – "we'll talk about this later"; "I need to think this through"; "why not talk to me when you've had time to cool down a bit"; "let's get a coffee"

- backing away from a conflict – possible violence, abuse or just an ugly scene. "I need a break from this"; "I don't want to get involved in this right now"; "I think you're being unfair"; "I'm not going to fight over this – where's a compromise"; "this is getting needlessly ugly"

- sticking to your guns or broken record technique – just keep repeating your point and not being bullied or drawn. If your point's not getting across then back away/ take a break

- being clear – saying no, saying yes, saying what you mean. Assertively saying what you want, need or feel and then walking away from the situation until you can be heard properly

- not being intimidated/threatened – behaving as if you're cool or confident, a smile not a fearful look

- suggesting a compromise or another way to deal with the situation

- try to solve the problem jointly

- saying that you have heard what the person is saying and can understand their point of view but that your position is ... because ...

- going into or staying in a conflict situation only if you are in control of yourself

- explaining why something has happened – sticking to the facts, being rational and truthful

- asking the person not to shout, swear, threaten, put you under pressure etc.

- suggest a solution will be found more quickly if, for example, the other person modifies his/her behaviour

- accept another person has a different point of view or other feelings, acknowledge these as being as real and as valuable as yours

- don't back someone else into a corner or an argument

- don't shout, don't use abusive language, don't make personal comments or be personally critical

- don't be negative about everything the other person says

- be positive about yourself before and during the conflict – repeat coping self-statements to yourself – "I won't give in"; "My point's just as important"; "I won't be pushed about" "this is important to me and I need to sort it"

Role-plays (30 min)

Put the group into two lines facing one another. In these pairs the learners should work out a potential conflict situation. Give them a situation, tell them to work out the script with one of the two trying to cool the conflict presented by the other role player. Suggested situations:

- taking a faulty item back to a shop

- damage to a car in the car park

- a work-mate blaming you for something he/she has done

- being over-charged in front of your mates and the shop assistant denying it

- being accused by a work-mate/co-resident of having stolen an item of food/clothing

Remind the pairs no physical contact and to moderate language. The aim is to cool the conflict not have full-scale battle.

Allow the role-plays to run for five minutes. Ask the pairs to stop. Tell everyone to sit down, select a few of the pairs and ask them to remain in role.

Ask one in the pair to describe the situation as it seems to them:

- what their part has been
- how the situation is developing
- what it feels like
- what they hope the outcome will be
- what emotions are involved

Go through the same sorts of questions with the other character in the pair. Invite the audience to ask questions and encourage a dialogue between the two characters.

Try to lead the two to a compromise; let them work out the details and ask them what it feels like. Ask them to compare this situation and their current emotions and feelings with those they felt earlier on.

If appropriate, work through a couple more role-plays. Ensure each pair is properly de-rolled at the close of its hot seating. Applaud and thank all those who took part.

Group review (15 min)
How did it feel to watch the role-plays and questions? What was the group's view of the role-play exercise? Was it useful to practice trying to cool the situation? What cooling strategies seemed most effective?

Individual review (10 min)
Ask the learners to use ME8, ask them to complete the planning boxes. Check on progress.

Closing round (5 min)
Ask each in turn to suggest one thing they have learned or gained from the session.

I have learned ...

I have gained ...

Ask the group to applaud itself for managing a taxing learning session.

3. EXPRESSING FEELINGS

 Trainer's notes

Engaging the learners in thinking about expressing their feelings is important for the following five reasons:

1. Many may not have the words to do so and many may feel that talking about feelings is 'soft' or 'sissy'. Some may hide feelings, push their own feelings or those of others aside or may let feelings out inappropriately

2. Expressing feelings may help learners to realise that others share similar feelings, that they are not alone

3. Expressing feelings is some of what binds people together in a situation or over an event. It helps break down isolation and helps to normalise situations and experiences

4. Learning what and how to express feelings may help the learners to avoid conflict

87

5. Expressing feelings helps the learners to distinguish between what is thought and what is feeling. This helps the learners to develop some perspective and to see things from others' points of view.

These are explored in the activities in this session. These five good reasons should be used at the close of the session to review with the learners why expressing feelings is of value to them.

Opening session: self assessment (20 min)

Ask the learners to work with the choice cards ME9. To select ones which apply to them or with which they agree.

Ask them to compare their pile of cards with another's and decide what conclusions can they draw about themselves?

- Do they show emotion?
- Do they manage emotions?
- Do they hide emotions?
- How might they like to manage their feelings in the future?

Group review (15 min)

What has been discovered? What surprises were there? How might members of the group like to manage their feelings?

Continuum (20 min)

Run a continuum with at one end having and expressing feelings as very important and at the other as not very important.

Ask the learners to place themselves according to their opinion. Ask for volunteers to explain why they have selected that position and to give some examples of why emotions are or are not important. Make some notes of what is said. Allow the learners to change positions if they wish.

Brainstorm (30 min)

Recap on some of the key ideas and then run two brainstorms as a whole group.

> **What are the benefits of showing feelings?**

> **What might be the disadvantages of showing feelings?**

These brainstorms will be revealing of many held prejudices and habits. Some may need to be challenged – but carefully. For example, "showing feelings is soft". Test the learners about what happens if feelings are not expressed. These may be issues about exploding with pent-up feelings or not communicating properly with a partner.

Some of the five key reasons outlined in the Tutor's Notes can be woven into this section.

I think, I feel (30 min)

Tutor's notes

Sometimes people do not express their feelings and do not say how and why they feel as they do but offer something which sounds more thought out or dispassionate. If people were more clear about what they felt they may on some occasions be more clear about what they really think or more able to make decisions.

As a group
Explore the differences between thinking and feeling with the learners. Ask for some to volunteer examples of occasions when they have said I think ... when really they meant I feel ...

The following example may help:
I think you don't spend enough time with me – could be translated into:
I feel undervalued, and that you do not think about me. I feel that you just take me for granted. I feel that you put everyone else above me.

Saying these I feel ... statements may present the speaker and listener with a lot of uncomfortable issues to tackle. It may be emotionally easier not to admit to feeling various things and to just make a simple I think ... statement.

It is also easier to make an I think ... statement to those who do not take feelings seriously, either their own or other people's feelings.

In pairs
Ask the learners to work in pairs to generate six examples of 'I think ...' statements which may really be about a set of feelings. They will need to then translate the 'I think ...' into 'I feel ...' statements.

As a group
Review these examples. Write them on the flipchart. Check if there are several which cover similar areas and explore why this may be so.

Brainstorming (10 min)

Brainstorm:

> **When do people use 'I think' ... rather than saying 'I feel' ...**

Role-play (45 min)

Ask the learners to work in pairs. To pick an ordinary domestic, work or relationship situation and to play:

i) a character who only wants to make I think... statements and to not engage in showing or exploring feelings

ii) the other character who is prepared to say both what they think and what they feel

This may be hard and some ideas of possible situations could be brainstormed before the pairs begin.

Allow ten minutes for the role-plays to be worked out and then ask for a couple of pairs to volunteer their scene.

After each role-play ask the characters still in role:

- to describe the situation as they see it
- to describe how it feels to be confronting the other character with their very different style
- to say whether they think the other character is right in what they are saying – or if they can agree with anything
- whether they would like to change their way of behaving, how and what would help

Thank the characters for taking on difficult roles. Applaud their work.

Review (20 min)

What comments would the group make about the role-plays? What lessons can be learned to improve communication?

Would any of those characters blocking emotions have given in? What would have helped them?

How might those discussing their emotions have got their points across more effectively?

Remind the group of some key communication strategies:

- being assertive – having equal rights to be heard
- planning what to say
- rehearsing what to say – visualising a conversation
- knowing what you will compromise over before you start the conversation
- using coping statements
- using breaks and time out

When might you not show your feelings? (10 min)

Run a brainstorm with the group on when feelings might not be shown. Examples might be when:

- it will unnecessarily hurt someone's feelings
- when it will undermine someone else for no good reason
- when it is possible to still reach the same outcome but without hurting/undermining someone
- when you need time to think about what you really feel rather than a quick reaction

Close (10 min)

Ask each learner to suggest something they have learned or will try in better managing and expressing their feelings.

4. MANAGING DISAPPOINTMENT

 Trainer's notes

Disappointment is a negative state to experience:

- plans and hopes are frustrated
- energy may be low
- someone else may be found to be blamed for things going wrong and this can spoil relationships
- confidence may be low
- there may seem little to live for

The disappointed person may take out his/her feelings on others around him/her or may become quiet or retreat from others. The ways in which disappointment is managed will have consequences for social relationships.

The reasons something is understood to be disappointing will also have consequences for social relationships. For example, disappointment may not be a reasonable response. It may be wrong simply to expect others to do what you want. It is not be reasonable to be disappointed at someone because you did not tell someone what you wanted or felt.

This session helps learners come to greater awareness of:

- how they manage disappointment
- why they may experience disappointment
- the ways in which disappointment affects their relationship with others
- how they can better manage disappointments and how they may seek to avoid disappointment

Introductory activities

Opening brainstorms (30 min)

1. Ask the learners to brainstorm as many ideas, thoughts and feelings as possible about disappointment. They should work in small groups for ten minutes.

2. As a larger group, pool these ideas.

What is disappointment?

Categorise these ideas as e.g.:

- Feelings about disappointment
- Causes of disappointment
- Effects of disappointment on self
- Effects of managing disappointment on others

3. Find any commonalities amongst the learners in e.g.
   causes of disappointment
   - not getting a job
   - relationship difficulties
   - not being listened to

   or in managing disappointments
   - getting in a temper
   - ignoring others
   - taking it out on others

4. Ensure that the differences between disappointments and tragedies are explored. Ensure that there is a sound working definition of disappointment. That disappointment:
   - is based on expectations and hopes
   - may be the result of reasonable or unreasonable expectations
   - that some disappointments may be preventable if people are more aware of events around them, e.g. things which lead to the breakdown of a relationship
   - that we can have a role in creating our own disappointments

Introduce the content of the session (10 min)

Explore with the learners some of the key areas of this session. That it is about:

- looking at their role in causing and managing disappointments
- looking at the ways in which better managing disappointment will improve relationships with others
- looking at what may be reasonable and the ways in which events may be interpreted.

Tell the learners that they will be thinking about disappointment in the ways they relate to others and best manage themselves.

In pairs (15 min)

Ask the learners to work in pairs to discuss what can happen when they are disappointed. They can swap stories about events or can just think of life episodes and list out what happens.

Ask the learners to work with their list and think about the consequences of their behaviour for other people and for their relationships with them. ME10 should help structure this activity.

Check on the progress of the pairs.

The spirals of disappointment (25 min)

As a group look at the handout ME11 and complete one example on the flipchart. Ask for a volunteer to supply the ideas. Starting at the widest point of the spiral note the initial disappointment and its causes and then the subsequent feelings, actions and their effects.

Link the discussion about managing disappointment into discussions about self-esteem, developing or diminishing feelings of confidence, getting on well with others, being assertive etc. There are ways in which one disappointment can lead to another. For example, deciding because one interview led to a rejection not to go to another ensures that a person does not get that job and the person can then feel low in self-confidence and self-esteem and feel bad about his/her future projects.

Ask the learners to work on their own spiral. The purpose is to demonstrate to the learners the ways in which events are linked.

Halting the spiral (25 min)

As a whole group work on the original example on the flipchart and decide where the downward spiral could be halted or reversed.

- What feelings could be better managed and how could this be done?
- How could the person try to do something differently?
- How could the person try to look at the situation differently?
- What should be done to stop further disappointments and their consequences?

Ask the learners to look at their own spirals alone or in pairs and decide how they could stop the downward spiral and disappointment.

Group review (15 min)

Consolidate work on the disappointment spirals with a group review of the strategies to halt or better manage disappointment. Examples of such strategies may include:

- phoning to find out why you did not get the job/training place and learning from what is said, e.g. going for a lower level job, doing volunteering to get relevant experience, practising how to do interviews
- finding out why someone made a decision you did not like, discovering that you had not expressed your views or ideas and that you could do so earlier on next time
- taking a more philosophical view "that's life" but not letting one knock stop you from trying again
- using coping self-statements
- discussing the situation with other people to get a broader sense of perspective

Depending on the group members there may be many different faiths and belief systems represented in the group. It will be worthwhile and interesting for the learners to discover how different faiths or belief systems manage disappointments.

Reasonable or unreasonable? (20 min)

Disappointments may arise because expectations are unreasonable. For example, that a certain job or person may be attainable. Expectations may be based on fantasy rather than a realistic understanding of the situation.

1. Discuss with the group the differences between reasonable and unreasonable. Ask the group to brainstorm the two definitions and to offer some examples of unreasonable and reasonable expectations.

2. Discuss with the group why reasonable and unreasonable are important issues when thinking about disappointment and managing disappointment.

3. Ask the group to work in pairs and to think of three examples of unreasonable expectations and disappointments and disappointments based on a reasonable expectations.

4. Share these examples with the whole group. Work out the consequences and the management of a few disappointments based on reasonable expectations and a few based on unreasonable expectations. Are there any differences in handling feelings of disappointment depending on whether expectations were reasonable or unreasonable in the first place?

Role-plays and hot seating (45 min)

The following exercise asks learners to explore and manage a disappointment. The objectives will be:

- to consider the reasonableness of expectations and hopes
- to think about the ways a disappointment may be better managed
- to consider the consequences of responses and behaviour

There are some examples of situations on ME12.

Ask the learners to work in threes with one situation. They should discuss it considering the points above. They should rehearse their scene and then to be ready to volunteer to perform it.

Ask for one or two scenes to be performed. After each one, keep the learners in role and explore a number of questions of the main character:

- describe the disappointment
- how do you feel about it?
- why has it happened/what should have happened in your view?
- are you pleased by the way you reacted?
- what else could you have done?
- do you think it was reasonable to expect what you did?
- do others think your responses are reasonable?
- how do you think others are feeling about what you are doing?

Check how the other characters feel about the disappointment, the responses to it and the ways their lives have been affected by the character's behaviour. How do they feel? What behaviour would they have preferred?

How does the main disappointed character feel about what they hear?

Allow some conversation between the characters to take place and resolve the situation if that is appropriate.

Ensure that there is a de-roling through applause and thanking the learners for a difficult role-play.

Take a break or introduce a game (10 min)

Group review (15 min)

Review the whole session with the group. Move from what had been gained from the recent role-plays and what they had learned to the other issues. Either run this session by asking for each learner to think of an important interesting or useful issue which had been covered or ask the learners to prepare in groups of three, four or so key findings from the whole session.

Thank the learners for attending and working on a difficult issue.

5. USING HUMOUR

 Trainer's notes

Humour has a role in helping people in social situations to work together, to cope with tense or difficult situations, to manage disappointments and to help them to cope with their own moods and feelings.

Expressing humour and feeling humorous is a positive feeling with beneficial effects. Smiling and laughter release tensions and help other people as well as yourself feel more relaxed.

Opening brainstorms (30 min)

1. Ask the group what they understand by humour. Run as a brainstorm to try to reach ideas about common features of humour and to reach an agreed definition.

2. Brainstorm:

> **How can humour help in relationships?**

Humour may:
- help get a sense of fun or lightness
- help get a sense of proportion
- bind people together in a situation
- create a sense of identity
- help people to see other sides of you – a childish side, a fun side, an approachable side
- help a group think about problems in other ways

3.

> **How may using humour upset/damage relationships?**

Humour may:
- upset people if used as an attack
- allow people to be racist, sexist, homophobic etc. under the cover of saying things as "just a bit of fun"
- be mocking and damaging
- lead people to think you do not take them seriously

In pairs (10 min)

Ask the learners to think about the
- types of humour they use in relationships
- the sorts of situations in which humour can be used and its effects

Ask the pairs to be prepared to share their ideas with the group.

Review (10 min)

Work through the ideas so far and summarise what has been discovered about humour. It can:

- *help bind people together:*
  - a common experience laughed about and re-told later
  - a difficult situation can be made funny at the time by seeing the ridiculous side
  - people can have shared jokes about events or other people – nicknames for colleagues etc. This however needs to be policed to ensure that it does not become bullying or undermining of others

- *help people to see each other in different ways* – as more approachable, more human, as easier to get along with. Examples might be a boss, or on joining a new group

- *help people to see other sides of a problem/situation*

- *help people to talk about things they find difficult*

- *help people to feel more confident* if they get others to laugh

- *help an individual see themselves in a different way*, self-mocking or to recognise they are over-serious

Brainstorming inappropriate humour (30 min)

Ask the group:
- when they would not use humour
- who they would not use humour with
- what types of humour they would not use
- what they would not joke about

Run this as four brainstorms. Try to seek a consensus view at the end of all four brainstorms to each issue.

Role-play (30 min)

Ask the learners to work in small groups on a role-play with the title 'A joke backfires'. There is no situation given, they will need to invent a situation and characters to explore humour going wrong.

Ask for volunteers to play their scene and discuss with the characters while they are still in role:
- the type of humour which was used
- what its intentions were
- why it went wrong
- the effects of what happened on all the characters – how did they feel? what might happen next?

Thank the learners for their role-plays.

Review (10 min)

Remind the group of the positive as well as negative role of humour in relationships.

6. UNDERSTANDING AND MANAGING GUILT

 Trainer's notes

Guilt is a most destructive emotion to experience. Guilt may be: self-imposed and it may be justified, or not; it may be imposed by others, "if you really loved me then ..."; or it may be something which society expects people to feel and may be "reasonable". Guilt is a difficult emotion to manage, it is sometimes hard to define, hard to share and within a relationship can play a very destructive role.

Guilt should be an area open to lively debate by the learners. There may be few agreements or resolutions. Guilt is something which needs to be explored because it impacts on the ways we conduct our lives, the ways we may try to manipulate or manage others and it is an emotional state we can become trapped within. Guilt can stop us doing what we want, stop us changing, and cause us to punish ourselves. Guilt can trap people into living in the past, making the future unbearable and the present a time of upset and reliving the past. Trying to understand what guilt is can be a key to unlocking set behaviours, attitudes and depressions.

The health warning applies to this as other modules. This is an awareness raising opportunity and a time for debate. It is not counselling. It is not a chance for individuals to deeply explore issues and seek to feel better. Appropriate support and referrals need to be available to support using these modules. Any learners who appear to be suffering should be spoken with on a one-to-one basis and referred to appropriate help.

Opening activities (25 min)

1. Introduce the session as an opportunity to think about guilt. It is a session to try to define what it is and what effect it may have on people's lives. Explain that this is not a session to look at individual problems.

2. Ask the group to work in small groups to try to define guilt. Ask them to record their ideas as a spider diagram and to consider:
   - what guilt may feel like
   - what happens if someone feels guilty
   - how guilt is used
   - what might cause guilt

   Check on progress of each group.

3. Whole group brainstorming of these issues. Again arrange responses as a spider diagram.

   Don't be critical or moralise about the learners' views of guilt or what may provoke guilt. There may be no clear-cut issues but the brainstorm will have opened up some issues.

Definitions and opening thoughts (15 min)

Guilt can be defined as:

   • the fact of having committed a specific 'offence' or act or having intended to

   • it is also the mental obsession with the idea of having done wrong

So, it may be a fact that someone has done something, or it may be that they feel they have done something or that they may actually be feeling remorse about having done something.

Discuss with the group why it is hard to define guilt. Is it hard because it may be breaching a personal standard? Are there absolute rights or wrongs? Can you be guilty for only thinking something rather than doing something?

Ask the group, and then list, what questions are raised in trying to define guilt. These questions will be referred to again in these sessions.

These may include:
- is feeling guilty damaging?
- what is the purpose of guilt?
- how long should it last?
- should people feel guilty?
- should you encourage others to feel guilt?
- how do you stop feeling guilty?
- is guilt a good thing?
- how do different religions think about guilt?

Stories (20 min)

If appropriate ask the learners to work in pairs or threes and to swap stories of occasions they have felt guilty or been with people who have. They can always make use of the 'fictional friend'.

Encourage a whole group-sharing of any of these stories and try to pull out any main ideas which help with the problem of defining guilt.

What problems can guilt cause? (15 min)

Ask the group to suggest problems which people may have with guilt. Ensure it is phrased so that they can talk in general terms and not feel they have to talk about themselves. List the responses.

What value may guilt have? (15 min)

Ask the group to consider some of the positives about the experiencing of guilt. Again list the responses.

Case studies (1 hour)

Ask the learners to work in small groups with ME13 and ME14. They are two case studies with one person feeling guilty and another not. The group should be asked to work on the two situations and be prepared to present their ideas to the whole group.

Whole group review. What were the common ideas between the small groups? What suggestions did they have for what should happen next? Did they feel more sympathetic to George or Mark? Why was this so? Ask the group as a whole to draw up three steps which George should take and three steps which Mark should take.

Would it have made any difference to their answers if George or Mark had been women?

Being guilty – what happens? (30 min)

Some people experience excessive guilt feelings over things which now do not matter, when the time for making the situation better or making reparation has gone (like George).

Work on an action plan with the group to decide how guilt feelings could be managed.

Questions the group might want to consider are:
- is the guilt reasonable?
- is the guilt created by someone else?
- did the person want to do the things he/she did? Does that make a difference?
- does on-going punishment help anyone?
- what practical things could be done?

Clearly the types of questions the learners may ask will be driven by the type of event which may lead someone to feel guilty. Some examples of cases can be taken from newspaper cuttings or made up events, e.g.

- unmarried 14 year old mother leaves new born on steps of church
- the murderer of three primary children laughs in court
- Francis told his best friend that he had been having an affair and really wanted to leave his wife whom he had never loved

Review (20 min)

Work back though the earlier exercises. Those, e.g. defining guilt, looking at the benefits and minuses of feeling guilty.

Emphasise the importance of moving on, of learning from the past and of owning your own guilt. Discuss the importance of not letting others impose guilt on you and the importance of making reparation but not living in a state of permanent state of self-punishment.

Thank the group and close the session with some activity, e.g. Shaking the Demon.

7. FEELING ANXIOUS

 Trainer's notes

Some people experience incapacitating panic attacks and severe anxiety. They do need to receive proper attention and advice. The following suggestions and exercises will help those experiencing less acute anxiety or irregular bursts of anxiety.

This session will link to some of the work on physiological changes and emotions and most naturally links to work on relaxation, meditation, time and leisure planning.

Ensure that the trainer has information on any local self-help groups and GP services available.

Opening exercise (20 min)

Explain the session will be about anxiety and ask the learners to consider how anxious they typically feel and to rank themselves on ME15. They should reflect quietly and try to complete boxes 1-3 on the sheet.

Group brainstorm (20 min)

Ask the group to work with you to build up a spider diagram of anxiety. e.g.

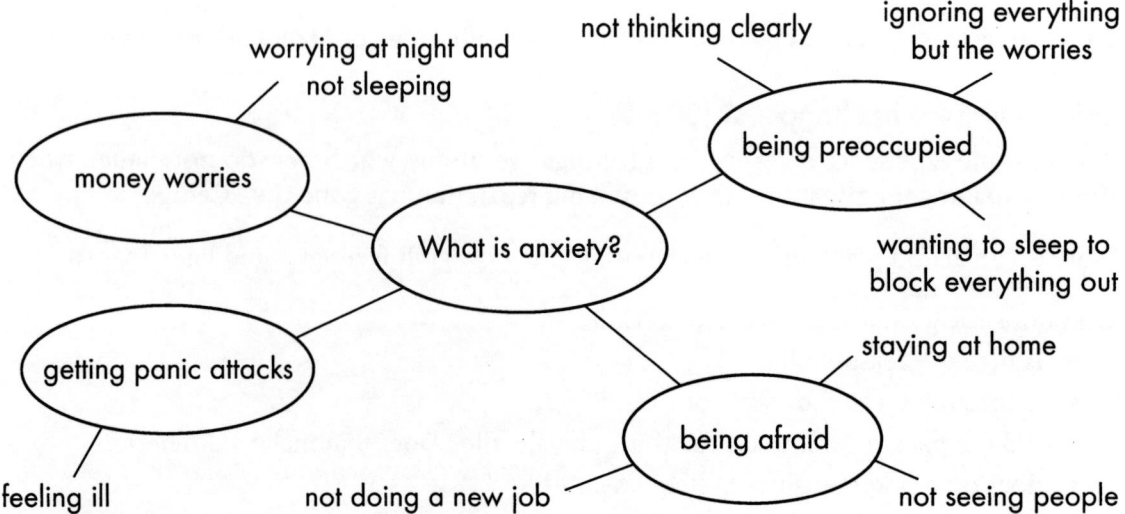

Try to cover the following areas:

- physical symptoms
- feelings about self
- feelings about others
- triggers of anxiety
- effects of anxiety
- whether it's always there or comes and goes

Don't challenge anything offered in the brainstorm but ask for clarifications or more ideas as appropriate.

Ask the group to review the completed brainstorm. Is there anything they want to add? Is there anything which has surprised them? Are there any comments common to many or a few of the areas?

Lecture – what is anxiety? (40 min)

Work from these notes to give a short talk. Draw the vicious cycles on OHTs/flipcharts paper. These notes look at four areas.

Anxiety has at least four dimensions:

- physical symptoms e.g. sweating, overbreathing;
- unpleasant mental anxiety e.g. recurring thoughts;
- avoidance, e.g. not doing things because they seem frightening;
- avoiding situations, people and experiences only makes them worse

1. Physical experiences of anxiety

Unpleasant physical symptoms and sensations can be experienced, e.g. dry mouth, blurred vision, palpitations, shakiness, chest pains, feeling hot/cold, dizziness, feeling light-headed.

Anxiety makes people ready for flight or to fight. This is useful if there is real physical danger but not if there is none. Because the release of adrenaline makes:

- People breathe faster, to get more oxygen to their muscles. This makes people feel giddy and short of breath because there is too rich a mix of air in lungs and blood
- The heart and lungs work faster, causing pounding of the heart, it may make people sweat to cool the body. This makes people cold. It can lead to draining the blood from the skin which can cause muscles to tense.

Adrenaline released but not needed makes the body tired and exhausted and can leave muscles feeling tense and even lead people to feel shaky.

It is important to exercise to get rid of the ill-effects of extra adrenaline in the body and then to find ways to properly relax, slow breathing and relax the muscles, e.g. relaxation exercises, meditation, soaking in a bath, listening to music etc.

2. Mental experiences of anxiety

Feeling vulnerable and anxious leads people to:

- interpret often minor things as dreadful and as part of a never ending cycle of doom
- fixate on certain worries and to go over and over them thinking that will all get worse
- imagine the worst in any situation. This may never happen or they may help it to happen e.g. "I'll forget what I am going to say if I have to speak to that group" or avoiding doing

something because it will be bound to go wrong. So, avoiding speaking to the group will make the person more anxious about the same or similar activity next time they are faced with it

3. Vicious cycles

The cycle of thoughts and symptoms becomes a vicious one, the unpleasant mental experience feeds fears and helps create physical symptoms as people get ready for flight or fighting. Each reinforces the other. People may get concerned about their state of health, e.g. this pounding of my heart is not natural, these pains in my chest are a heart attack; the feelings cause panic and tension and are likely to increase the heart rate or the pain and so reinforce the health concern. People may get concerned about work or domestic issues, e.g. loss of job, therefore loss of home and status; they then experience the physical symptoms of panic and anxiety which helps to reinforce their fears.

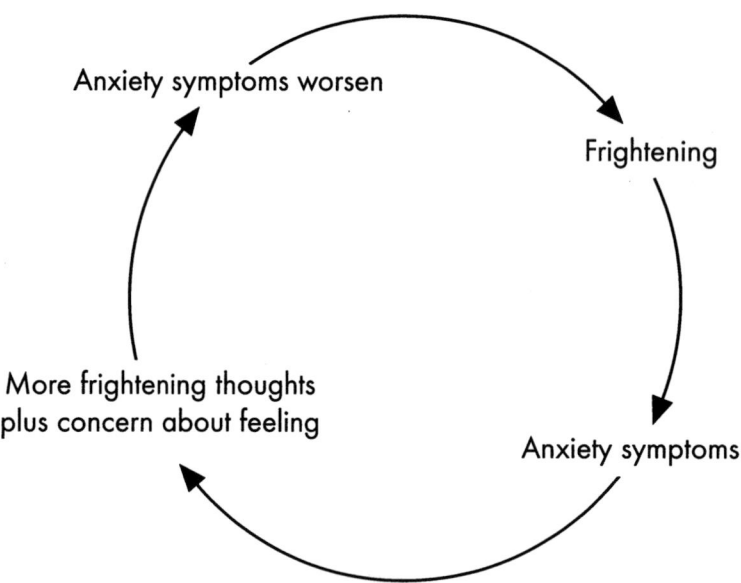

4. Avoiding situations, people and experiences only makes them worse

People can get so anxious about things they damage the quality of their lives and their life potential. They may opt to not change jobs "it's safer here", "I would fail". They may get anxious about leaving a poor, dysfunctional relationship "well no-one else would want me and I couldn't cope with the kids, money and life's knocks on my own". People may get so anxious that they withdraw from people, withdraw from public situations, e.g. ones which should be enjoyable "everyone will be looking at me" "they'll all see I'm nervous". "I'll do something stupid and they'll all laugh".

Anxious people will also avoid tackling those issues which make them anxious

- this may mean not being assertive and challenging a partner, friend or workmate's behaviour
- this may mean not looking at money problems and so letting them get worse
- not visiting a doctor to check on a possible problem

Avoiding may make people feel better in the short-term, in the longer-term it may worsen the situation and will undermine people's sense of confidence, self-worth and faith in their own abilities to solve their own problems.

The other danger of avoidance is that of becoming dependent on others. This may make them frustrated and resentful. It certainly puts the dependent individual in a low power and low esteem position within the relationship.

The avoidance vicious cycle works as do the others so:

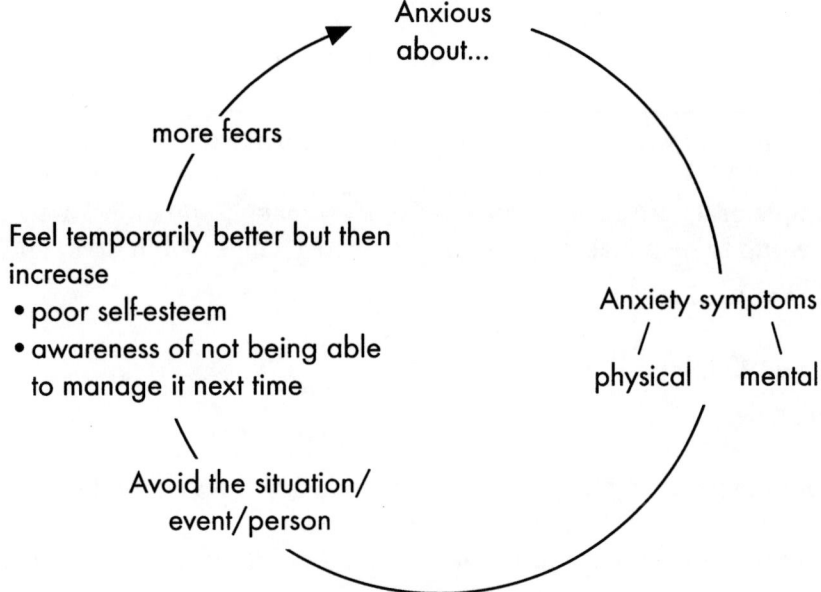

Checking on understanding (30 min)

Ensure that the lecturette has made sense to the learners by:

i) recapping on a few of the key points – use the quiz questions ME16

ii) use activity sheet ME17 to apply the ideas to their own situations

The learners should try the quiz on their own and then share their answers as a group. This will allow the trainer to check understanding and clarify any points.

The application of the ideas to personal situations should be rehearsed with the group so everyone is clear about what is required. Individual's progress will need to be checked upon.

Someone may volunteer an example of an anxiety to help the trainer draw out a cycle on the board.

Then ask the learners to work on ME18.

Making changes (40 min)

 Trainer's notes

This session will be partly a talk by the trainer, asking for examples and partly a practical relaxation session. Draw on the following suggestions.

Part of the problem is acknowledging that:

- the physical symptoms are part of anxiety
- there is probably a pattern to the symptoms
- tackling the issue may make someone feel worse in the short-term but each time an anxiety is worked on it is easier to manage
- confidence building is a slow thing
- feeling bad will be part of feeling better

In tackling anxiety there are some pointers on ME19 which can be used with the learners. The points can be added to and discussed as the group works through them.

Emphasise the importance of breaking the cycles:

- deciding to walk away from a worry will reduce it for a while, getting professional help will get it in perspective. Tackling it will give the learner greater confidence. The learner will find it probably was not as bad as he/she thought. This will help in dealing with a later anxiety.
- confronting a problem will give confidence and may change the nature of the problem

Work through a couple of the learners' examples of anxiety making situations, draw them out as cycles and ask the group to help make suggestions of where changes could occur and what changes they could be.

Practical relaxation (20 min)

Ask the learners to sit/lie.

Ask them to try not to think of anything but to concentrate only on their bodies.

Ask them to tense all the muscles from feet to face and to hold this for a few minutes.

Ask them to be aware of what this tension feels like.

Ask the learners to then relax their toes, balls of their feet, ankles, calf muscles ... up to unclenching their cheek muscles, opening and shutting their jaws etc.

Ask them to sit/lie quietly now they are physically relaxed and spend a couple of minutes thinking about a quiet place they like.

Draw the learners slowly out of the relaxation. Ask them how they feel and emphasise:

- they can do this by themselves
- they could relax in silence or with some appropriate music
- after relaxing they could quietly sit looking at an object concentrating on its detail
- to relax is to do many beneficial things for one's body, mental health and overall well-being. These include:
  - reduced heart rate and rate of breathing – the opposite effect of physical stress and anxiety
  - improved concentration
  - an improved sense of personal well-being
  - a sense of being better able to cope

Making changes (30 min)

Ask the learners to work alone on their own vicious circle diagrams (ME18). They have had some suggestions from you as trainer and from the rest of the group about ways to decrease anxiety making situations. Ask them to look at their own circles and mark in another colour things they could do to make changes. Check on progress.

Ask the learners to share their circles and to make extra suggestions for tackling anxieties.

Check all are making good progress then ask the learners to complete their own change plan (ME20).

Anxiety log (10 min)

Before closing the session review with the learners the use of and role of the Anxiety Log (ME21). Simply, the learners should use the Log to record actions they take – small target steps –

and to record how they feel and what went well. It is important that the Log is used to 'talk themselves up' and to affirm that they are trying. The end column can be used for actions they may try differently next time.

The log is their tool. They may only be able to do part of what they intended – e.g. talking to a group for the first five minutes then handing over to a workmate. The Log is to help them not to add to their anxieties by adding pressures and concerns about failure.

Closing (5 min)

Thank everyone for dealing with a difficult area of life and wish them well. Have available addresses for further help or support.

Session Four: Review and conclusions

Review (30 min)

Ask the learners to review the whole module in small groups:

- What was particularly helpful?
- What new ideas do they have?
- What areas would they like to change?
- What do they feel unsure about?

Ask each group to feedback their thoughts. Add any particular points which you as trainer found beneficial.

Discuss the ideas which have been suggested, explore why something was good. Try to answer any areas of concern.

Individual work (20 min)

Ask the learners to review notes, plans and worksheets from the sessions they have attended. Ask them to pick a few action plans or exploration of issues which they would like to use in a final action planning session.

Work with the learners as they do this. They may want to share their plans and worksheets with another in the group.

Action planning (15 min)

Ask the learners to then use an action plan sheet (ME22) and to think about how they may continue to better manage their emotions.

Some learners will need assistance with this, some may want more advice on strategies, others with agencies for referrals.

Close (5 min)

Bring the group together for a final time. Thank them for their hard work.

See any learners one to one who need additional help.

ME1a: Case and consequences One:

1. You have gone to an interview for a job which you really want. You think you have a good chance of getting it. You know you have the right skills and the right experience for the job. You've got the usual interview nerves.

Think of a couple of words to describe how you feel:

You're waiting to go into the interview and someone who's had it in for you for some time turns up for interview too. You know he knows the boss and you begin to think the situation's a stitch up.

What emotions do you feel?

How might you respond to the situation?

List the actions you might take	List their consequences

Look back at your list, how many of your actions have been driven by your emotions? List which ones.

Have you done the best thing for yourself in trying to get the job?   Yes/No

What could you have done to give yourself the best chance?

ME1b: Case and consequences Two:

2. While you were in the pub with some friends a bloke on the other table started to interfere in your conversation. He began to join in and began to make a nuisance of himself. A lot of what he did was to make jokes at your expense.

How do you feel?

What might you do?

What are the consequences of this?

Your friends tell you to ignore it. You try but it's hard. You have to drive your friends home and have stayed completely sober. As you are reversing your car out of the pub car park, the other chap who has been drinking cycles into your car.

What might you do?

What are the consequences?

Look back and decide what emotions you felt when he ran into your car. List them.

What other emotions could you have experienced?

What else could you have done?

What would the consequences have been then?

*Read through these four situations
and think how you would respond to them*

1. Your friend borrowed £100 and now seems to be denying he/she ever took it. How do you react?

2. As usual all the conversation at the pub is dominated by one person. You'd like some attention and to talk about the awful day you've had. You're feeling het up. What do you do?

3. You'd been hoping your luck would turn and you would get this job. The letter in the post this morning said you hadn't. How do you feel? What do you do?

4. Again Steve's dumped his two kids on you to look after. It's the third time this week. You know he's got problems but ... how do you react and what do you say?

Re-read your answers. If you were an outsider looking at yourself how would you describe yourself?

ME2: Acting in the manner of ...

Angry	Intimated	Sad
Accepting	Happy	Fearful
Surprised	Aggressive	Remorseful
Depressed	Miserable	Disappointed
Optimistic	Disgusted	Submissive

Cut out each emotional state/feeling and give to learners

ME5: Getting angry

1. Complete a list of things which make you angry – about six
2. Then think about each one, what is it which makes you angry and what could you do to stop this

Situations/ Events which make me angry	Why does it/what is it that makes me angry?	What could I do to stop getting angered?

ME4

Read through the statements below and ✓ any which apply to you

	✓
My life goes from crisis to crisis	
I tend not to stick up for myself	
I don't really think I've much to say that's interesting	
It's silly to talk about feelings	
I find it hard to say 'no'	
I do fly off the handle easily	
I find it hard to do things for myself	
I'm always falling in love with someone - then I get hurt	
I am quick to use my fists	
I don't really know what I feel most of the time	
It's always easier to do things for other people	
I can't pick myself up after someone dumps me	
People know not to push me too far	
Sometimes I'm just too anxious to do anything	
I don't get over knocks very easily	
I'm too scared to really try anything different	
If I'm happy I feel guilty	
People sometimes say I'm only happy when I've got a problem	
I don't show my feelings much	
I often get into arguments	

Look at the statements you have ticked.

What does this tell you about you and how you manage emotions?

ME7: Getting into conflict

List the sorts of things you get into conflict over e.g. a car parking spot; a knocked over pint; wanting to go out and your partner does not

Who do you get into conflict situations with?

Do you know when you're going to get into conflict?   Yes / No / Sometimes

What happens to you?

How do you feel?

How do you feel if you 'win'?

What does 'winning' mean to you?

How do you feel if you 'lose'?

What does 'losing' mean to you?

ME6: Action plan

Please complete the following questions

1. A key thing I know about anger is:

2. A key thing I now know about anger and me is:

3. Making changes

I intend to change the way I react to:	I am going to do this by:	I can best help myself by:

Feelings make you feel bad	I'm always told I'm over emotional	Emotions should be at home not in public	I get embarrassed about other people being emotional	I know what's going to make me angry and I back away
I hate it when people don't tell me how they feel	When you know how you feel about something it's easier to make a decision	I think I can manage my feelings	I often don't say what I feel. I just criticise people	People say I'm a wet fish
I can't talk about my feelings	Not talking about how you feel is being dishonest	I don't mind telling people how I feel	Even if someone's angry with me I like to know	I find it hard if people don't show their feelings

---

ME8: Cooling conflict

1. On a scale of 1 to 10 (with 10 highest) I would rate myself as _____ for getting into conflict
2. I think I get into conflict with:
3. The situations which cause me most bother are:
4. I would **like** to rate myself as   1   2   3   4   5   6   7   8   9   10   for not getting into conflict (1 is the lowest score)

ACTION PLAN

The Cooling Conflict strategies I want to use are:	I will apply these to... (list the people and situations by each strategy)	Other notes (who can help me and special reminders of what to do)

My target date for lowering my score is ....

Event/Reason for disappointment	How you felt	How you reacted	How others felt your disappointment

	I prefer not to think about my feelings	Showing emotions is about being weak	People say I wear my heart on my sleeve	I'm not a very emotional person
	I'm a very emotional person	How you feel is more important than anything else	I tell my kids to keep their feelings to themselves	If I don't think about my feelings then maybe they'll go away
	I keep my feelings to myself	I'll do anything not to have to talk to my partner about how we feel	I think I don't really control my feelings	I find it hard to get in touch with my feelings

ME11: The disappointment spiral

What other things happen?

What are your feelings?

How does it feel now?

Where will it end up?

ME12: Disappointment

Dave had been a caretaker at the community centre for two years. He liked his job but had been told a few times that he needed to speed up his work and not take so many breaks. Today he was told he was going to be cut down to half time as the management thought the workload was not a full-time job. Dave goes back to his family and...

Winston had agreed with his keyworker that it was time to think about moving on into his own flat. He had wanted this for some time. He had done lot of preparation - knew about managing his money, had some good ideas about making meals and had got a lot more confidence after taking a basic computer class. He had gone for an interview with a landlord and really liked a small flat by the river. He thought the interview went well, but...

Sarah had had enough. Damen just didn't pull his weight at home. She was doing everything for the kids, the home and taking a part-time training course to try to get a better job. She had told Damen enough times that he had to change. He promised but it just wasn't happening. This evening she told him....

ME14: Mark

Mark is a salesman selling medical equipment. He is away on the road for most of each week. He stays in expensive hotels because his firm pays.

He married a year ago to Sally, a girl he'd known since he was seventeen. They have a boy, Simon.

Mark says he loves Sally. He buys her something most weeks for the house or for herself.

Mark always finds someone when he is away for clubbing, dinner or for sex. Mark thinks that none of these affairs matter far much. Mostly he only sees the women a couple of times.

1. What is your view of Marks' behaviour?
2. Should he feel guilty? For what?
3. If he felt guilty what do you think he would do?
4. Do you think Sally would think he should feel guilty - why?
5. What do you think will happen to Mark and Sally - why?

ME13: George

Thirty years ago George had been left in charge of his boss' clothing shop. He had earned their trust after working well and honestly for eight years. For two years he worked hard as the manager of the shop. He increased the sales, helped all the shop assistants and always had a till that balanced.

George got himself into debt and then had to find a way to pay the debt off. He began to take from the till - small amounts, but something most days. For a few weeks he even took some stock to sell in the pub.

Thirty years later George lives alone, does not have friends, does not go out much and works in a low-paid factory job. He is working below what he could do and earns far less than he could. He has a rented bed-sit.

George suffers everyday from the guilt of what he did, and that he was caught by people who trusted him.

*   What do you think of George?
*   Do you think he should still feel guilty?
*   Why is he working in the factory?
*   How might George's life have been different?
*   What would you have done if you were George?
*   If you were now told that his bosses forgave him, paid off his debts and asked him to repay them £2 a month, what would you say?
*   Has being guilty helped George?
*   What has George given up because he felt guilty?

ME16: Understanding anxiety

1. Physical symptoms of anxiety could be?

2. When you are anxious how well do you think?
   Very well, not so well, badly.   Why is this?

3. What do people often do when they are anxious?

4. What happens when people avoid situations /people?

5. List up to 10 situations which may make some people anxious

---

ME15

Look at the triangle and write down on either side of the triangle things which cause you little, some or high anxiety.

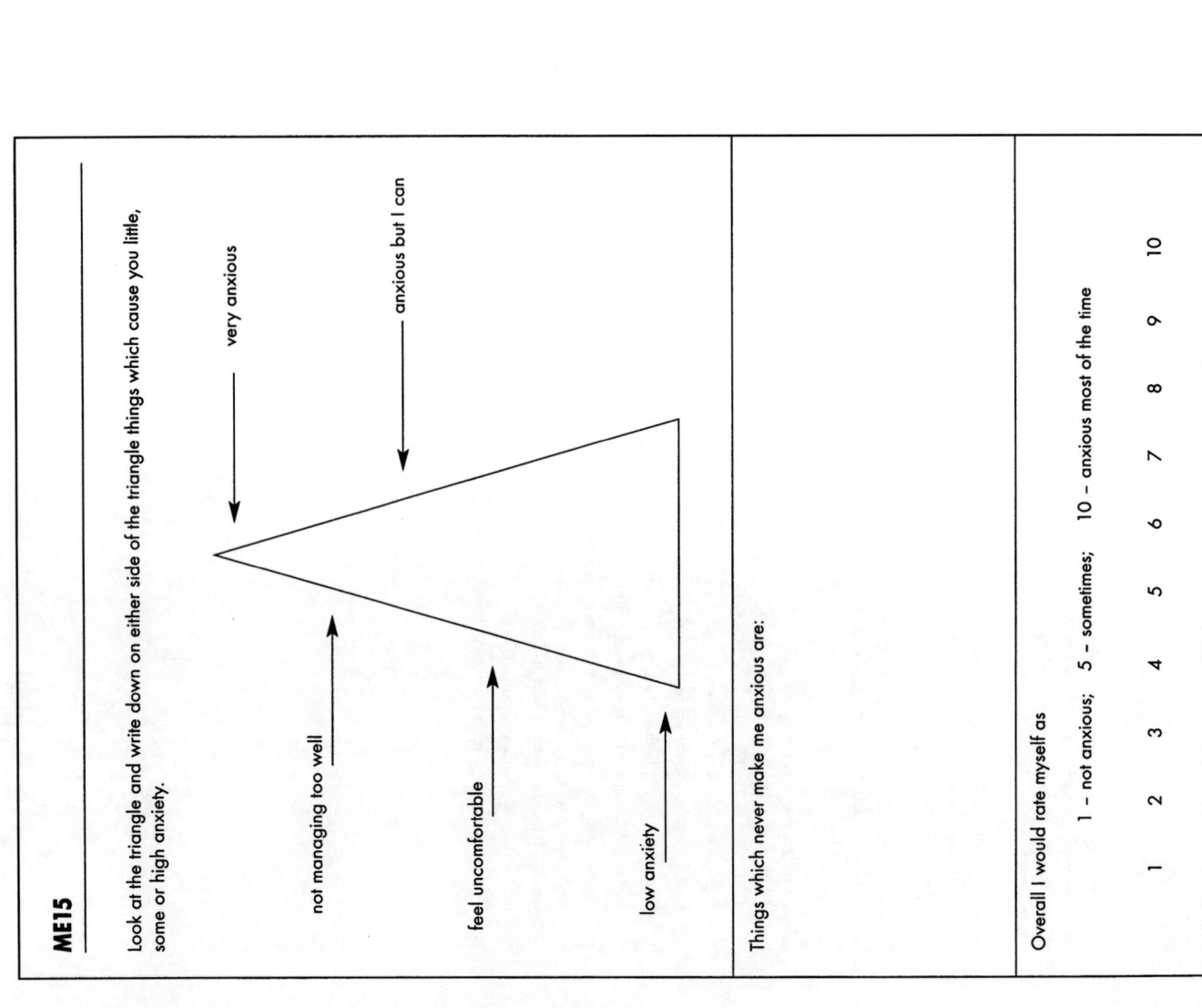

very anxious

anxious but I can

not managing too well

feel uncomfortable

low anxiety

Things which never make me anxious are:

Overall I would rate myself as

1 – not anxious;   5 – sometimes;   10 – anxious most of the time

1   2   3   4   5   6   7   8   9   10

ME18: Vicious circles of anxiety

Use Activity Sheets ME16 and ME17 to remind you of what makes you anxious and what you do. Now, pick an example and draw your own circle of anxiety. Put in as much detail as you can

---

ME17

Look at the four questions below and write a few words about each

When I am anxious I feel:

Things which make me anxious are:

People who make me anxious are:

The things I do when I am anxious are:

ME20: Change plan

The most important things for me to change are:

They make me anxious because:

I am going to:

I will do this by

Date I shall check on progress:

ME19: Getting less anxious

Things to do to make you feel better - do some or all, there is no right order.

1. Stop what you are doing/thinking and go somewhere else

2. Breathing exercises. Slow breathing and concentrate on saying to yourself one thousand as your breathe in, two thousand as you breathe out

3. Try some relaxation exercises. Lie down/sit down. Tense all your muscles from feet to face and slowly relax each part of your body

4. Accept you are anxious. Know the worst could not be as bad as you imagine. You haven't yet died from embarrassment, gone shopping and been laughed at ...

5. Decide that if you let being anxious go on then nothing will get better. Sort out a plan of action - a small step and a date to try it

6. Decide if you don't like a situation then you can leave or stop it. It's up to you to leave the pub, tell someone you'll talk about it later, say you'll ring back when you've had time to think ...

7. Slow down. Plan what you need to do and the order you will try to do it in. Reward yourself for things done. Don't beat yourself for things not done.

8. Know that everything you try which is difficult is helping you to overcome your anxieties.

9. Talk to someone about your fears and how you feel. Try to get it in perspective. Get a list of professional people who can help - CAB; GP; Debt Counsellors.

10. Plan to eat well, get enough sleep, take breaks, plan leisure time.

11. Don't self medicate – more alcohol, coffee, drugs, shopping, gambling etc. will not make problems go away even if things are better temporarily.

ME22: Better managing my feelings and emotions

Which areas would you most like to improve upon?

List your reasons why?

Now take one area and decide on several smart steps which you can take

Step	What needs to be done	Who/what can help

I will check this plan again on:

ME21: Anxiety log

Knowing what makes you anxious is half the battle.
Use this log to help you to make changes – every little you do will help in the long run

Date	Action taken	I felt:	I was pleased because:	I will:

Managing myself

 The module is divided into:

1. Introducing self-management (1 hour 50 min)
2. Self and self-management skills (1 hour 40 min)
3. Managing time and setting goals (2 hours)
4. Managing pressures and emotions (2 hours 30 min)
5. Encouraging others to see me positively (1 hour 30 min)
6. Conclusions (1 hour)

It may take 10 hours 30 minutes to complete.

 The module will touch upon issues which are covered in other modules in this manual and in *Developing Life Skills*. These include:

- time management and goal setting
- assertiveness
- developing personal support networks
- understanding and developing self-esteem
- managing emotions and feelings

The module helps learners develop some skills and to heighten their awareness so that they can become more adept at managing the ways in which they impact on others, and so the ways in which others respond to them.

 It uses:

- brainstorm
- various self-assessment exercises
- whole and small group discussions
- role-play
- hot seating

Trainer's notes

This module has been written to encourage learners to reflect upon

- their usual behaviours and patterns of response
- their reactions to situations
- the ways in which they manage their resources, such as time or personal support networks
- their presentation of themselves to others

The module seeks to encourage learners to be more conscious of the ways in which they interact with others and others respond to them. It encourages learners to consider the ways in which such reactions may be shaped by their own behaviours, responses and projections of themselves. Just as learners may negatively affect people's perceptions of them, so they can encourage positive responses. Appreciation of and developing some self-management strategies will give the learners greater control over interactions with others.

Session One: Introducing self-management

Opening brainstorm (10 min)

Brainstorm with the whole group what:

> **Managing myself**

means to them. Allow a wide range of ideas – from money management, time management, looking after health, clothing etc. through a range of more obvious aspects of effective social skills. These may include managing emotions, presenting myself well, not getting hostile but getting my point across etc.

Once the brainstorm has ranged widely ask the learners what they mean by some of their comments, ask for examples or for clarification.

Working alone (15 min)

Ask the learners to take some time on their own to look at the group brainstorm and to note any areas which they think they would like to work on in order to develop more effective self-management. This should be written on MM1.

Group review (25 min)

Ask some learners to volunteer some of the areas they would like to work on and some of their reasons. Keep a running list on the flipchart.

Ask for some learners to volunteer their hopes of the course. Again, record some of these.

MM1 should be kept so the learners can check their expectations and hopes against what they feel they have achieved. This early exercise will help them to think about what they want and will, with some tutor guidance, help them shape learning goals and focus their attention. This tutor-aided individual planning should take place early on in this module.

The group review of the key areas will help the trainer plan the module, its content and emphasis.

The group review should be used as an occasion to help steer the learners into thinking about:

- the differences between social skills and life skills
- the value of developing their life skills and using them as building blocks for their social skills development
- the importance of managing themselves in order to avoid hostile interactions or conflict and in order to promote more satisfying encounters with others
- the links between the various skills and qualities they have listed

Explain to the learners that Managing Myself will be concerned with developing *social skills* but will also demonstrate how *life skills* such as improving time management can impact on social skills and improve interactions with others.

Sorting out some key ideas (50 min)

The following four brainstorms will highlight some important ideas.

1.

> **List the types of people you may meet or deal with in a week**

At the close of the brainstorm ensure that encounters with all types of people are covered.

2.

> **What does getting on well with others give you?**

Ensure that all types of people are covered when considering feelings, sense of self-worth, belonging etc.

3.

> **What happens and how do you feel when you do not get on well with others?**

Again ensure the range of people is covered. Keep a good balance between the feelings and the possible consequences of interactions going wrong.

4.

> **How does how I manage myself affect how I get on with others?**

If the learners get stuck, review some of the ideas from the previous brainstorm about what may go wrong and its effects and use the first brainstorm – Managing Myself.

Review all the lists and encourage the learners to see the importance and value of self management for getting on well with others. Encourage the learners to appreciate why developing self management skills are important, and to consider the consequences of not developing such skills.

Ask for some volunteers to tell a story about themselves or another and an occasion when they did not manage themselves well and the consequences.

Close this introductory session with a game which encourages movement and awareness of others.

Session Two: Self and self-management skills

Jim (30 min)

Remind the learners of a few key links between self management and getting on well with others. Introduce the web (MM3) as a way of looking at these links. This exercise will help the learners think about their priorities and the links between developing aspects of their self management and improving their social interactions.

Give the learners MM2 and MM3. Ask for a volunteer to read out the case of Jim on MM2. Ask what seem to be his main problems and list a few of these on the flipchart.

Ask the learners to work in small groups to decide what key areas of self-management Jim needs to tackle. Once the group agrees they should complete MM3.

Ask for feedback from each group to discover:

- how much agreement there is between the groups

- where and why there may be differences between the groups

Tackling issues (20 min)

Take one or two of Jim's problems. Ask the group to break down each problem into its various parts. How do these impact on other people? What might Jim do to tackle his problems? Which other people might help him and how and why? Build up a spider diagram for each problem discussed.

Creating personal webs (30 min)

Ask the learners to think about themselves, their own situations and the self management skills they would like to develop. They can refer to MM1. They should make use of MM4 for this activity.

Ask the learners to work in pairs to discuss aspects of their webs.

- Taking one of each of their key areas, they should explore all aspects of the problem and work out how it impacts on others

- What solutions might they have?

- How do these solutions impact on others?

- Have they similar key areas?

Group review (20 min)

Ask for any volunteers to share part of their web and explore some of the ways a problem impacts on others and how solutions might impact on others.

Session Three: Managing time and goals

 Trainer's notes

This area has been dealt with extensively in *Developing Life Skills*. So for those learners experiencing severe problems, additional sessions based on the module in *Life Skills* will be beneficial.

This session sets out to address four key areas. These are:

1. Why time management and goal setting is important for better management of self and improved interpersonal relationships

2. Analysing what might be wrong and why

3. What can be done to better manage time and the impact of this on self-management and interpersonal relationships

4. Strategies to improve time management and goal setting

Why is time management and goal setting important?

The learners may be employed, unemployed, on a training programme, doing some study or learning or may be in a residential setting. Some may feel they have little control over their time. Others that they have too many demands or too few demands on their time. Some may feel they have all the time in the world, and feel bored or directionless. Some may have a sense of purpose, or feel overly busy.

During this session the trainer may need to manage complaints that time is not an issue because someone is unemployed, or that there is nothing which can be done because someone is in prison or has little control over what can be done in a residential setting. These issues will need working with. The trainer will have to demonstrate how important it is to manage time and how it is possible to set personal goals and time manage whatever the learners' circumstances.

Checklist (10 min)

Ask the learners to complete checklist (MM5). Find out what they have learned from the exercise. Explain that a score of 4-7 may mean that there are some issues but none too serious; 7-14 is getting serious and requires that they make real efforts to think about changing their use of time. 14 and over means that they are probably making life hard for themselves and for others.

Brainstorm (10 min)

Lead on from the checklist by brainstorming as a group how poor time management and goal-setting affects:

i) the individual, and

ii) others around him/her

Run these as two separate brainstorms one after the other on the same spider diagram but use two different colours. Once both topics are exhausted ask the learners to suggest any links between the two groups of suggestions. Use a third colour to put in the links.

Chains of consequences (15 min)

Explore with the learners the implications or chains of events involved in poor time management by drawing them on the flipchart.

Take a starting point and then trace through the implications, events and the ways these consequences may make things worse for the individual, and how they directly impact on others and worsen an individual's social skills.

An example is worked below.

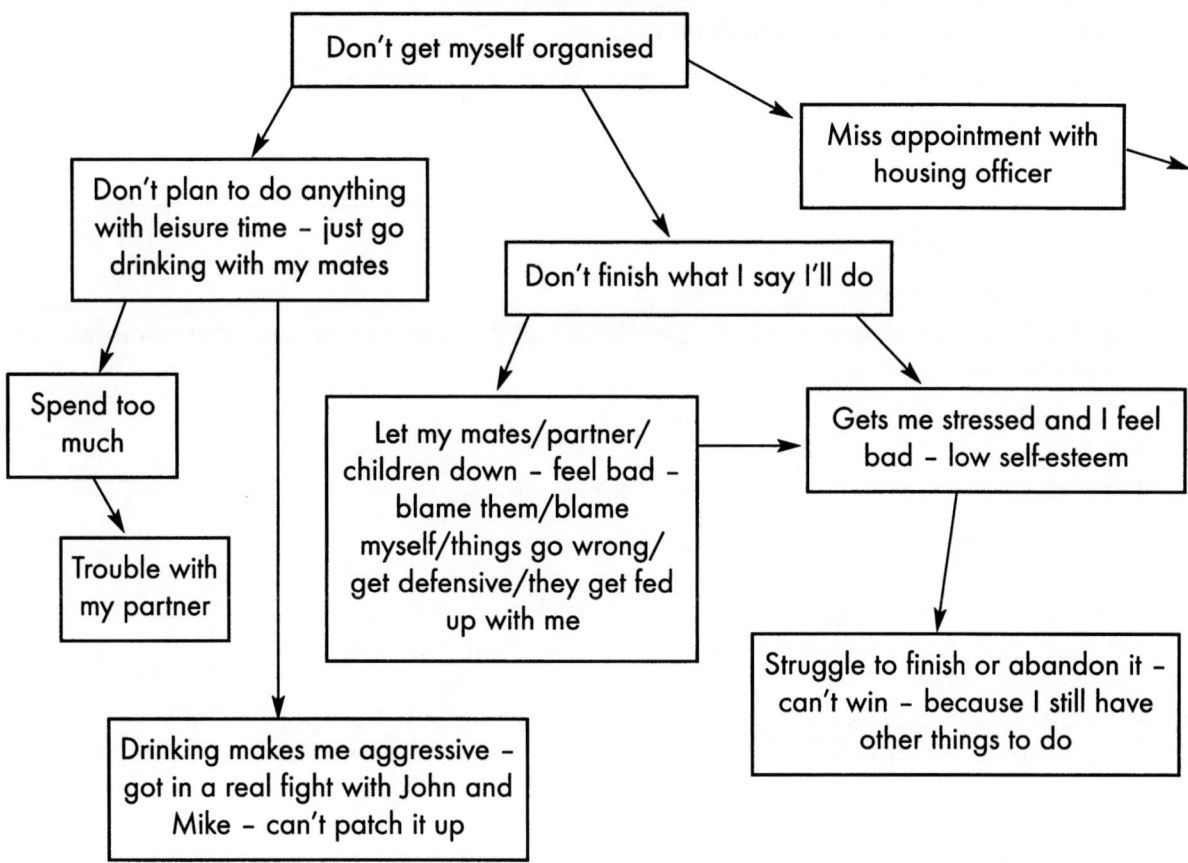

Working alone (20 min)

Ask the learners to use A1 sheets and coloured pens to draw out some of their own chains of consequences using a time management/planning problem as the starting point.

Once this is completed the learners should add in another colour, any ideas for stopping the chains of consequences or stopping the chain from starting.

In pairs (20 min)

The learners should share their charts. Each taking the other through their chains of consequences.

The pair should help each other with suggestions about ways to break the chains, or to stop the chain starting in the first place.

Each pair should make up a list of problems with time management and the possible solutions.

Feedback (15 min)

Share the problems and solutions with the whole group. Ask what the learners gained from the exercise.

Strategies (20 min)

Review with the learners some strategies for better time management to them in improving on the ways in which time management, planning and goal setting can support social interactions.

1. Plan what to do with your time:
   - lists for the day
   - plan outings etc. with friends/family don't expect it to organise itself

- don't put off jobs and then fail to do them
- know when there are deadlines, when you have promised things for people
- keep a list of important dates, appointments, birthdays etc.

This way:

- you won't get stressed and feel bad about letting people down
- people won't feel you are unreliable
- people won't feel that you have no time for them, that you do not value them or think that you can't be bothered
- you will be more likely to achieve more

2. Break large tasks down into realisable targets – be SMART

   This will ensure that things get done and not put off.

3. Plan to do some new things. Experiment and develop other interests. Other people will find you more interesting and you will meet new people by breaking your usual habits.

4. Having goals at home, work, or a training course or for personal development will be more likely to mean that an individual enjoys their life better, does not regret or resent having wasted time and will appear to others as a purposeful person.

5. Knowing where you are going, why and what you hope to achieve will mean you are more able to present yourself in a positive way and not as someone drifting through life. This is seen by many people as more attractive.

6. Having a direction and having daily plans mean you are less likely to drift along trying to take up other people's time and being someone who wastes others' time. You respect the fact that others have things to do, that time is of value and you have things to do yourself.

Closing round (10 min)

Ask the learners to each think of one thing they could do to better manage their time and so their ways of getting on with other people. Ask each to volunteer their suggestions and have a group list. There is no need for comment.

Session Four: Managing pressures and emotions

Opening role play (20 min)

1. Ask the learners to work in pairs or threes. Ask them to devise a short scenario in which one person is either very stressed or very emotional and is not handling themselves well. The reason for the stress/emotion can be anything they choose.

2. Check each group is working well and understands the task. Encourage the learners to develop their ideas and characters by questioning them. The scene will develop as they explore its consequences.

3. Once the learners have a short scene prepared ask them to role-play it. The learners should know they will have to role-play or talk about their scene to the whole group.

Whole group (40 min)

Ask for a few pairs/threes to perform their role-plays. While the learners are still in role ask them questions such as:

Of the stressed/under pressure person:
- Why did you react like that?
- What pushed you over the edge?
- How did it feel to behave like that?
- What do you think it felt like to be on the receiving end of such behaviour (eg shouting)?

Ask those on the receiving end as appropriate:
- Why do you think he/she gets so het up?
- Does it often happen like this?
- What usually sets him/her off?
- What do you usually do to calm him/her down?
- How do you feel being on the receiving end of this sort of behaviour?
- What have been the consequences for the family, the person him/herself, others?

Such questioning will continue the role-play. Having got the characters discussing their feelings, guide them into a conversation with each other *still in role*. e.g.
- Ask the person who is being stressed/under pressure to tell the other how it feels to hear how their behaviour is affecting other people
- Ask the recipient to say what they would really like the stressed/under pressure person to do knowing that this time they will be listened to

Try to encourage some dialogue. Draw in the audience. How did they feel watching the situation? What did they feel about how the situation came about and how it escalated? What would they have done?

The audience can be encouraged to ask questions of the characters while they are in role.

This experience and the likelihood of stirring up uncomfortable feelings of past experiences of pressure, stress and conflict may have been an intense experience for those in role. They need to be properly de-roled. Devices for this include:
- remind everyone it has been a role-play
- congratulate the people, use their real names, for playing the role of X so successfully and putting so much into it
- invite everyone to applaud the performance
- ask the learners if they would like to make any comments about their characters
- complete the de-roling with more applause and praise

The time taken for the role-play, hot seating and de-roling process will probably only permit a couple of such role-plays. In order that everyone has a chance to comment on the scenes they produced ask for examples of other things which create stress/pressure and how it felt to be stressed or to be on the receiving end of such. Generate a list on the flipchart. Ask for suggestions for better managing such pressures.

It gets me stressed (30 min)

Thank the group for the hard work so far. Explain that the session is looking at stress, pressures and the ways that not managing such feelings affect interactions with others and ourselves. The following exercise requires A1 sheets and coloured pens.

Ask the learners to work individually on spider diagrams, using 'It gets me pressured/stressed' as the starting point. Work an example through with them.

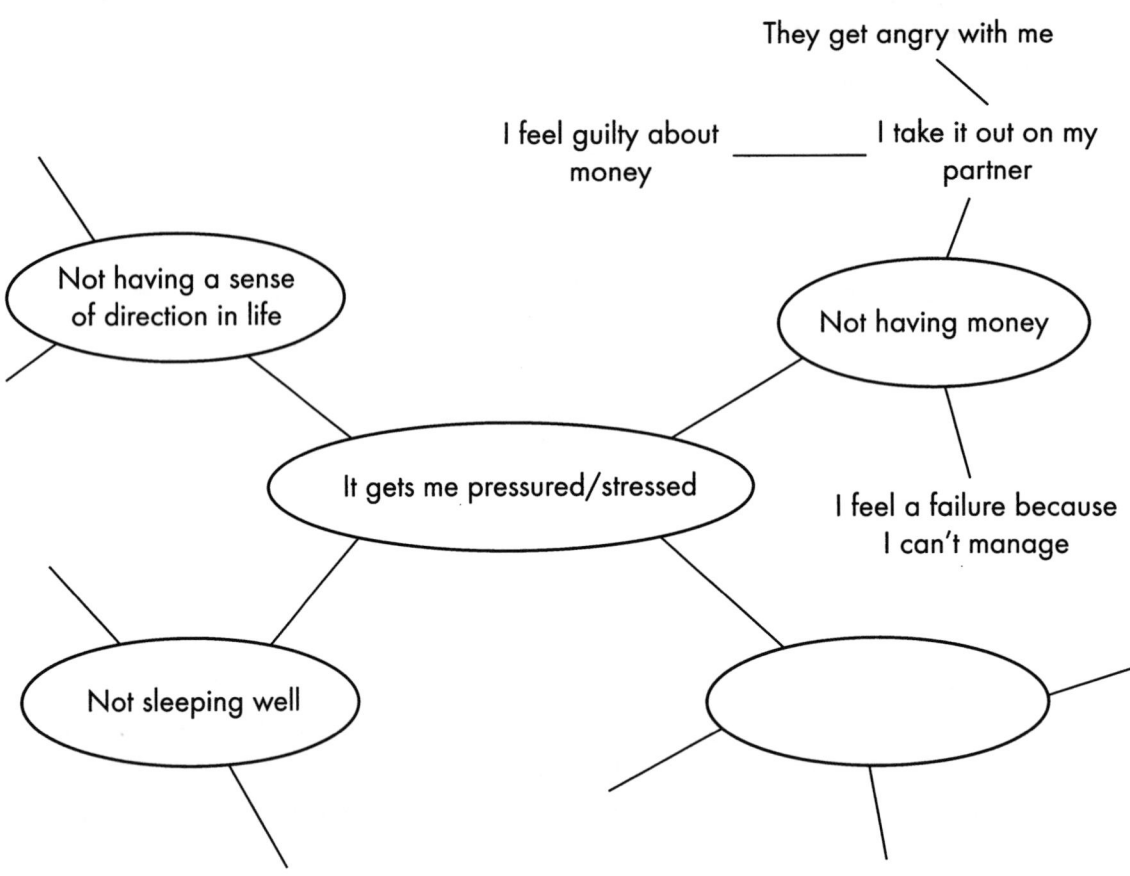

They get angry with me

I feel guilty about money

I take it out on my partner

Not having a sense of direction in life

Not having money

It gets me pressured/stressed

I feel a failure because I can't manage

Not sleeping well

In the smaller circles record the key pressures/stressors. Then on the lines record what this makes the individual feel, how they try to make others feel and the consequences of this.

Group review (20 min)

Draw the group back. Find out what has come out of the exercise: e.g. were they surprised:

- at the numbers of pressures/stresses?
- at the consequences of being under pressure?
- at the fact they provoked people to respond in certain ways?

So what do we do? (10 min)

Brainstorm:

> **What do I do to handle pressure/stress ...**

The group list may include:

- talk about it
- realise when I am getting stressed
- go out more
- hide away

- spend money I haven't got
- drink more
- get in more fights/rows

The list will probably include negatives and positives. Once the brainstorm is complete ask the group to consider if all the strategies seem good ones or if there are any they would regret and why.

Trainer lecturette and group discussion (25 min)

At this point the trainer may want to refer to modules in *Developing Life Skills* and to the preceding module in this manual. The trainer will need to steer the group to considering functional and affirming ways to manage pressures and stresses. The session could also include a practical relaxation period at the close of a lecturette (see Notes MM6).

Involve the learners by asking for comments on the various points, or for examples of things they have tried to better manage pressures.

Action plan and close (10 min)

This session closes by asking the learners to consider what they can do to deal with one or two of the stressors they identified in their spider diagram in the earlier exercise and to implement some of the strategies that have been discussed. The emphasis should be on positive and functional ways to manage stress. A proforma is found at MM7. Check on individual progress.

Session Five: Encouraging others to see me positively

Introductory brainstorm (15 min)

Introduce the title of the session and write it on a piece of flipchart paper. Ask the learners to brainstorm why this may be important in terms of managing themselves and their interactions with others.

They may generate reasons such as:

- being seen to have something to offer others
- appearing interesting
- not seeming a waster
- people would want to be involved with me
- people would find it attractive
- people are more likely to help
- people would want to be involved if they thought I knew what I was doing
- being energetic and positive attracts others
- being asked to do things/help
- people are more likely to say yes to me
- I would feel better about myself, have higher self-esteem
- I would come to feel more confident even if I did not feel confident to start off

Presenting poorly: small groups and group review (30 min)

Ask the learners to work in small groups and think of at least thirty ways in which people can make themselves appear in a negative way or appear badly. Encourage them to consider:

- clothing
- body language
- style of speech
- the way they present themselves
- attitude

The learners should think of concrete examples.

Each group needs one person to record the ideas and one person to present the group's findings to the group.

Create a running list of the small groups' suggestions:

- Was there much similarity of ideas?
- Were there things offered by one group others had not thought about?
- What surprises were there or things which the learners hadn't thought of before?

Pick a couple of the ideas and ask for a show of hands if any of the learners think they do these things. Check why they do them and how they feel doing them.

Group list (20 min)

As a group, brainstorm as long a list as possible:

> ### What happens if people do not see you positively

Encourage the ideas and ask the learners for some examples or experiences. Explore the consequences of what may happen if people do not see others positively.

Practical exercise and discussion (40 min)

Ask the learners to pick a card from a shuffled pack. Ask them in turn to move around the room as if they are that number. The rest of the group has to guess the person's number. Each learner takes it in turn to move in their role. A low number card feels bad about themselves, doesn't care much about appearance, is not bothered what other people think etc.

A high card thinks much more about themselves, spends a lot of time on clothing and personal grooming.

Ask the learners for ideas about how the high, low, medium and picture cards might behave before they begin the exercise.

Some interesting issues should emerge – e.g. Is being arrogant and full of oneself about presenting oneself positively? The learners might like to distinguish between high numbers and the picture cards. The learners may like to think about how attitudes are presented.

Definition (15 min)

After this exercise return to the original brainstorm about getting others to see you positively. Ask the learners to work up a definition of what it means. Seek a group consensus.

Self-assessment and planning (30 min)

In light of the previous discussions and exercises, ask the learners to now consider themselves and work on MM8.

Ask the learners to volunteer any areas they would like to work on about their own behaviours, attitudes, presentation and any reasons for their decisions.

Work through three or four of these asking for the group to brainstorm suggestions for things which the individuals could do.

Ask the learners to return to their sheets and to complete MM9, an action plan. Stress that this is very much about starting points for them to consider what they might try to do.

Check on any areas which learners have identified and suggest sources of help to assist the learners to reach their goals. Ensure this is noted as part of individual action plans.

Session Six: Conclusions

 Trainer's note

This final session should review the key ideas of the module, ensure the learners have understood how self-management links to improved self-esteem, better interpersonal relationships and improving their life chances. The final session should check for any areas which learners have not understood, should encourage some planning for change and enable the trainer to direct learners into other learning activities which will support them in this.

Group review (40 min)

Draw out the spider diagram as below; insert the titles of each session in each circle.

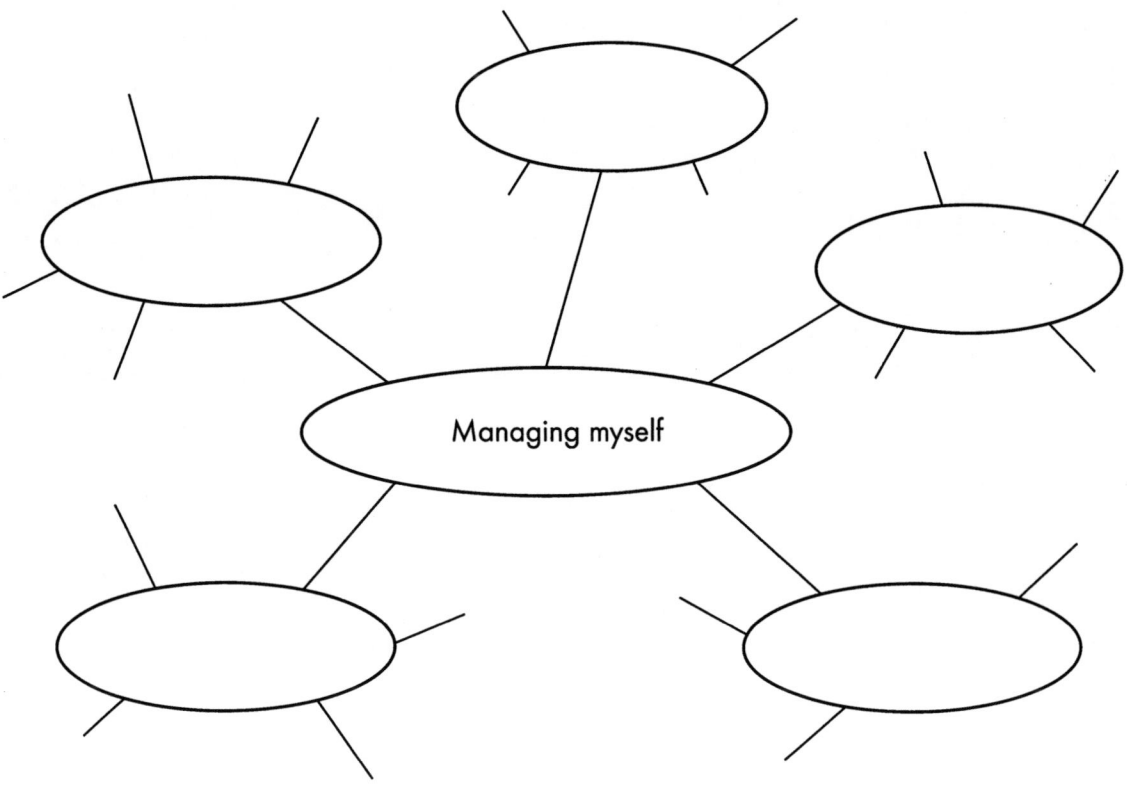

Ask for volunteers to offer key ideas from each of the sessions. Record these in one colour. Record in another any areas which learners did not understand so well or find so useful. Try to tackle any issues raised in his way.

Take a poll on the areas which the learners think they are most likely to work on and why. Record this.

Take a poll on any further help which the learners need. Record this.

Working alone (10 min)

Ask the learners to complete an evaluation and check this against their earlier expectations. Check on learners' progress and make a note of anything to follow up. Note any areas the learners would like to follow up.

10 min

Thank the learners for their work and close the session with a final game.

MM2: Jim

Jim's 27. He's been married once and is now living with Sally. He has three children, two from his marriage, one with Sally and now another's on its way. Jim's been in trouble with the police and spent some time inside for car crimes and burglary when he was younger.

For a long time people thought he was just trouble. He is still quick to anger. He has had a very unsteady work history - more time on the dole than in work. He has tried most of the government schemes to get people re-trained and back into work.

Last time he was employed, three years ago, he lost the job for always being late and for being abusive to colleagues and the boss. He's done some cash-in-hand work since then, mainly barwork.

At 27 he can't work out what's wrong. He feels tense about money, bothered that he and Sally aren't getting on. He's fed up being unemployed. He's fed up with his own fits of depression and temper.

MM1

Look at the ideas from the group brainstorm and pick those you would like to work on to develop better self management.

Areas I would like to work on are:	My reasons for this are:

From this course I would like to find out more about:

By the close of this course I would like to be able to:

MM4

Put yourself at the centre and use the blanks to fill in areas of self-management skills which you need to or want to develop. Again, link areas of problems together.

How many lines linking different areas do you have? What does this tell you?

MM3

Work round the web filling in Jim's problems and use coloured pens to show how one problem links to another.

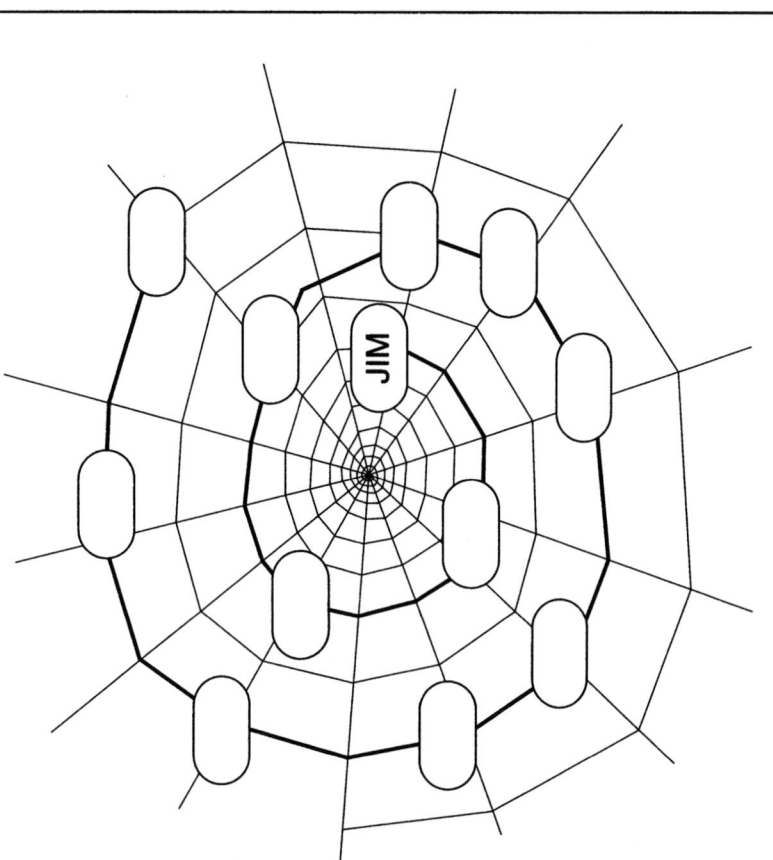

JIM

Any surprises?

MM6: Managing pressures/stress

1. Identify the cause. Check it really is the cause. Decide what action could be taken to change the situation or to deal with it better.

2. Think about your reactions. Can you better manage how you respond in order to upset yourself less?

3. Who can help you manage pressure/stress? Who could talk it through? Who could offer advice, e.g. debt counsellor, AA ...

4. What actions do you take which make the situation worse? What could you do to improve things? Remember taking drugs or drinking won't help.

5. Take up other activities/interests. Do something for someone else.

6. Explain your situation to those who matter - ask for help. Don't just take it out on them.

7. Plan your time.

8. Learn to relax, concentrate on something else, take a break from the stresses.

9. Think about how others are feeling.

10. How would a friend advise you? Is the advice good?

11. What small things could you do to make things better?

MM5: Time and me

Read the statements.

✓ for yes or no – Be honest with yourself!

	Yes	No
Do you plan what you are going to do?		
Would you say you had a goal in life?		
Does your partner complain you just can't be bothered to finish things?		
Do you know how long something will take to do?		
Do you find your life interesting?		
Are you often rushing a job?		
Do you often feel bored and restless?		
Do you get stressed because you run out of time?		
Do you often do the same things out of habit?		
Do you take your boredom out on other people?		
Do you leave things to the last minute?		
Do you make time for friends?		
Do you make time for your partner?		
Do other people get fed up with you getting in their way?		
Will you look back on your life and wish you had ...?		
Think back over the past week. Have you wasted time?		
Are you too rushed to spend time with your children?		
Do people think you are interesting with lots of ideas, hobbies, interests and activities?		
Have you wasted anyone else's time this week?		
Do you sometimes wish you had planned what you were going to say a little more carefully?		
How many ✓ in the Yes column?		

MM8

Complete each circle with an example of something you do. Then think about the consequences, add these to the lines coming out of each circle. Add as many circles as you want.

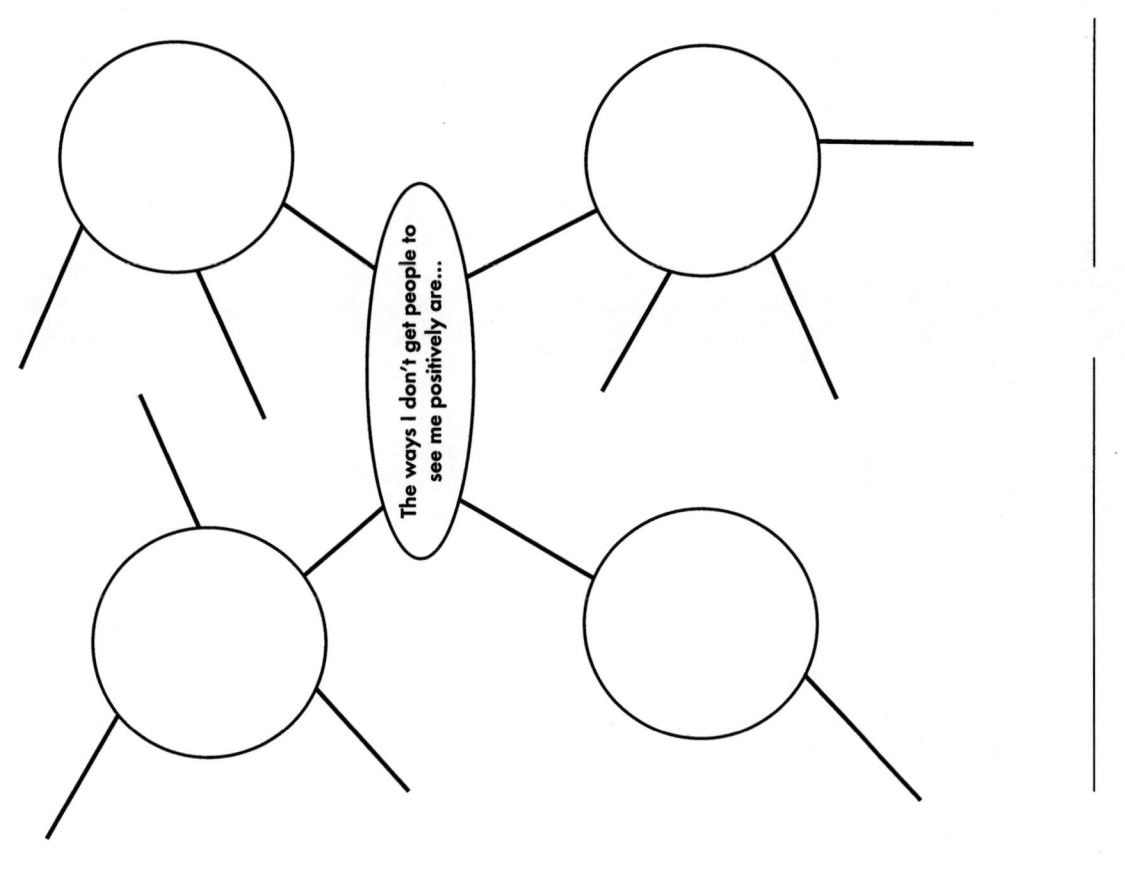

The ways I don't get people to see me positively are...

MM7: Action plan

A Key Pressure for me is:

I want to tackle this because:

A Key Pressure for me is:

I want to tackle this because:

Goal 1	Goal 2
I will:	I will:
Who can help?	Who can help?
I measure my success by:	I measure my success by:

Dated: ....

MM9: My plan to encourage others to see me positively

The areas I want to work on are (list 2–3):

My reasons for wanting to work on these are:

1.

2.

3.

Area to Improve:	Area to Improve:	Area to Improve:
Action I'll take:	Action I'll take:	Action I'll take:
I'll measure my success by:	I'll measure my success by:	I'll measure my success by:

Developing assertiveness skills

The module is divided into seven sessions.

1. Introducing assertion (1 hour)

2. Exploring a range of behaviours and choices (3 hours 30 min)

3. Assertion versus aggression: the benefits of assertion (1 hour)

4. Developing assertion skills (4 hours 30 min)

5. Looking at personal triggers to passivity or aggression (1 hour 30 min)

6. Self-confidence and self-esteem (1 hour 30 min)

7. Planning to keep confident, to keep a sense of well-being and to stay assertive (1 hour)

The module takes 14 hours to complete. However you may wish to make use of some activities from the first four modules in this manual. This will add to the time it takes for completing this module.

The module links well with and is an underpinning part of many of the skills and behaviours which this Social Skills manual seeks to develop. Developing Assertiveness Skills links with:

- Developing communication skills (both verbal and non-verbal)

- Seeing it from others' points of view

- Instituting and maintaining relationships

A clear appreciation of what constitutes assertiveness and individual rights links into the heart of understandings about communities and relationships.

Developing Assertiveness Skills has links with modules in the other companion manuals. For example with Developing Positive Attitudes in *Developing Life Skills*, Valuing Others and Valuing Myself in *Addressing Anti-Social Behaviour*. Much of the work in this module will be on developing positive attitudes, an awareness of self and an awareness of the impact of behaviours on others in both the short and long term. There will be some role-play practice and work on the types of skills to develop to effect better communications with others. Some of the specific work on communication skills has been addressed in the first two modules in this manual and you are referred to those when planning work from this module.

 This module uses the following learning and training techniques:

- role play, mimes and sketches

- brainstorm

- discussions

- feedback and presentations

- self assessment

- pair work

- magazines or newspapers used to stimulate ideas

- information giving, including use of OHTs

- action planning

Trainer's notes

This module is intended to help learners to:

- develop an understanding of what it means to be assertive and the benefits of assertiveness both for themselves and for others

- understand the different ways in which people may behave, what may motivate such behaviours and the impact of such behaviours.

- understand the differences between assertion and other behaviours such as aggression and the consequences of each type of behaviour

- gain some insights into their own behaviours and to realise why their interactions with others may go wrong

- experience through role play the differences between passive, passive-aggressive, aggressive and assertive behaviours

- appreciate the importance of developing self esteem and self confidence as part of developing as a more assertive person

- understand the types of situation in which their self esteem and self confidence may be undermined

- understand how to protect themselves and their sense of well being in personally difficult situations and understand how to avoid slipping into aggressive, passive or passive-aggressive responses rather than being assertive

Work on developing assertion skills is essential for those who lose control of themselves and the situations they are in, by becoming either too passive and accommodating or becoming too aggressive. People are often able to be assertive in some situations, those in which they feel more comfortable and confident. It is important to develop assertiveness skills and therefore more appropriate responses to situations in which people feel more threatened or vulnerable. This will help give them greater self-control, greater control over personal destiny and a greater sense of well-being. Being able to be assertive is likely to mean that interactions and relationships will be more satisfying and that decisions or actions are likely to be better grounded and so less likely to have long-term negative consequences.

Session One: Opening activity: introducing assertion

Brainstorm with the whole group (15 min)

Ask the group to consider:

> **What does it mean to be assertive?**

Write up everything the group members suggest using their own words. Explore the group's suggestions, teasing out what they mean by some of their suggestions. This process of exploration should highlight the differences between aggression and assertion. Looking at the differences between assertion and aggression is essential to the process of defining assertion, and an appreciation that being assertive is both about an individual knowing what he or she wants, then being able to ask for it but not undermining anyone else's rights in so doing. It will be important to explore with the group such statements as the following:

- getting what I want
- saying what I think
- having my own opinion

- having my own way
- other people listening to my point of view
- not being forced into actions I do not want to take

Such exploration needs to highlight assertion as also about respecting the rights of others. It is not simply about an individual getting their way. Words such as compromise, negotiation and discussion can be introduced at this stage as being an important part of the process of developing assertiveness skills. Some challenge may be needed if the learners consider these words are signs of weakness.

Defining assertion (25 min)

Ask the group to work in pairs to define assertion. Ask them to illustrate this with some examples. Each pair should write their definition on a sheet of A1 for display.

After fifteen minutes ask the pairs to offer their definitions and examples to the whole group. The A1 sheets should be taped to the walls as a display. The group may decide to adopt one of the definitions.

Round up the first session (20 min)

Use the flip chart to record the ideas which have been introduced so far. Check that everyone has a clear idea about what assertion means. Ensure that the following points have been covered. Explain that being assertive is about:

- knowing what you as an individual want, think, feel and understand in any situation
- taking the time to find out what you think, feel etc.
- being able to communicate those feelings or thoughts in a clear way which does not undermine someone else but which allows you to feel that you have been heard
- having the opportunity to try things out, to change, to make mistakes and to develop as a person
- having respect for other people so that they are equally able to realise their wants and wishes and to change and to make mistakes
- being able to like yourself most of the time and to feel comfortable with what you are doing and have done
- feeling that you are able to be consistent in your responses to others in a range of situations and that you do not get backed into a corner and give in to pressure or become aggressive

Go through the key learning points the module will cover and ask for any comments from the group. Explain that this module on developing assertiveness will be about:

- developing an understanding of the differences between different types of behaviours and the effects that such behaviours have on others and themselves
- understanding what they want in certain situations, how to gain this and how to better go about getting it. For example through clear communication, through negotiation and compromise rather than by being bullying or being manipulative
- understanding how and why they may react differently in different situations
- developing greater respect for themselves and for others

Use OHT 1 for a clear visual illustration of the importance of balance, equality and respect which is necessary in an assertive relationship.

Outline what will take place in the remaining six sessions.

Session Two: Exploring a range of behaviours and choices

 Trainer's notes

This session introduces a range of behaviours: passivity, assertion, aggression and being passively aggressive. These behaviours may be actively chosen or may be ones into which the learner 'falls' out of habit, a lack of a sense of what else may be done or because they allow themselves to be pushed by others.

The session should help the learners to discover if they have a particular type of response to many or only certain types of situations. These sessions should help the learners to decide if these responses are appropriate ones, how responses will impact on other people and to explore other ways to respond to and so to manage situations.

The session makes use of self-assessment activities, information giving, role-play and hot seating.

Information sharing: working as a whole group (up to 60 min)

Explain, there are four types of behaviours and responses called:

1. Passivity
2. Aggressiveness
3. Passive-aggressiveness
4. Assertiveness

Write up the first three behaviours as titles on three sheets of flipchart paper. Ask the group for a description of each. Tell the group that you will look at behaviour four, assertiveness, at the end of the session. Magazines and newspapers will help the group to think about body language, facial expression, use of physical space, proximity to others etc.

Passive behaviour

Ask for some descriptions of passive behaviour and responses. Use the following questions to help steer the group to think about a range of issues.

- What do people do when they are passive?
- What might it feel like to them?
- What might it feel like to others?
- Why might someone be passive?
- What short-term gains might there be from being passive?
- What might be the longer-term effects of being passive?

Ask for examples to illustrate some of the answers. Ensure that the group covers the following points.

People may behave in a passive way when:

- they feel that they do not have power in a situation
- they give another person power
- they have been powerless in other similar situations
- with a particular person they assume passivity
- they seek to avoid conflict
- it is easier
- they do not expect to be heard
- they have little regard for themselves

- they have little or no real awareness of their own wants or opinions
- they do not want to take responsibility for themselves or their destiny

People show they are passive by e.g.:
- not making choices
- not taking any part in decision making
- saying they have no power in a situation
- being apologetic about their needs or wishes
- helping other people to discount them
- claiming someone else has power over them
- they feel forced to do something

They are passive when they say they are not able to do something when in reality they have chosen not to do something.

Being passive may offer short-term gains because people:
- avoid conflict
- avoid making a decision
- can avoid making mistakes
- do not have to take responsibility for themselves or anything else and can blame someone else later
- do not have to feel guilty if they have done what someone else wants
- can feel good because they have made someone else happy or done the right thing according to someone else
- may be praised for putting up with something or doing what the group wants and putting others before themselves

Passive people may be easy to be with because they are not demanding, they are not challenging, they seem to just fall in and they may be relied on to do things. They need not be considered as having feelings or wants.

In the longer-term passive people may resent that they have given in, they may blame others and may become hostile – see below – passive-aggressive behaviours). In the longer-term their self-image becomes reinforced as being weak, perhaps of little value to themselves or others, as having few opinions and as not needing to be counted or considered. They may have a limited sense of self-worth or self-esteem.

Likewise, in the longer-term others may not have any respect for passive people. They may be taken for granted, dropped for someone who has ideas, opinions or personality to offer. Relationships may become complex with the passive person being resented for always giving in, for not taking the initiative, the person getting their way may feel that they are a bully or of limited value because they can only attract weak people.

Self-image for both the passive and the dominant person may become distorted, the decisions may not be of the best and the longer-term relationships may be dysfunctional.

Aggressive behaviour
Consider aggressive responses or behaviours. Ask questions to guide the group.
- What do people do when they are aggressive?
- What might it feel like to them?

- What might it feel like to others?
- Why might someone be aggressive?
- What might the short-term gains be from being aggressive?
- What might be the longer-term effects of being aggressive?

Sum up the group's responses and add to them if necessary. The following points should be covered.

In becoming aggressive people may domineer or close down others, they may deny that others have ideas, points of view or wishes. Those around them may become stifled or avoid them.

In being ready to be aggressive such people are tense and experience all the physical consequences of being ready to fight or to defend a position (see Managing Emotions and Feelings).

Aggressive people may feel powerful, that they have got their way or have been listened to. They may feel that they have not been walked over. But they may be limiting themselves and their experiences of others by pushing weaker people, not accepting challenges from others or allowing that there are other ways of doing things.

The aggressive response may become a habit. People not wanting to face such aggression may avoid them, leaving them to the company of those who will submit or with people who share similar behaviours and views on life.

Poor solutions to problems may be adopted because there was no-one who felt able to challenge. They may become victims of their own aggressive behaviours and attitudes because others will respond to them as aggressive and expect them to be so.

Passive-aggressive behaviour
Passive-aggressive behaviour means people start out responding passively and then become resentful, hostile and aggressive or manipulative in order to gain what they want. Explore with the group what this behaviour type is like, its effects on the person behaving in that way and on others around him or her. Use the questions to guide the group's thinking. This set of reactions and behaviours may be harder for the group to think about.

- What do people do when they are passive-aggressive?
- What might it feel like to them?
- What might it feel like to others?
- Why might someone be passive-aggressive?
- What might the short-term gains be from being passive-aggressive?
- What might be the longer-term effects of being passive-aggressive?

The group may come up with some examples of behaviours and ideas which cover such points as:

- agreeing and going along with an idea or situation and then kicking out against it. This can cause confusion for other people because the time to have said "no" or to have protested has passed.
- the hostility or aggression which is offered may be about something else or long after an action has been taken
- people may come to not trust what an individual says expecting that they will react badly later

- they may find the person unreliable or difficult to be with
- the person may blame everyone else but not themselves for things which are done
- those around the passive-aggressive person may fear spitefulness at a later point
- the person may become manipulative and devious in an attempt to get something after having agreed to something else
- a fight or conflict may be created to let off steam or frustration
- the passive-aggressive person may experience feelings of self-dislike or self-disgust at having behaved in ways which seem weak or to gain little respect from others
- the person may know that they are hard to be around and may feel and be increasingly excluded from other people and activities, because the others prefer to be with straight talking people

Having explored these three types of behaviours, the next three activities use this information. The first activity asks the learners to work alone thinking about their own behaviours. The second, some role-play situations ask for these behaviours to be tested and analysed. The third activity asks the group to work on the benefits of being assertive rather than falling into these other ways of behaving.

How do I behave? A self assessment activity (30 min)

Use DA1, ask the learners to read it and then ensure that everyone understands what is wanted. Ask the learners to work alone for ten minutes.

Depending on the group ask the group to come back together as a whole or to work in pairs to look at some of their answers to the questions below.

Find out if anyone has a particularly common response to situations. Could they therefore call themselves more passive, aggressive or passive-aggressive?

Are there any who seem to have a range of behaviours depending on the situation? Are they prepared to share some examples of these different behaviours and discuss what motivates such differences?

Are there particular situations in which they are more likely to be passive or to be aggressive?

Are there any types of behaviour which they wish they did not exhibit or would like to change?

Ask the learners to note this.

Role-plays: choosing different responses (up to 60 min)

Divide the group into three and give to each one a role-play situation, use DA2. Ask them to work on their role-play for ten minutes and then perform it. Go from group to group, helping them to develop their role-play.

While each group performs, ask the audience to think of some questions to ask the characters. At the close of each role play, ask the audience to question whichever character they wish. Be clear the audience knows they are questioning the characters not the group members. The following may help steer the questioning.

- What did you want from the situation?
- How did it feel to respond in that way?
- Did you know how your response would be received by the other characters?

- How do you think they view what you did/said?
- How do you think it felt to be on the receiving end of what you said/did?
- What else might you have done/said?
- What impact would this have had on the others?
- Which behaviour would have gained you what you wanted?
- How did it feel to be on the receiving end of what was said/done?
- Was he/she right in what she/he said it felt like?
- What was wanted from you?
- Was this the right way to get it?
- What other behaviour could have been tried?
- How would you have preferred him/her to have behaved? Why?
- What did you think of what he/she suggested as an alternative behaviour? Would that have worked better for you? Why?

The questioning will help the group experience the effects of the behaviours which were played out and to consider the possible effects of alternative ones.

Thank all the learners for playing their parts and answering the questions in role. Applaud the role-players.

Looking at assertion: pair work and whole group feedback (up to 60 min)

The exercise looks at assertiveness. Recap on the group's definition of assertiveness.

In pairs, the learners look at the situations on DA3. They need to work out what are the aggressive, passive, and assertive responses to each situation and to describe the short and long term benefits and disadvantages of each one. They will need three copies of DA4.

After 30 minutes of working in pairs the learners should be ready to feedback to the group as a whole.

To prevent boredom ask one pair to outline one of their responses for a situation and then ask the other pairs to add anything more or which is different. Do not ask each pair to outline every response to every situation. Ask as many different pairs to take the lead in offering feedback. Put the advantages and disadvantages of each type of response on the flip chart.

The group should have decided that the assertive response is most likely to attain a better outcome and to leave more people with a stronger self-image than adopting either passive or aggressive responses. Tease out the reasons why assertiveness is better.

Session Three: Assertion versus aggression: the benefits of assertion: role-plays and finding alternative solutions

This session focuses on the advantages of assertion over aggression. It asks the learners to work through three role-play situations. The audience helps the players to find ways other than aggression to deal with the situations.

Divide the learners into three groups and give each group a situation. Use DA5. Give the groups ten minutes to think through their situation and to manage the problems they face by being aggressive.

Ask each group to play their scene. Ask the audience to watch the scene and then to make suggestions to help the players better manage the situation by being assertive rather than aggressive. The players should make use of the suggestions to re-play their situation. If those watching feel that the players are not working the situation through successfully they can interrupt the second role play to offer further suggestions. It is important to encourage the audience to be very specific about what they want done and what consequences they expect. This will make them more thorough and more reflective about what they want to see achieved.

At the end of the second version of the role play hot seat some of the characters and ask them, while continuing in character, to consider the differences between the two scenes. Ask such questions as:

- which way of behaving felt better and why?
- which did they prefer and why?
- which ways of behaving seemed to them to be likely to lead to better longer-term outcomes and why?
- which type of behaviour was harder for them, and why?

Ask the audience and the role players to come up with a list of the skills which were used when being assertive rather than aggressive. Record these.

Ask the group at the close of all six of the role-plays if it became easier to think about being assertive rather than aggressive and why this was so? Ask the group to look at the list of assertiveness skills which have been suggested and then to add more. This list is needed for the next session.

Session Four: Developing assertiveness skills

Remind the group of the key points they have discovered about assertiveness. These should include:

- an individual knowing what he/she wants, thinks, feels and understands in any situation
- being able to communicate those feelings, thoughts or wishes clearly in such a way which will not undermine someone else and which allows him/her to feel heard and respected
- being treated and treating others with respect as having equal rights in a situation
- having the opportunity to try things out, to make mistakes and to develop
- having respect for other people so they are able to develop, voice opinions, have their needs met
- being able to like yourself most of the time and feel comfortable with what you are doing and have done
- feeling able to be consistent in responses to others in a range of situations. Not to lapse into passivity or giving in to pressure and not becoming aggressive
- knowing how to reach a compromise position and to negotiate

Use these thoughts and the list of skills from the last session as the group's starting points.

Brainstorm activity (25 min)

Ask the group to brainstorm:

> **What skills, qualities or understandings do people need to bring into situations so that they can be assertive?**

Write the learners' responses onto a flip chart. They should cover:

- a sense of self
- knowing what I want to do and why
- having self knowledge
- knowing how what I do affects others
- treating others as equals
- being able to negotiate
- managing change and not being afraid
- knowing how to compromise
- knowing what I am prepared to compromise about
- wanting to be treated as an equal
- taking responsibility for myself
- letting others take responsibility for themselves
- not trying to control others or manage their lives
- being thoughtful about others
- knowing others' limits
- listening to what others say and want
- developing communication skills
- knowing how to say no and be heard
- knowing how to get my point of view across
- thinking about the implications of things
- not being dependent on others

While much is about being treated and treating others well and as an equal there are skills which individuals need to develop to be assertive. Use the list which the group has made to work out what these skills or qualities are. They should cover:

- good communication skills; e.g. asking clearly, listening and not assuming
- being able to accept criticism or rejection without coming apart or becoming aggressive
- learning how to manage conflicts
- having clear and confident body language
- having a clear sense of self

At this point you may want to use some of the exercises in the first two modules of this manual on developing verbal and non-verbal communication skills. You may also wish to select some activities from the third and fourth modules on understanding and managing emotions and oneself. The sixth session in this module looks at developing self-confidence and self-esteem.

Other skills which help in developing assertiveness are the skills to manage time, to set goals and to manage change. These are covered in Developing Life Skills. These are skills about setting and working to personal agendas.

The rest of this session looks at:

- communication skills (2 hours and 5 min)
- managing criticism (1 hour)
- managing conflicts (1 hour)

Communication skills

This section looks at two aspects of communication: not using words and phrases which construct an individual as passive, and saying what you mean and meaning what you say. Other communication skills which need to be considered as part of developing assertiveness are addressed in Modules One and Two in this volume.

NOT APPEARING AS PASSIVE

A key way to encourage people to disregard an individual or what he or she says is for that individual to undermine him or herself by appearing as very passive. There are a number of ways to offer clues about passivity to others.

Mimes and sketches (20 min)

Ask the group to work in threes to think up a couple of mimes, poses or brief sketches to present to the whole group to illustrate a passive person. They have seven minutes to come up with some ideas and then the remainder of the time should be used to present the ideas to the rest of the group. Keep a running list of the ideas on flip chart paper.

Continuing the brainstorm (10 min)

After the mimes and sketches review the whole list of suggestions and ask the group if there are any more which can be added. The list should include such as:

- apologising before speaking
- apologising for being
- cringing away
- being deferential
- letting personal space be invaded
- speaking very quietly or not clearly
- body language and posture which makes the person seem to have shrunk as small as possible
- hesitating
- the person changing their mind about what is wanted
- agreeing quickly to anything anyone else says
- saying someone else is always right, can always make the best decisions, knows best
- putting him or herself down – silly me, I'm so stupid about money, I can't ever do anything practical

Ask the group are there differences in the ways in which men and women may appear as passive?

Analysing the brainstorm (15 min)

Once the group feels that they have no more to add to the list then ask everyone to reflect on the list and decide which apply to them. Ask them to make a list on a blank sheet of paper and keep this.

Work through the flipchart list as a group and decide what responses passive behaviours provoke in other people. E.g. annoyance, irritation, a desire to talk over the person or complete disregard. It is important that the group can see that the passivity provokes responses in others.

Turning passivity round (25 min)

Ask the group to work in pairs for 10 minutes and to select five things from the list and to think of ways in which a person doing such things can be encouraged to do something else. Offer some examples. For example: looking someone in the eye instead of looking at the floor; having written out what is to be said so they are sure to be able to say it; asking the other person to listen rather than interrupting or jumping to conclusions.

Ask each pair to feedback to the group, try to cover all the items on the flipchart.

Completing the personal lists (10 min)

Ask the learners to look again at their own lists of their passive behaviours and to note suggestions they can use to challenge their passivity.

SAYING WHAT YOU MEAN AND MEANING WHAT YOU SAY

Information giving (10 min)

Explain that a way to ensure others do not take you seriously is to frequently change your mind or be easily swayed to change your mind. Distinguish between reasonableness in changing a point of view and simply giving in or doing it to please others. It is important for the learners to understand that:

1. they need to know what they want to say before they start, even if this means writing some notes of the few key points they want to make
2. they need to know what is involved in a situation before they agree or refuse. This may mean standing back and thinking before they speak, asking for more information, getting someone else's advice or ideas or checking that they understand what they have been told
3. their body language, the way they speak and what they say all need to give the same message
4. agreeing to something or saying what you do not mean to avoid conflict or to buy time may only lead to greater difficulties later on

Offer DA6 for further information.

Pair work (20 min)

In pairs ask each to tell the other about an occasion when they either did not mean what they said or they were not clear about what they meant. It is important that in telling the story they think through:

- why the communication went wrong
- why they were vague in what they said
- what they hoped to get from the situation
- what the consequences of the situation were
- what they wished they had done

Feedback (15 min)

For the feedback session.
Either i) ask for one or two in the group to volunteer to tell one or two of the stories and the consequences
or
ii) begin a group brainstorm of the reasons people may be vague or not communicate clearly and the consequences of this

It is important for the learners to realise they could avoid getting into situations or causing themselves and others difficulties by being more assertive.

There may be commonalities in the types of situations which learners were swayed. For example in close relationships, over emotional matters, over money or meeting housing needs. Discuss any patterns and some strategies for being less vulnerable.

MANAGING CRITICISM

1) Self criticism (20 min)

Criticism is a powerful tool which people use to disable themselves and to disable others. If people have low self-esteem they are more likely to hear criticism where none exists, to believe critical comments without question and to see criticism as applying to them as a whole person rather than to something they may have done. They are not likely to challenge critical comments and are more likely to be do something they do not want to do rather than attract more criticism.

They are also more likely to be critical about themselves. Undermining oneself leaves the way open for others to be critical. The management of criticism is linked to self esteem and self-confidence and to communication skills.

The learners should work through DA7 marking any of the comments they make about themselves and to consider what this says of themselves. They should keep a log of self-critical comments for a week to see how frequently they make such comments to undermine themselves and the consequences of this.

2) Taking criticism (20 min)

The learners should consider how often others make critical comments about them and how they deal with such comments. Again use DA7, tick comments which people make about them.

In pairs discuss the comments which they hear others make about themselves and their responses. Their partner should suggest ways to challenge comments.

Remind the learners that criticisms can be challenged to find out:
- if they are really accurate
- why they are being offered
- whether it is just an attack
- how they could be helpful
- if something could be said in another way

The learners may also not mind about things which others see as faults.

3) Being critical of others (20 min)

It is important that the learners are aware of the ways they are critical of and may be undermining others. Raising awareness of the ways in which the learners use criticism is important but may be difficult. A group brainstorm may be one way to explore a number of the issues in a less accusatory or personal way. Ask the group to consider:

> **Why do some people criticise others? How do they do it and what effects does this have for the criticised person or group and for the person doing the criticising?**

Depending on how well the group functions you may want to ask if anyone is prepared to speak about the ways in which and reasons for which they have criticised others or you may chose to leave the group to reflect for a few minutes on the ways in which any of the material explored in the brainstorm has a bearing on them.

MANAGING CONFLICTS

Many people fail to be assertive because they are concerned that to stand up to someone or to voice their own wishes will lead to conflict.

Group brainstorm (20 min)

Ask the group to brainstorm what concerns them about conflict. The list may include such as:

- being laughed at
- experiencing aggressive behaviour
- feeling weak
- being criticised
- being abandoned or left
- being threatened

Ask the group to brainstorm why people may avoid conflicts. The suggestions may include:

- making life easier
- avoiding unpleasantness – verbal or physical abuse or attack; silence or exclusion
- stops upset
- leads to a quiet life
- stops difficult issues having to be dealt with
- stops mockery
- stops aggression
- stops criticism

Ask the group to brainstorm the consequences of avoiding conflict. These may include:

- always giving in and being expected to do so, thereby making it harder the next time to resist
- not dealing with serious matters and letting situations go on
- not giving other people a chance to see things from your point of view
- not giving the other person a chance to understand what something means to you
- always making the other person feel that they have to take decisions
- lowering your own sense of self-worth by not doing what you want
- feeling angry or upset later

Individuals will have to decide whether it is better to accept the consequences of avoiding conflict or confront it. Ways to manage conflict include:

- trying to face the real issue rather than side issues and discussing that
- trying to negotiate so that both parties can be happy with a solution

- being open about the ways in which you have given in the past and the reasons for this

- the importance of the current decision to be taken and the strength of your views

Pairwork (20 min)

Ask the group to work in pairs to explore a conflict situation. This may be one which they have experienced or think that they might experience. The pair needs to:

- think through the situation

- untangle the issues from both sides

- decide what outcomes both sides would like

- find strategies for dealing with the potential conflict

- reach the outcome which would be acceptable to both people

Group feedback (20 min)

Ask for a pair to volunteer to role play or to talk through their conflict and the strategies which they have thought of to deal with it. The pair will need to outline the conflict, the solution which they want to reach and the steps to reaching it. The rest of the group may want to add other suggestions or to find ways to strengthen the pair's strategies.

As a group list out some ways to deal with conflicts and the reasons for those suggestions.

Session Five: Looking at personal triggers

 ### Trainer's notes

It is likely that people will be able to be assertive in some situations but not in others. It is likely there will be some occasions when they become overly aggressive or unnecessarily passive. In order to stay assertive it is important for the learners to work out what causes them to feel less assertive, to identify what situations and with which types of people or person they may find it hard to put into practice that which was outlined in Session Four.

This session builds on DA1 in which the learners listed situations in which they were less assertive than they would like.

Working alone: using DA8 (30 min)

Give each learner DA8. This asks them to identify four situations in which they feel they have not been assertive. They may look at particular situations with a specific person, for example, partner, child or boss or they may pick a type of situation such as complaining about a faulty piece of merchandise or dealing with the demands of a line manager.

DA8 asks them to work out why they are not assertive and what could be done to enable greater assertion. Ask the learners to work on their own for up to half an hour.

Once they have completed the exercise or if they become stuck part way through then ask them to work in pairs to help one another or to share ideas.

Practising skills: pair work (30 min)

In pairs the learners should each pick one situation, go through with their partner what makes them less assertive and what they feel they should do to be more assertive. The partner may have other suggestions. Once both are happy with the list of what can be done, they should then work together on a role play so that the learner can practice how he or she will be making use of the skills, thoughts and reminders about the situation. The other half of the role play partnership should test the resolve to be assertive and should as realistically as possible make the situation hard for their partner. Once both feel that they have managed to work through a situation with sufficient assertiveness, they should make a note of any areas of difficulty and then swap roles.

Whole group feedback (20 min)

The pairs can be asked to share what they have learnt and how they have experimented with developing assertiveness skills and responses in a safe situation. Some pairs might like to explore one of the situations with the whole group and explain what was learnt and what will be tried. Individuals might like to comment on what they found difficult and will have to remember in future.

As a group, make a list of situations and responses which could be recorded on the flipchart so that all in the group could have their awareness raised of ways to manage situations more effectively in future.

This work needs to be kept for the final session.

Session Six: Self-confidence and self-esteem

 Trainer's notes

One of the keys to becoming and remaining assertive is having a good sense of self, feeling at ease with oneself, feeling able to cope and to take responsibility for oneself and events which happen. This section seeks to raise the awareness of the learners about the value of developing a good sense of self.

Brainstorm (40 min)

Brainstorm with the group the following three questions. OHTs DA2/3 help explore self-esteem.

> **1. What does it mean to have good self- esteem?**
>
> **2. What things would help someone to have a sense of self-esteem?**
>
> **3. Why does self-esteem help someone to be assertive?**

This exercise should help to make clear for the learners the links between a robust view of oneself and managing to be assertive. A good sense of self will help people to cope with:

- criticism
- rejection
- negative comments
- difficult situations e.g. dealing with authority, making a complaint, asking for help
- people who want to apply pressure
- the threat of loss of friendship, love, jobs, promotion etc. if something is not done

For people who have a strong sense of self such experiences will not:

- undermine them unduly
- be a threat
- cause them to be diminished in their own eyes
- leave them completely dependent on someone else for a sense of self and well being

Explain that working on developing self esteem is a large and on-going task. The learners will need to be able to identify what makes them feel less good about themselves and to tackle those aspects of themselves. Such work will involve significant honesty, soul searching and perhaps activities such as counselling. There may be particular issues to be resolved such as problems with addictions which may lead to problems with maintaining family relationships and friendships or retaining employment.

There are many exercises and self-assessment activities which the learner can try in order to consider aspects of self and to consider where there may be areas which could be more effectively developed. It is important for each person to be aware of the ways in which they view themselves and the assumptions they hold about themselves. Without such knowledge there can be little moving forward. There are many exercises for considering self esteem and developing self-knowledge. See for example Positive Attitudes in the *Developing Life Skills* manual, Self Management in this volume and some self assessment materials in *Becoming an Effective Trainer*.

The importance of considering self-esteem in relation to becoming more assertive is illustrated by OHTs 2 and 3. OHT 2 shows good self esteem which means that individuals are less likely to be dented and diminished by others and when things go wrong in their lives. OHT 3 shows the steps to lower self esteem. These aspects of lower self esteem leave people more likely to be knocked off balance and to be less likely to be able to take risks and so be assertive with others, less likely to be clear about their own wants or unable to stand up to others' demands.

Self assessment exercise (30 min)

DA8 and DA9 are self-assessment exercises. The learners may want to refer to DA7 and consider some of the criticisms they made of themselves and the ways in which they might like to change. They may like to work on such areas as part of improving a sense of self. Work on self-esteem and self-confidence will take time and may require specialist agencies to assist. A list of referrals may be needed.

What breeds greater self-esteem and self-confidence? (20 min)

Close this session with a brainstorm about the ways in which the group thinks that it can improve self-esteem and self confidence, e.g.

- Being comfortable with myself
- Not being ashamed of what I have done or am but coming to terms with myself
- Taking myself seriously and making an effort to develop the skills I have and to learn new ones
- Tackling some of the things I do not like about myself or my situation instead of letting it drift on
- Taking responsibility for what I do next and what happens to me
- Setting some goals and achieving them. These may be directly related to working on matters of assertiveness. For example, being able to take a compliment or being able to stand firm and not do something someone else wants through fear of rejection, managing to deal with a conflict situation instead of just burying it
- Having energy and motivation and succeeding makes people feel better about themselves

Session Seven: Planning to keep confident, to keep a sense of well-being and to stay assertive

 Trainer's notes

This final session pulls together the ideas and activities in this module. There is an Action Planning activity – DA11.

Summary (15 min)

As a group closing activity ask each member of the group to offer one thing which they found of interest from the module and some reasons for its value. Write these items and reasons on the flipchart. Encourage everyone to try to pick something different, but to say if an item already selected was also important to them. Make a note of all of the times a single item had been selected.

Action planning (35 min)

Explanations (5 min)

Ask the learners to use DA11.

Remind the learners that in thinking about making changes they need to set themselves **SMART** goals. That is they need to be realistic, to have small steps, they need to be targets towards which progress can be measured and they need to be timebound.

Planning (20 min)

Ask the learners to work alone for twenty minutes on their action plans. They will need to look back over some of the earlier activity sheets where they noted things which they would like to change or could change.

Sharing (10 min)

Ask the learners to work in pairs for the final 10 minutes to outline their goals and what they hope to do to achieve those goals. They can be as detailed and revealing as they choose. The other person should listen carefully and offer any suggestions which may help towards the realisation of a goal.

Closing game (10 min)

Bring the group back together and finish with a wind down and re-grouping game. Thank the learners.

PASSIVE

You are OK

I am not OK

I give in to your wants

AGGRESSIVE

I am OK

You are not

You give in to my wants

ASSERTIVE

I am OK   You are OK

I have the right to be me
You have the right to be you
I have the right to be listened to
You have the right to be listened to
I have the right to be treated as an equal
You have the right to be treated as an equal

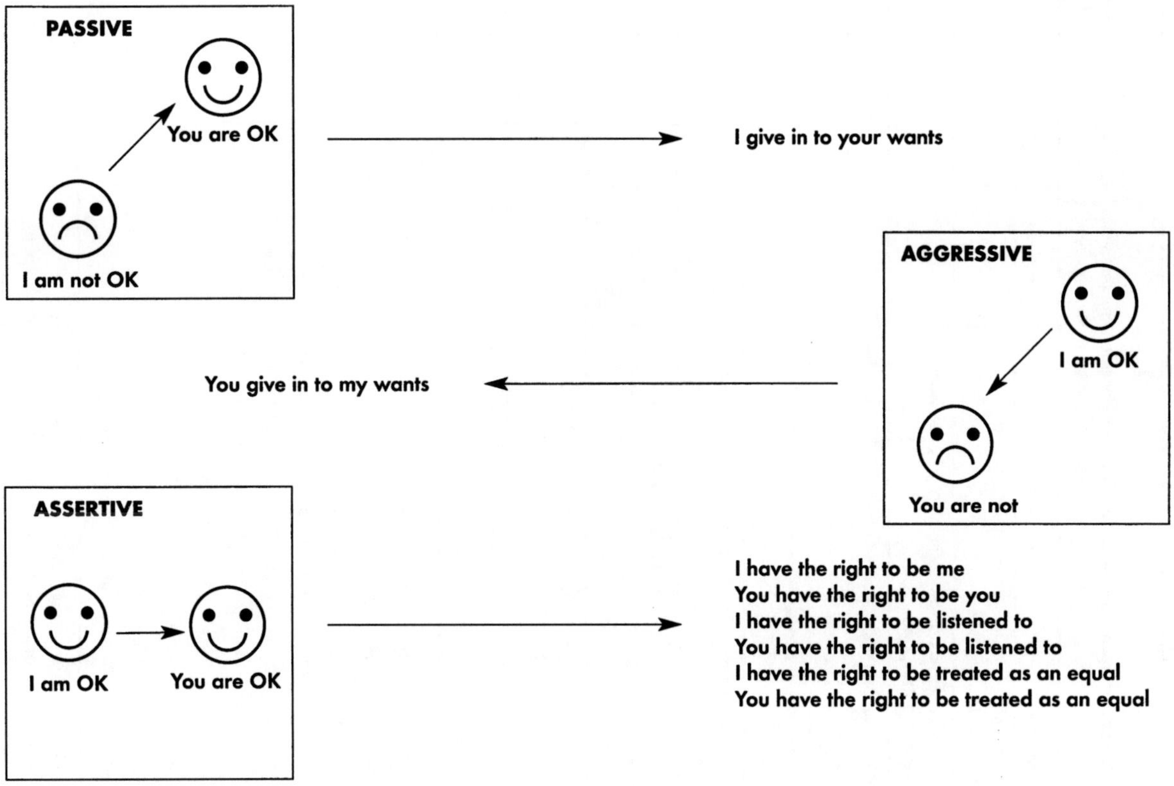

OHTDA2: Steps to higher self-esteem

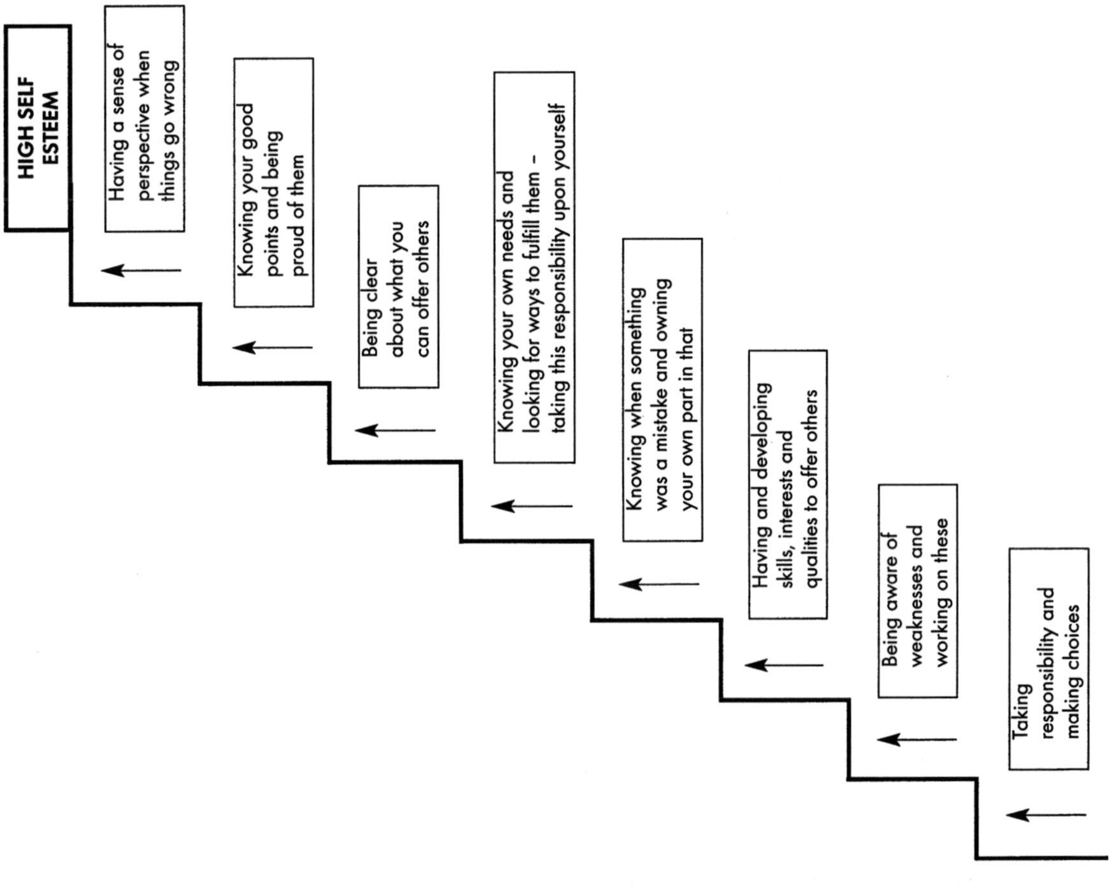

HIGH SELF ESTEEM

Having a sense of perspective when things go wrong

Knowing your good points and being proud of them

Being clear about what you can offer others

Knowing your own needs and looking for ways to fulfill them – taking this responsibility upon yourself

Knowing when something was a mistake and owning your own part in that

Having and developing skills, interests and qualities to offer others

Being aware of weaknesses and working on these

Taking responsibility and making choices

DA1: How do I behave?

Read through the following situations and decide what you would do. Then thinking about your response tick the column which applies to you.

Situation	Passively	Aggressively	Assertively
A person pushes in front of me in a queue and I react...			
A friend asks to borrow something I do not want to lend and I respond...			
When dealing with people in authority I tend to be...			
When I take back a faulty item I am...			
My partner wants me to do something I do not want to do so I am...			
At work I am asked to do more than is in my job contract. I am ...			
I had to phone the Benefits Agency again and yet again I spent ten minutes in a phone queue, when I finally got through I was...			
When I feel I am being bullied by others I am...			
Total up the ticks			

Tick any of the following which apply to you   ✓

I often apologise if I want something
I usually just take what I want
I don't find it hard to ask for what I want
I find it easier to tell people what to do - it's quicker
I like to get on with things without being told by anybody else
If you want something doing right you have to do it yourself
I don't debate with my kids - I just tell them
I don't like to ask for anything
I prefer to be told what to do
I have to check with others on how I am doing

Look back at your responses – are they mainly passive, aggressive or assertive or a mix? Underline the one which applies.

List any situations in which you would like to behave differently and why

---

OHTDA3: Steps to lower self-esteem

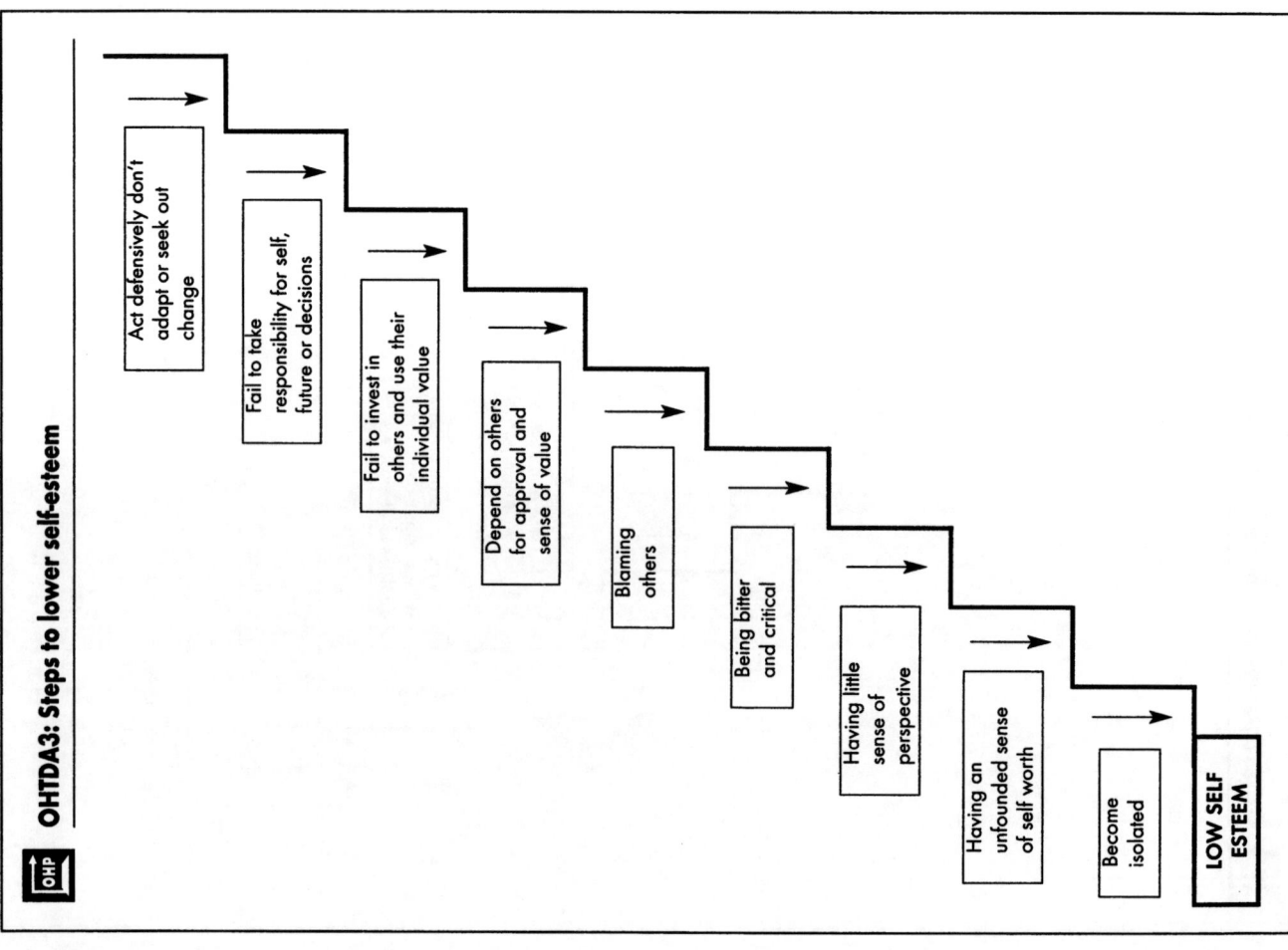

DA3: Situations

Read through the following three situations. Decide how a passive, an aggressive and an assertive person would respond to each situation. Decide what would be the longer-term and short-term advantages and disadvantages of each type of response. Use DA 04 to write down your answers

Situation One:

In order to make things work out better for you, you had decided to make changes to the ways in which you had been conducting your life. You've made some changes including: less drinking, making better use of your time and money, looking seriously for a better job and trying to get in better physical shape.

It had been important to you in trying to make these changes for you to stay away from some of your old friends. It's the weekend and you are feeling a bit bored. Two of your friends come round to get you to go out. They are not keen to take no for an answer.

Situation Two:

You've recently started going out with someone and want to make a go of the relationship. The person is everything that your previous partners have not been and everything you have always wanted.

Increasingly you find that your ideal person is asking you to do things which you do not want to do and to make changes to yourself which you are not keen to make.

Situation Three:

After much difficulty you have got a new job. The pay is reasonable and you like your workmates. The work is not bad but your immediate boss is becoming a pain. She keeps expecting that as you're the new one into the team, you will pick up any extra work and will stay on after hours to get many of the rush jobs finished.

DA2: Scenes for role play

Give each group one of the following scenes

1. Ben had been working as a delivery driver on a casual basis for the past two months. Some merchandise had been returned by a dissatisfied customer – at least that's what the customer said. It should have been amongst the goods in Ben's van. There is no record of the merchandise and Ben denies seeing it.

2. John had had a bit too much to drink and let his bad temper get the better of him. He had been suspicious that Alex was trying to go out with his ex-wife. He had accused his ex-wife of who had denied it and then he turned on Alex in the pub and begun to shout at him.

3. Four people were working behind the bar on Friday night. When the takings were cashed up they were £30 down. No-one knew anything about it. The Manager was called back to the bar from his night off with his new girlfriend. He was angry about that and even more angered when no-one would own up to knowing anything about the shortages in the takings.

DA5: Role plays

Each group needs one role play. Each role play is about a problem. The main characters should decide how they are going to approach the problem. One character should be aggressive. It may be that the other becomes aggressive and there is conflict or it may be that someone is passive and just gives in. There should be no attempt to sort the situation out by being assertive rather than aggressive

1. Bobby and Jeanette had been living together for a couple of years. Things had not been going so well. One big source of tension was Jeanette's son, Jon. He was a teenager who could not stay out of trouble despite promises that he would stop. He had begun to drink heavily and this made a difficult situation worse. Bobby was already at the end of his tether when there was a knock at the front door one Tuesday night to say...

2. The people in the flat above had been difficult since they had moved in. They had never bothered to carpet the floors, turn down their music or to keep quiet on the stairs. They often had friends in and people they met in the pub. Often there was shouting, swearing and fighting on the stairways and loud music in the middle of the night. This had been going on for just too long and having been woken up for yet another night Jo decided something had to be done.

3. Everyone knew that he had had a reputation for chatting up women and trying to get as much as he could from the situation. There had been some ugly scenes in the past but it didn't seem to stop him. Jan and her friends were out to celebrate her birthday. He'd had a few and, not sensitive to anyone else at the best of times, just wouldn't take 'no' from Jan for an answer.

DA4: Response sheet

Number of the situation . . . .

A passive person would:

In the short-term this would have
Advantages

Disadvantages

In the longer-term this would have
Advantages

Disadvantages

An aggressive person would:

In the short-term this would have
Advantages

Disadvantages

In the longer-term this would have
Advantages

Disadvantages

An assertive person would:

In the short-term this would have
Advantages

Disadvantages

In the longer-term this would have
Advantages

Disadvantages

DA7: Criticisms

Read through the following comments and ✓ any which you say about or to yourself in column 1 and then ✓ any which are made about you by others in column 2.

Fill in any that you want to in the blank spaces.
Then complete the questions at the bottom of the page.

Comment	1: I say	2: Others say
I can't manage money well		
I need someone else to make the decisions		
I always seem to do the wrong thing		
It's just the way I am		
I can't keep a job for long		
I just say the wrong thing too often		
I can't hold my drink		
I don't know when I am well off		
I just don't treat people properly		
I've let myself go		
I'm selfish		
I'm too fat/too thin/too old/too young		
I'm stupid		
I'm careless		
I can't meet deadlines		
I'm bossy		
I'm a waster		
I don't put effort into other people		

Other things you say about yourself
What sorts of things which you say about yourself do you think you want to change?

Look at the things others say about you - do they get said by a range of people or just one or two?

What does this tell you?

Do you think that the comments are true?

Do you want to change?

What changes would you like to make?

DA6: Saying what you mean and meaning what you say

Being vague, allowing your mind to be changed or not saying what you want is not being assertive and won't get you what you want from a situation. Remember the following points for clear and assertive communication.

1. Decide what you want from a situation before you start thinking about what to say.

2. Decide on a few key things you want to say. Keep them brief and simple. Write them down if it helps you remember.

3. Check that what you have said has been heard and understood.

   Before you agree to anything, step back from the situation. Check that you have understood really what is asked of you and then ask yourself:

   What are your gut feelings?
   What does the situation involve?
   What would you recommend to your best friend to do?
   What more information do you need?
   Can anyone offer you sensible advice or help?

4. Does your body language, the way you are speaking and what you say work together to give the same message? Or are you looking like you do not take yourself seriously and can be encouraged to change your mind?

5. Don't agree to something or say what you do not mean just to avoid conflict or to buy time. It only leads to greater difficulties later on.

DA9: Rating your self esteem

Read through the following statements and tick the column which applies to you.

	Yes	No
1. Do you see yourself as a worthwhile person?		
2. Can you admit to making mistakes?		
3. Do you enjoy your relationships with other people?		
4. Do you welcome new experiences?		
5. Are you willing to trust people and give them a chance?		
6. Can you forgive yourself?		
7. Do you give yourself the chance to enjoy yourself?		

More Yeses than Nos? ... The more Yeses the higher your self esteem

	Yes	No
1. Do you feel bad when people criticise you?		
2. Are you your own worst critic?		
3. Do you feel a failure if something goes wrong?		
4. Do people ever say you have no sense of proportion?		
5. Do you feel bad about your appearance more often than good about it?		
6. Do you spend time thinking more about what has gone wrong than right in a day?		
7. Do you feel that you spend a lot of time pleasing others?		

More Yeses than Nos? ... The more Yeses the lower your self esteem

---

DA8: Situations or people when I find it hard to be assertive

Complete the sentences below for 4 people or situations when you find it hard to be assertive

The situation or person when I find assertiveness hard is:

1.

2.

3.

4.

Rather than being assertive I tend to:

1.

2.

3.

4.

I think this happens because:

1.

2.

3.

4.

In the future I would rather that I:

1.

2.

3.

4.

DA11: An assertiveness action plan

My key areas for change are:

1.

2.

THE PLAN TO TACKLE THESE AREAS

List SMART Action Steps

Start Dates

_____

Who can help and with what?

I will know I have made progress when:

I will review my progress on:

Date plan made:

DA10: Portrait of yourself

Spend some time thinking about yourself in order to come up with a description or picture of yourself. You may want to use pictures taken from magazines or draw yourself or you may just want to use words. Include all your good qualities e.g. sense of humour, punctuality, honesty, being warm hearted, etc. Come up with two pictures, one of how you see yourself and the other of how you would like to see yourself. Fold the page lengthways and put the two side by side

What are the differences between your two pictures?

How much of yourself do you really want to change and why?

Seeing it from others' points of view

 The module takes 6 hours 10 minutes to deliver and is divided into:

1. Introducing the issues (2 hours)

2. What prevents seeing it from others' points of view? (1 hour)

3. New skills, new strategies: making changes (3 hours 40 min)

4. Conclusions (30 min)

It is a module which emphasises role-play and hot seating to better encourage the learners to actively experience situations from another's point of view.

 The module uses:

- role-play

- discussion

- hot seating

- self-assessment

- brainstorm

 Trainer's notes

This module links with many others in this manual. It is designed to focus the learners' attention on the importance of appreciating others' points of view. It encourages learners to become aware that others have feelings, expectations, prejudices and concerns, and that these will be brought into any social interaction and have a bearing on the outcome. Learners may fail to see others with whom they are in close contact as people in the round, as people with preoccupations, concerns and preconceptions. For learners who have spent time in socially isolated situations, have withdrawn into themselves, have been homeless or leading chaotic lifestyles or have lived in some residential contexts there may be failures to see themselves as well as others as whole people, and to appreciate themselves as impacting upon and interacting with others. Raising awareness of such will be a significant area of work.

The module aims to raise learners' awareness of the value of seeing situations as others may see them and appreciating that there are several possible outcomes to many problems and situations. The importance of developing such awareness should be emphasised for:

- decreasing conflicts

- developing skills in negotiation and reaching compromise

- reducing hurt to others

- helping learners to experience a better quality of life because they will be able to:
  - share others' experience
  - appreciate what others say and do and why this is so
  - understand the impact of personal actions and decisions on others and the ways in which these may be perceived

A greater appreciation of others and realisation of others' needs and views will help an individual to feel that they belong, that they are part of a group and to feel less isolated.

Developing the skills and sensitivities to appreciate others' situations and circumstances are ones which people usually develop as they age and mature. However, it is easy to lose sight of others' viewpoints or fail to appreciate their experiences, rights and individuality:

- at times of stress
- at times of preoccupation
- when people have not been encouraged to consider others' feelings or reflect on their own behaviour
- if people are unduly self-absorbed – e.g. facing personal difficulties
- when there have been few incentives to value others
- when someone is socially and emotionally isolated
- when a living or working environment does not encourage such behaviour

Seeing it from others' points of view depends on:
- developing the skills to imagine someone else's experience and why they may act in certain ways
- thinking about and appreciating how an individual's behaviour may impact on and affect someone else
- having concern for others sufficient enough to encourage and motivate an individual to want to modify or change their behaviour
- an individual developing a sense of responsibility towards others and feeling part of what happens to and for other people

Session One: Introducing the issues

Trainer's notes

This session introduces learners to some of the reasons why individuals fail to see things from another's point of view, what they miss by doing this, what they would gain by looking at situations from others' points of view and ways to use such insights. Subsequent sessions look at skill development.

Opening activity (10 min)

Ask the learners to move their chairs to the sides of the room. Then in the clear space to move around the room, they should not knock into each other, they should try to be aware of where other people are and not get in their way. At intervals tell the learners to stop, to move anti-clockwise, to walk faster, slower and so on.

This warm up session will make the learners very conscious of themselves, of each other and of the need to know where people are in the room.

At the close of the exercise ask the learners what they thought the activity was about and draw out the points as above.

Brainstorm (20 min)

Having reformed the group, ask the group to brainstorm what the following phrase means to them.

> **Seeing it from others' points of view**

There should be no censure or attack on what another says. The brainstorm may reveal that they think it wimpy or what 'good people' do or that it stops you getting on or makes you soft. They may think it's something they are good at or bad at. The trainer should draw out: feelings about seeing things from others' points of view, the benefits of this and any perceived weaknesses of doing this.

Once the brainstorm is exhausted ask the learners to try to group their responses as:

- benefits
- weaknesses
- their feelings about seeing from others' points of view
- why it may be hard to see things from others' points of view

Ask what is meant by a few of their responses.

This opening brainstorm will provide much basic attitudinal information for the trainer. The trainer may want to refer back to the opening activity and to the value of knowing where others were in the room in order to prevent accidents, possible conflict, upset, to be fair about use of space and so on.

The benefits (10 min)

Develop the earlier brainstorm and focus on the benefits of seeing things from others' points of view. This may include:

- better able to control my behaviour
- more able to be acceptable to others
- feel I share more with others
- feel more accepted
- know when I ask for things I am likely to gain them because requests are appropriate
- avoid upset
- know when to back down
- can compromise

If the learners cannot think of benefits and can only focus on weaknesses try to find out why, ask them for examples and for reasons for their replies.

Role-plays (1 hour)

In small groups ask the learners to rehearse one scene and then to role-play it to the group (OPOV1). At the close of each scene, keep the characters in role and ask them questions such as:

- what does it feel like when he/she wouldn't listen to what you had to say
- what do you think of his/her attitude
- what would you like him/her to have done
- what do you think is going through his/her head now
- what was he/she thinking when they started speaking
- what do you think they think is in your mind

Encourage the others in the group to ask questions. Then ask the audience for:

- their views on what each character thinks the other is thinking
- why they think the situation is developing as it is
- what they think will happen next
- what they think should happen and how this could come about

After each role-play allow the characters to de-role by making some comment on the situation and on their character's behaviour.

Ask for the learners to volunteer points which they had gained from the exercise.

Thank everyone for working hard.

Review (20 min)

Refer the learners back to the brainstorm of the benefits of seeing situations from others' points of view and ask if after the role-plays they want to add any more points, expand any points or prioritise any of the points as being particularly important.

Session Two: What prevents you seeing from others' points of view?

Starting from the premise that there is value in seeing situations from others' points of view this session focuses on why individuals often don't or are prevented from seeing things from others' points of view.

Activity One (20 min)

Ask the learners to work alone (10 minutes) and then in pairs (10 minutes) on OPOV2. This is a brainstorm activity which will require some thought about themselves and their experiences of others. It requires the learners to compare their brainstorms.

Whole group review (10 min)

Bring the pairs back together and ask them what they have discovered about why people do not always see things from others' points of view. Ask for a few examples from each pair. Tick any suggestions which come up repeatedly.

Self-assessment exercise (10 min)

Give the learners OPOV3 and ask them to work alone and respond honestly. No-one else need see their responses.

Review (10 min)

Ask for any volunteers to say what they have found about themselves from doing this exercise. Were there any surprises? How did they feel about the checklist? What else might they have added to it if they had written it?

Alone (10 min)

Ask the learners to reflect on the discussions and their completed checklist (OPOV3). They should then work through the questions on OPOV4. This asks them to consider what they might like to change and why. The next session works on how. Ask them to keep OPOV4.

The trainer should walk around helping and checking on the learners as they progress this exercise.

Close the session with a game to bring the group back together in a sharing exercise and emphasise the importance of awareness of others.

Session Three: New skills, new strategies: making changes

Trainer's role
Recap that:
   i) the group has considered the value of looking at situations from others' points of view and imagining how others may see you or your actions – provide specific examples of such benefits

ii) the group has thought about what may prevent people from seeing it from others' points of view. Offer reasons, e.g. being stressed about something, forgetting a close friend or partner also has rights and concerns etc.

Explain this session will consider the skills and strategies which individuals can develop to help them become more effective in seeing themselves and situations as others see them. This will help them to:

- avoid conflicts
- share experiences with others
- build more equal relationships
- feel better about themselves

Doing it better (1) Seeing

Activity One (15 min)

Give the learners the diagram OPOV5. Ask them to read though the steps and comment on what may be valuable, hard or easy to do, or what seems to not make sense to them.

Emphasise:

- the value of standing back
- asking how you see a situation and how they may see the same situation and why
- asking what is important to you and to them
- considering how your behaviour and wants may appear to others
- asking yourself how important the situation is to you and to your overall values
- using your communication skills to good effect

Working in pairs on situations (30 min)

Set the learners to work through the four situations on OPOV6. Ask them to consider the situations from both people's points of view. At the close of the exercise one of each pair should be ready to summarise the key issues from both parties' points of view. Go round and check on progress.

Review (15 min)

Ask for volunteers to go through what they think are the key issues. Record these. How much consensus is there? Did some pairs have difficulties – why? Was one situation harder to tackle than another? Why?

Alone (15 min)

Ask the learners to spend time thinking about some occasions when they failed to see a situation from someone else's point of view. What were the consequences? What could they have done? Use OPOV7.

In pairs (20 min)

Ask the learners in pairs to talk to each other about an occasion when they failed to see something from another's point of view. OPOV7 will act as a basis for this. Can the other person help them to complete more ideas on OPOV7?

As a whole group (15 min)

Ask the group to reconvene:

- how did they find the exercise?
- how much harder is it to discuss their own situation than work on the fictional ones and why?
- what gains did they make looking at a situation in pairs?

Look again at the diagram (OPOV5) and ask the learners how valuable it is. Ask how important it is for the learners to consider a situation against the backcloth of:

- their values and what else is important to them?
- what may be important to others?

Doing it better (2) Communicating well

Review with the Whole Group (30 min)

Brainstorm as a group the important communication skills and their key features which would help two people to explore and perhaps to reconcile their differences. Record the group's thinking in a structured way. For example:

Communication Skill	Key Features
Ask what he/she thinks	
Listen carefully	Pay attention, don't interrupt, ask if something's not clear ...
Show the person you have listened	
Check you understand	Say back the key points "so you are saying ..."

Take time to complete this group discussion thoroughly. Refer back to other modules for detailed accounts of communication skills; e.g. Module 1 and 2 in this manual.

Doing it better (3) Compromise and negotiation

Trainer's role

Learning to compromise and the value of compromising will help the learners to resolve their differences. Learners may see compromise as weakness or as backing down and this will need to be tackled. Learners may need help to understand compromise as an immediate term strategy but one which may help their longer-term goals and life values.

Opening brainstorm (15 min)

Ask the learners to brainstorm the word compromise.

- How many thought it to be a negative thing?
- How many spoke of backing down or not getting their own way or losing a battle?
- Use the brainstorm and its outcomes as a way of developing key learning points about the importance of compromise.

How do you compromise? (15 min)

Ask the learners to think briefly in pairs about how they see a compromise happening. They may be able to give an example from life experience.

Give out the statements (OPOV8) and ask the learners in pairs to think about them and to select those that they think are important. They may pick all or a few. Ask them to put them in order of sorting out a compromise.

Review (20 min)

Collect the group's ideas about what makes up a compromise and create a flowchart to include all the steps which the learners may go through in reaching a compromise.

Session Four: Conclusions

Review (10 min)

Without labouring the various learning points recap the areas which the module has covered. Note these on the flipchart. If appropriate, use some of the group's earlier brainstorms as a way of demonstrating their starting points and how their thinking has developed.

Working in pairs (10 min)

Ask the learners to work in pairs to create two statements about two aspects of the programme which have been of value to them.

Closing rounds (10 min)

Ask each learner to give one of the statements to the whole group. Record them but do not comment during the closing round.

Ask the group to look at the collected ideas. Add any things which as a trainer and individual you have thought particularly important.

Thank the learners for their hard work.

OPOV1: Things go wrong because...

Give each group only one situation to consider. The learners should each take on one of the main characters and should work out how the scene will develop. One or both characters may fail to understand the other's point of view

Any additional members in each small group may help shape the role–play or may join in the role–play as a minor character.

Lesley feels she has been trapped at home for the past three days with baby Paul who has a bad cold. On top of this he has been teething. Lesley has not had much sleep, has been worried about the illness and feels that you don't really care or even realise she's doing her best.

You think Lesley has it easy staying at home with the two kids or meeting her mother or friends when she wants. You're fed up after three nights of Paul's crying and want to go out to a darts match. You're going to make her see you have it tough.

You'd moved to a new town four weeks ago. You'd done it to break with your old mates and to start again. Everyone said it'd be hard. It is. The only thing going for this place is the girl at the petrol station who's on the shift before yours. She always smiles and you know she fancies you really. Tonight you're going to try again to get her to agree to go out with you even though she said 'no' yesterday.

It's not fair. You've been in the job for nearly three years and this bright spark college lad has just come in and got promoted. Your boss needs her head tested – you know the job inside out so why can't she see her mistake? You storm into her office to sort it out.

OPOV2

Use the spider diagram below to help you to think of as many reasons as you can why you or other people may fail to see things from others' point of view

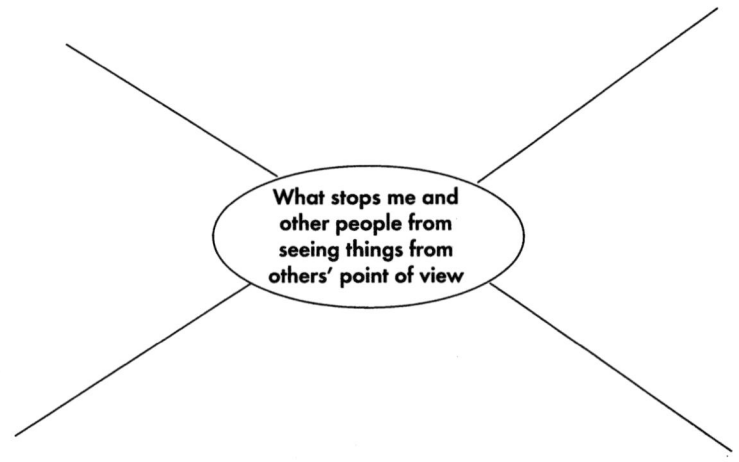

What stops me and other people from seeing things from others' point of view

OPOV4: I think I am ...

Where 1 is really poor and 10 is good I would rate myself on seeing things from others' points of view as:

1   2   3   4   5   6   7   8   9   10

I think I am best at home/work/where I live/in a training situation/with people I know well ... at seeing things from others' point of view. List the situations you are best in – think of some reasons

List the situations you are worst in and list some reasons

The situations I would like to do better in are:

The reasons for this are:

The people I would like to improve with are:

My reasons are:

OPOV3: I think I ...

Read through the statements below and ✓ those which apply to you

I know I don't take my partner's view into account	
I think I don't see things the way my kids do	
I can never see why people make the decisions they do	
I never really understand how my boss sees things	
I'm better at considering other people who are at work	
I get an idea in my head and want it to happen	
I take more notice of strangers' views than people close to me	
I think my friends think I am stubborn and don't take them into account	
I am more concerned about how strangers see me than people close to me	
I like to see what I want to happen happen	
I often challenge what people say about me	
I do talk over people sometimes	
I know I'm not very sympathetic to others' problems	
I don't think I have to change my behaviour for anyone	
I often wish I could just get on with things by myself	
If people don't like me … tough	

Read through the statements you have ticked.
What does this tell you about yourself?

Is there anything you would like to change?

OPOV6: Others' points of view

Read though the four situations and think:

- what are the key issues for each person?
- how does each person see the situation?
- who wants what from the situation and why?
- what would you advise each to do?

1. They had been married for two years and perhaps should never have been married. However there was the baby to think about. He was the only thing which they had in common. Sally has not met someone else. She has decided that all the arguments they have are doing neither of them any good. Phil won't hear the truth of this or anything else Sally says. He just wants it to go on as "normal". If they split it would be just like his parents all over again.

2. "For God's sake – get out of the house and find a job." Bev had heard this everyday for the past few months. There were no jobs she could do. Going out meant sitting about in the cold or waiting in lines at the Job Centre. She didn't feel very confident about anything just now. Losing that job had really upset her, she still didn't understand why it was her who was made redundant.

3. Darren had been to see his boss again about his problems with being bullied on the shop floor. The boss called them practical jokes – he accused Darren of not being a good sport. Really he thought Darren was just not as good or just as fast as the others. He had decided that he was not going to upset a good bunch of lads for Darren. Darren was getting more stressed, sleeping badly and fearing to go to work.

4. He knew he shouldn't have done it. He couldn't explain why. Just lately the only way he was coping was doing stupid things – spending too much on clothes and CDs; drinking too much; staying out with his mates; he'd even had a fling with a girl he's met at a club last week. He knew none of this was helping his marriage. He just couldn't bear the noise of the baby, Sharon being so depressed and the constant need to find more money to pay for household stuff. He wanted to be single again.

OPOV5: Seeing it from others' point of view

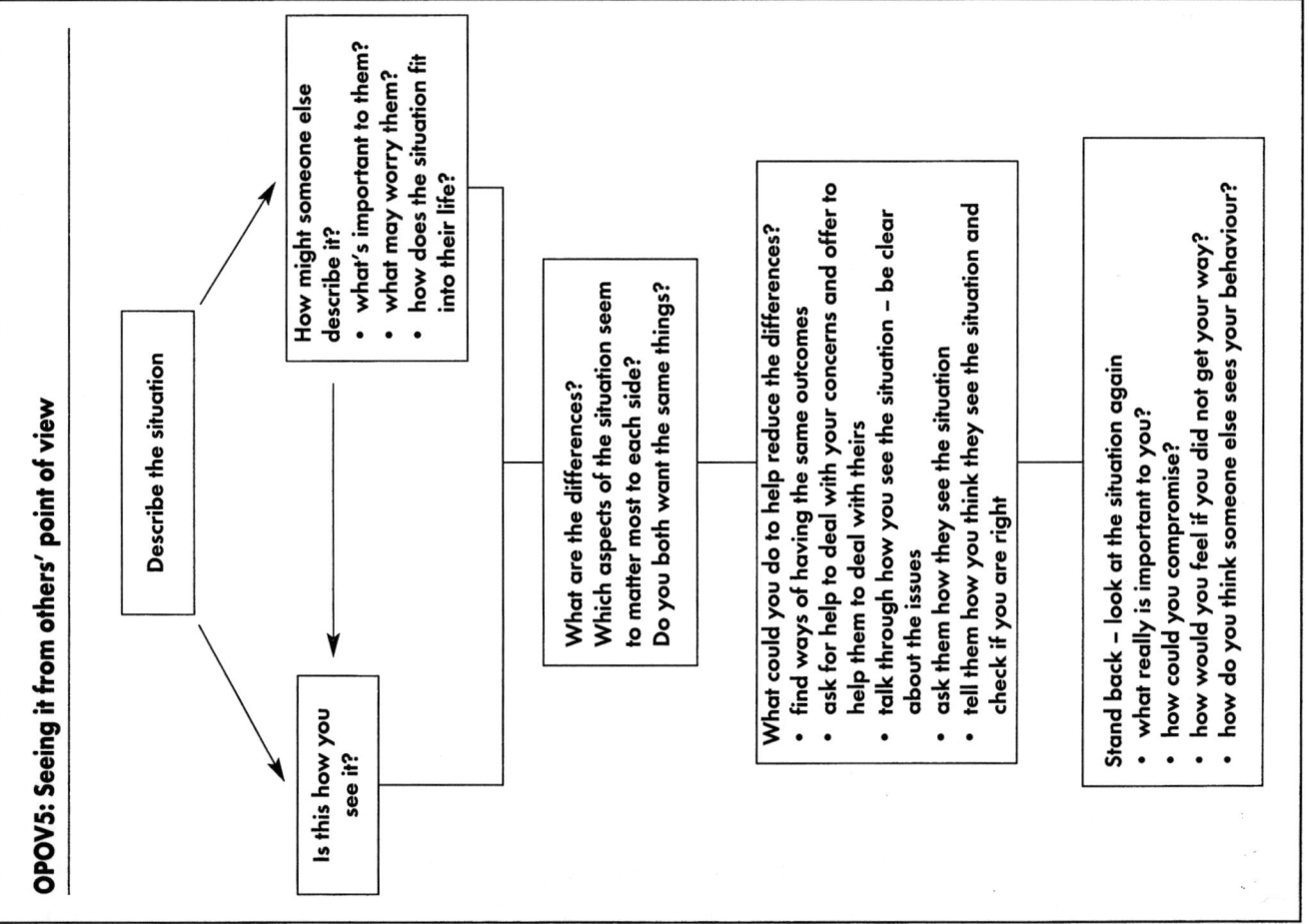

Describe the situation

Is this how you see it?

How might someone else describe it?
- what's important to them?
- what may worry them?
- how does the situation fit into their life?

What are the differences?
Which aspects of the situation seem to matter most to each side?
Do you both want the same things?

What could you do to help reduce the differences?
- find ways of having the same outcomes
- ask for help to deal with your concerns and offer to help them to deal with theirs
- talk through how you see the situation – be clear about the issues
- ask them how they see the situation
- tell them how you think they see the situation and check if you are right

Stand back – look at the situation again
- what really is important to you?
- how could you compromise?
- how would you feel if you did not get your way?
- how do you think someone else sees your behaviour?

OPOV7

Think back and remember a couple of situations when you did not see a situation the same as someone else

Describe what the situation was	How did you see it? What was important?	How might they have seen the situation? What do you think was important to them?	What was the outcome? How did you feel? What else could have happened? What would you now have **liked** to have happened?

OPOV8

Select the statements you think are important to reaching compromise

- What's really important in my life?
- What is the situation – as I see it?
- How do they see the situation?
- What do they want from the situation?
- What do I want from the situation – ideally?
- What would I be unhappy about as an outcome?
- What would be okay for me as a result?
- I need to clearly think about and write down what I want and why
- When I talk to the others/him/her I need to express myself clearly, reasonably and positively
- I need to ask what they/he/she wants and show I am listening
- I need to present my compromise carefully and not just expect them to agree
- I need to have some discussion and not just tell people what I think

Relationships with partners

 The module may last for 19 hours and is divided in the following way:

1. Relationships with partners (3 hours)
2. Starting relationships (1 hour 50 min)
3. Keeping relationships healthy (2 hours 30 min)
4. Phases and changes, including endings (2 hours 35 min)
5. Men and women: attitudes and expectations (4 hours 10 min)
6. Communication (3 hours 40 min)
7. Close of module (1 hour 15 min)

 It links with developing assertiveness skills, learning to say 'no' and learning to ask clearly for what one wants.

The module addresses many serious and important issues. These include:

- expectations about having a relationship
- expectations of self in a relationship
- expectations of a partner in a relationship
- defining personal values
- defining boundaries and reasonable behaviours
- gender expectations, beliefs and values
- maintaining dysfunctional relationships and why this happens

The module does not set out to provide solutions to relationship difficulties or to tell people how to make successful relationships. The module does not require the trainer to take on the roles of a relationship counsellor or marriage guidance worker. There are many professional agencies better equipped to take on such work. A list of some such organisations is supplied at the close of the module.

The sessions and activities should encourage the learner to become more aware of:

- why he or she enters certain types of relationships or finds certain types of people attractive
- why he or she feels a need to be in a relationship
- why he or she maintains relationships which may be damaging
- why he or she may fail to sustain relationships
- his or her expectations of self and others in relationships
- personal values and expectations
- the role of gender expectations in relationships

The module aims to provoke some self analysis and to encourage thinking about areas for personal development or change. The module is not a 'relationships quick-fix-kit'.

 This module makes use of the following learning styles:

- role play
- discussion
- self-assessment
- diary-keeping
- small and large group discussion
- collage work
- letter writing
- action planning

Trainer's notes

This module links with those preceding it, such as Developing Communication Skills, Developing Assertiveness, Seeing it From Others' Points of View and those following about developing relationships with others. The module draws on many aspects of skill development – questioning, listening, making sense of what others say and taking action.

Trainer's warning

The trainer should be aware of the potential dangers involved in discussing close relationships.

1. Some learners may be seeking satisfying relationships, others may be in poor relationships or just finishing relationships. Learners may, for many reasons, be feeling very vulnerable and in need of great sensitivity on the part of trainer and fellow group members. Establishing some group groundrules is essential. These should cover confidentiality, no personal attacks or personal criticism and respect for diversity. Many of the activities assume heterosexual relationships but this should not blind the trainer to the likelihood of working with learners in same sex relationships.

2. The module may touch on difficult matters. While trainer and group members will want to be supportive sessions should not be dominated by the problem of a group member. Appropriate help should be sought or referrals made.

3. If learners feel vulnerable or certain issues touch sensitivities then time out or ways to take a break should be established at the outset. However, the module is not setting out to do one-to-one work or counselling.

4. The intention of the module is to raise awareness and provoke thought. This should be reiterated. The fact the module is no 'quick fix' to relationship matters must be emphasised.

Session One: Relationships – why do we have them?

 Trainer's notes

This introductory session opens up discussion about why people enter relationships, what they expect to gain from them, give to them and may move them to consider how reasonable their expectations may be. It introduces:

- values
- reasonableness
- expectations
- gender based expectations
- alternatives to coupledom

Opening brainstorms (20 min)

Open the session by explaining that these early activities ask them to think about why they have close relationships.

Brainstorm:

> **Why do people have close relationships?**

Responses may include:

- friendship
- company
- being better off
- sharing resources
- sense of belonging
- not being lonely
- sex
- children
- what everyone does

Run two further brainstorms either as two small groups concurrently, then pooling ideas and as two simultaneous brainstorms:

The advantages of close relationships	**The disadvantages of close relationships**

These early activities may highlight group members' assumptions. Some contributions to the brainstorms could be explored for meaning and for examples.

Why do I have close relationships? (15 min)

Ask the learners to use checklist RWP1. Ask the learners to look through their checklist and see if there are any patterns in what they have ticked; e.g. do they want someone to do things for them or to do things for someone else? do they seek and have balanced relationships?

Ask the learners to think about a relationship they have recently had or have and to consider whether it gives them the things they have ticked. (RWP2)

Definitions: small groups (10 min)

Having provoked some thinking about close relationships ask the learners to work in small groups to try to define what they mean by a close relationship.

Collect the various groups' definitions and check for similarities and differences. The trainer should add a further definition as appropriate. Encourage discussion about the various definitions. If consensus is possible note this. Keep these definitions for later sessions.

Expectations (10 min)

Explain that we all enter relationships with expectations about what they will give us (refer back to RWP1 and RWP2) and about the other person. Expectations may be reasonable or unreasonable ones. Ask the learners to think about what expectations they have of close relationships. Learners can work alone or in pairs and make a list of expectations they have of relationships.

Working alone (20 min)

Ask the learners to work alone to consider what they think partners *expect of them and of a relationship with them*, use RWP3 to help structure their thinking.

Ask the learners to compare their own lists of another's expectations of them with their expectations of others. Ask:

- How close are the two lists?
- Are there things which the learners expect of others which they may not want to give to others or would not expect others to require of them

Ask the learners to mark their brainstorm list with ✓s and *s for things they expect of others and others may expect of them. They might like to also consider what they are prepared to give others.

Small group discussion (15 min)

Ask the learners to work in small groups to discuss the findings from their brainstorm RWP03 list of expectations.

Ask the learners to decide as a group why there are:

1. differences between what we expect of partners and what we expect them to expect of us
2. similarities between what we expect of others and what we expect them to expect of us

Ask the learners to consider why they do not want to meet partners' expectations of them.

Collage (20 min)

Ask the learners to create a collage using magazines of the types of things they hope for from a close relationship. The activity will help draw out ideas and will help discussion.

Words can be added to the collage as well as the images.

Allow time for the learners to look at each other's collages and to decide what they think they represent in terms of expectations of the person, the relationship and its outcomes.

Group discussion (15 min)

Ask the learners to brainstorm a list of expectations people have about relationships and of the other person in the relationship.

```
Expectations of partners and relationships
```

The brainstorm may include:

- consideration
- security
- excitement
- take an interest
- a future
- share money
- a good home
- feeling safe
- sharing faith/values

- money
- honesty
- sex
- be good looking
- help around the house
- protection
- nice things
- look after me
- having a family

These ideas could be reviewed in light of what seems reasonable or unreasonable.

Men and women: roles and relationships (15 min)

The trainer will need to be aware that some learners will be or may be in same sex relationships. As a group ask the learners to brainstorm:

Women's Roles in a Relationship	Men's Roles in a Relationship

Encourage as many ideas as possible without comment. This flipchart sheet should be saved for later sessions. At this stage check back with the learners what they mean by certain of their suggestions, whether only women or only men can do certain things and why there may be differences or similarities.

Check:

- To what extent had gender already had an impact in their earlier work on expectations?
- To what extent was this something that the learners had not yet considered?

Small group work (15 min)

Ask small groups to review the types of expectations they have of others and which others may have of them and decide if some of these expectations are based on sex role expectations or behaviours/attitudes based on different gender expectations.

Ask the learners to look at their lists and at the collage work.

Encourage group feedback and record what observations the small groups have made.

Continuum (15 min)

Draw an imaginary line diagonally across the room. One end represents fixed views and expectations of women's and men's roles and the other very flexible ideas and expectations about women's and men's roles. Ask the learners to place themselves along the line to demonstrate whether they consider themselves as flexible or traditionalist in relation to gender expectations.

Ask for some learners to explain why they have adopted a particular position. Discuss reasons and any definitions of sex roles. Allow for any changes in position. Record the learners' places.

Review (10 min)

Recap on the activities to date. These have covered:

- reasons for relationships
- whether personal relationships – current or recent 'match' these reasons
- expectations about what a relationship and a partner offers
- expectations being or not being gender specific

Work around the group, asking each to offer something they have not thought about before or consider interesting from the session.

Session Two: Starting relationships

 Trainer's notes

These activities encourage the learners to think about why they enter relationships and to consider their own values and expectations. This session encourages learners to become aware of the reasons that relationships may fail because they start off on the wrong footing.

The key messages are:

- having realistic expectations
- taking time to discuss important issues
- taking time to get to know the other person and knowing him/her in a variety of situations before marriage or living together
- setting up good communications

- knowing oneself
- being personally mature with a life of one's own

Opening session (15 min)

Introduce this area of work as about starting relationships. Explain that it is an important area to consider because if the start goes wrong then a relationship may not last very long or may not be a healthy one if it does survive.

Ask the learners to brainstorm:

> ### Why do people start relationships?

Review the suggestions. Assign positive, negative or neutral values to them. For example, boredom or loneliness may not be positive reasons, having seen someone around and liked them is positive.

Role-plays (35 min)

Ask the learners to work in pairs or threes to consider a short sketch in which one describes to a friend(s) why he/she is planning to start relationship/has just started a relationship. The reasons may be positive or negative or a mix. There should be several motivating reasons. The friend(s) should encourage or question what has taken place and the basis for the decision. The other character should try to answer these questions. Allow ten minutes for this.

Ask for a couple of pairs/threes to enact their role-plays. At the close of each ask whether the role-play has changed the character's mind or whether he/she will still go ahead. Discuss with the group the possible consequences and course of the relationship. Take about 25 minutes for this.

Self assessment and discussion (20 min)

Use the Starting Out checklist of statements (RWP4) for the learners to determine what may drive them to start relationships. After the lists have been completed ask for any volunteer to describe what they have found.

All the statements are fairly negative reasons for starting a relationship and may if not balanced by positive reasons mean that the learners are:

- fairly immature or not independent – getting into relationships because everyone else does
- not being thoughtful about why they want a relationship – just drifting into it
- not being assertive about their own wants or needs

Discussion and brainstorm (20 min)

Discuss with the learners the importance of their own maturity before starting a relationship and knowing fairly clearly what they want. Explore as a brainstorm with the dangers of perhaps being immature, becoming dependent and not knowing what they personally want. Their suggestions may include:

- getting too dependent on someone
- doing things they don't want
- getting into a relationship they wish later they hadn't
- wasting time going out with the wrong person
- feeling uncomfortable with values being undermined

Small groups (20 min)

In small groups ask the learners to draw up a hit list of six main points to consider before getting into a relationship. Share these lists with the whole group. Suggest any further points and use this as a group summary.

Session Three: Relationships staying healthy

These activities encourage the learners to consider why they consider a relationship to be good or bad; what keeps relationships healthy and how they may work to support or to damage a relationship. The learners will need to be reminded about effective communication skills. The ways in which communication skills support, help the development and add to a relationship are outlined.

Introductory activity (10 min)

Ask the learners to decide how good they would rate themselves at relationships on a 1 to 10 scale (see RWP5). Ask the learners to then decide what 'good at' means to them and to consider their strong points and areas to develop

Feedback (20 min)

Ask for some volunteers to share what they have written. Emphasise they don't have to be too self revelatory.

Brainstorm of what 'good at' means. This may include:

- honesty
- talking
- interest in each other
- making time

- offering friendship
- caring
- being concerned
- being supportive

Then list what they think constitutes being 'poor at' relationships. Some may be simple opposites, other items may spark fresh thinking about what constitutes a good relationship. Items may include:

- not having time for each other
- not listening or ignoring someone's needs
- taking a person for granted
- not seeing the other person as having rights

Lecturette (15 min)

Explain that by the close of the session the learners should be aware of the ingredients for keeping a relationship healthy and that they may like to think about any changes they want to make to the ways in which they run relationships and the ways in which they expect others to relate to them in a close relationship.

Use the notes (RWP6) as pointers for keeping relationships healthy. It could also be used as a handout.

Role-plays and discussion (50 min)

As a way of reviewing this material put the learners in small groups and ask them to work with one of the three case studies (RWP7). They should discuss the situation and prepare a role-play.

After each role-play, hot seat some of the characters and find out:
- how they felt about the situation
- what they wanted to happen
- what they thought was happening
- whether they were happy or not
- what else might have happened
- how changes could have been made
- what problems the couple faced
- how they thought the other main character was feeling
- how did it feel to do the role-play. Ask the learners to come out of character and to say what their view was of their character and the situation

Give all three situations to the whole group. As a group consider what other issues and concerns there may be in each of these situations. Collect ideas under such headings as:
- the problems
- how the situation could be saved
- whether the situation could be saved
- what advice they would offer the couple to deal with their problems
- what advice they would offer to prevent problems or to deal with problems in future
- what points did those role-playing miss? Are there alternative solutions?

Small groups (15 min)

Ask the learners in small groups to write a menu of things which help to keep a relationship healthy. These could be written on A1 sheets as a poster display.

Compare the lists, listing any items which appear frequently. These can be compared to the suggestions on RWP6.

RELATIONSHIPS GO WRONG

Small groups: relationship wreckers (15 min)

Refer back to the lists of good and bad relationships. Ask the learners to work in small groups to write a list of fifteen things which can be done to help a relationship go wrong. Allow fifteen minutes for discussion.

Whole group discussion (20 min)

Ask each group to read through their list and create a whole group list of all items. Tick any which appear on several lists.

Their lists may include:
- money problems
- destructive habits – gambling, drinking heavily
- not spending time with each other
- prioritising people outside the relationship and ignoring a partner
- jealousy and giving cause for jealousy
- having different values
- not being sympathetic

- not being there
- poor sexual relationship or different expectations of sexual relationships

Ask the group to select their top five Relationship Wreckers. During the course of discussing the various issues which may damage a relationship try to draw out:

- attitudes of one partner to another which may make something unreasonable or a problem e.g. once two people get married or live together one takes another for granted and forgets to bother
- poor communication which may cause or increase a problem e.g. financial problems are not shared so one partner feels resentful of another's behaviour and expenditure
- assumptions being made about an issue without it having been discussed, for example having children as the next step in a relationship, or moving jobs/house without much discussion, ways of spending money
- issues which were not discussed at the outset of a relationship: for example, personal values or goals, attitudes to money or families

Try to emphasise with the group that a relationship is not wrecked simply by a problem but by the ways problems are created, recognised or managed. Encourage the learners to consider that relationship wreckers can be tackled and sometimes effectively. Some sources of help are listed at the close of the module and work on developing communication skills should better help the learners to manage their relationships.

The learners may want copies of the Relationship Wreckers list and of the list of ingredients for successful relationships.

Self assessment (10 min)
Ask the learners to work alone on self-assessment and planning activity (RWP8).

Feedback (10 min)
Draw the group back. Ask for any volunteers to say what they have learned about themselves or found valuable from the session.

Ask for examples of things which the learners may do differently in future.

Session Four: Phases and changes in relationships

Introduction (15 min)
Relationships have life cycles of their own and go through phases and changes. Ask the learners to brainstorm all the things which may happen in a relationship which may create high points and low points.

Lifelines of relationships (20 min)
Work with the learners to try to draw out the lifeline of one of their personal relationships, with its high points low points, plateaux and the reasons for such. An example OHT RWP1 may help.

Review (20 min)
Refer to the first brainstorm and changes they have drawn on the relationship line and review with the learners which changes may be:

- planned
- stressful but good
- stressful and bad
- a result of other problems
- likely to be very damaging
- ones which can be got over with time, a willingness to do so, appropriate help and support

List the changes and types of changes relationships may face and strategies to manage them. Discuss with the learners:

- Agencies which help e.g. Relate, Family Planning Cry-sis (organisation helping parents with excessively crying children) AA or NA (to help with substance abuse), Debt Counsellors etc.
- Improved communication skills (See Session Five and earlier work in this manual)
- Taking time out of the situation, thinking about or do something else and try to get issues into perspective
- Talking with others to gain opinions, ideas, support and others' perspectives
- Setting aside time for discussion and not taking decisions in the 'heat of the moment'
- Accepting that changes and issues in relationships are normal, natural and inevitable. Understanding that a relationship is not 'broken' because it faces changes or problems. Accepting that a relationship will never be 'perfect', or stay at its 'in love' phase for ever
- Considering a pros and cons exercise on a relationship and deciding what an individual wants from it
- Having a clear action plan for confronting changes

Working alone (20 min)

If appropriate, the group may like to try the relationship lifeline exercise to reflect back on their own relationship and to consider what learning points there may be or areas for change.

MANAGING EXITS

Lecturette (20 min)

This session and the next one on 'being left' may touch on difficult emotional issues and areas. However trying to unravel these difficult areas and find better ways to manage these types of changes are important for the learners to develop better relationship management strategies.

Relationships do finish or should finish. The partners may not be able to face further changes, they may have faced too many difficulties in the past and feel 'ground down' or exhausted. One partner may not want to forgive the other any more – for infidelities, deceptions, creating financial problems, substance abuses, mental, emotional or physical abuse. The two may have grown apart or just not have been a good fit in the first place. The reasons for starting the relationship may have been the wrong ones – simple physical attraction, boredom, loneliness, drifting into a relationship or just not paying proper attention to the fact that there were so many differences between the two people.

Ideally ending a relationship should be managed to keep dignity of both partners. There should be some explanation of why something is over and a chance for discussion. If there is a possibility for reconciliation it should be acknowledged, if there is none, false hope should not be held out.

Key points

The person ending the relationship should:

- plan what to say and stick to it
- set a time limit on how long to spend going through the issues
- warn the other person that they need to have a serious discussion
- undertake the meeting where they feel safe
- not be pushed to make promises about e.g. future meetings or sharing or giving up jointly owned items because they are made to feel guilty
- remain assertive and not become angry or make personal attacks.

Those ending relationships need to be prepared for irrational responses – threats of self-harm or suicide; abuse; personal attacks; attempts to blackmail or attempts to make them feel guilty.

Role-play (30 min)

Use RWP9 with its three possible situations. Give one to each of the groups and allow ten minutes to explore the role play issues. Ask for one or two groups to volunteer to enact their role-play.

While still in character ask the players:

- how they felt
- what concerned them most about the situation
- what they thought would happen next
- what was the hardest part of the situation and why

Discuss with the audience how they felt. What they might have done differently.

BEING LEFT

Brainstorm (10 min)

Those who have been left need to take steps to rebuild their lives.

Brainstorm with the group:

> **What does being left feel like and lead to?**

- rejection
- a chance to start again
- a relief

- not coping
- being alone
- feeling guilty at deciding it's a good thing

Discussion (20 min)

Explore with the learners that there are many different feelings which may be involved in being left. These could include hurt, anger, feel loss of confidence, confusion, not knowing what next, relief and a sense of adventure.

Explore with the learners the various stages to grieving for a relationship and the importance of not getting stuck in a pattern just thinking about the relationship, talking about it, trying to contact the person or getting so angry with the person that vengeance is sought.

It is right to be hurt, to feel bad, to blame and to feel angry. Perhaps writing these out in a letter may help. Explain the cathartic function of letter-writing in expressing and exploring feelings. Often there is no need to send the letter.

Ask the group for other suggestions for working out and working off hostile, angry or hurt feelings. Note these down for the group.

Rising to the challenge (15 min)

Explore with the group its ideas on how to manage being left. What opportunities does being left present?

- a chance to think about who I am and who I want to be
- new chances to make relationships with other people
- a chance to take a new job or move
- the chance to have another intimate relationship but on a different basis
- the chance to do things I've always wanted – spend more time with friends, an interest group or take up a hobby more seriously. List these on the flipchart.

Ask the group what they think are the worst things to do if they were left. List these on the flipchart. How bad are these fears or concerns? Members of the group might like to consider them and perhaps challenge or offer strategies for dealing with them.

Review in small groups (15 min)

Ask the learners to produce five key points to remember to handle the difficult stage of a relationship of being left/leaving someone. Collect in these ideas.

Thank the learners for their hard work and close the session with a cooling down activity.

Session Five: Men and women: attitudes, expectations, values and being reasonable

 Trainer's notes

These activities may well need to be handled differently if the client group is all male, all female or mixed. The session aims to further explore issues about gender-related expectations, valuing the opposite sex, gender roles in relationships and what may be reasonable expectations and behaviours. It introduces learners to ideas about gender stereotypes and expectations and the damaging effects they can have on close personal relationships.

The session does raise some issues of violence and bullying within close relationships. This is however not the focus of this session. Information and referrals will be needed for people dealing with such issues, problems with anger or temper control and with being abused by a partner.

I'm a man (30 min)

Ask the group to brainstorm in small groups under the two headings

Real Men Do	Real Men Don't

Bring the groups back together and record the whole group's answers. Emphasise that there should be no criticism of each other and if an idea appears under both headings it can be explored later. After the listing exercise review the various items. This should generate discussion and the group should reach a point when they are able to try to define what they mean by being a man. The group may need several definitions – a man in public life, a man with his mates, a man at home with partner and family.

Explore the importance of stereotypes and gender expectations at this point.

A woman is ... (50 min)

In small groups give out a selection of magazines – not just women's magazines and ask them to build up a collage. A woman is ...

At the end of twenty minutes ask them to list the key words about what a woman is.

Each group should share their collage and key words. Check after each group presents their work whether their collage is really their view or whether they have created it just because they were all the images they could find in the magazines.

Ask the groups to look again at their collages and to consider:

- do the collages really represent what a woman is? How much of what is in the collage are popular ideas of being a real woman?
- how fair are the images of 'real women'?
- what are the expectations of a real woman which are set up by such images?
- what are the effects on real women of such images?

Brainstorm (15 min)

Ask the group to brainstorm:

Real Women Are	Images of Women Are

Images of men (15 min)

Look again at the brainstorm *Real Men Do: Real Men Don't*. Ask the learners to look at the two lists and decide what are ideas or ideals and images of real men and what real men really do.

How much do men miss out if they stick to the image of a real man is/does?

You might like to have a collage or OHTs of images of men from magazines.

In small groups
Expectations 1 (15 min)
Ask the learners to think of and tell each other of some occasions when they feel they have had unreasonable expectations imposed on them or been measured against the image of an ideal man/woman.

Ask for one or two to volunteer their story and ask what it felt like.

Expectations 2 (15 min)

Again, in small groups ask them to share any occasions when they made unreasonable demands or measured someone again the ideal man/woman.

Ask for one or two to volunteer their story and ask if they have any idea how it felt to the other person.

Review (10 min)

Draw the discussion together by explaining that ideas about:

- looks
- staying at home
- being the strong silent type etc.
- doing certain jobs
- not showing emotions
- earning money
- behaving in certain ways
- sexual performance
- keeping house

are all ways to stop people being who they are or communicating effectively. Such expectations can damage a relationship.

That's her job/his job

Key areas for domestic conflict are over money, how it is spent and over who should do what jobs/spend their time in certain ways. For example, a man may not want a woman to work but to look after his children – or may want a woman to work and look after his children. A woman may expect help with certain domestic tasks but a man may expect not to do those sorts of jobs in the home. The following exercise asks the learners to consider any expectations they have and whether or not these are fair.

Small groups and discussion (30 min)

In small groups ask the learners to brainstorm a list of jobs – at home or at work. Ask them to consider the list and add to it by working in small groups and deciding which are male jobs, female jobs or both. Then ask for one group to volunteer its list of jobs as male, female or jobs for both.

How much agreement is there in the group?

Do people agree or disagree and why?

Ask the learners to volunteer any examples of jobs they would never expect to do and why?

What dangers or difficulties are there in expecting a partner to do certain jobs?

What problems may arise if you don't know how to do certain things?

Explore with the learners the ideas of fairness, empowerment, feelings of self-confidence and control.

Brainstorm (10 min)

Ask for a list of any jobs, skills or tasks at which the learners would like to develop so as to be able to do better. As a group think of ways this could be done. Keep a note of such skills/jobs so these can be built into the learners' development plans.

Expectations, bullying and abuse

Sometimes relationships go wrong because partners have unreasonable expectations of the other, don't see their partner as a person with feelings, identity, rights and freedom of action. This activity explores what can happen in such situations. It is meant as an awareness raising exercise. Individual problems will need to be dealt with out of session.

Role-plays (40 min)

Ask the learners to work in pairs or threes and to develop a short scene on one of the following themes:

- she made me do it
- I did it for him
- it's all her fault
- why won't he just listen to me
- so I hit her- so what- other men do
- she's just my wife
- I'll never do it again

Ask for a couple of pairs/threes to enact their scene. With the characters still in role ask them:

- how the situation happened
- what's been going on before
- how they think it will all end
- what it feels like to be them in the role
- what advice they would offer their character

Check with those watching what it felt like to be watching. What advice they would offer and how they think it felt to be the characters in the scene.

Brainstorm and discussion (30 min)

What sort of situations get out of hand?

Why do situations get out of hand?

Ask the learners to consider what people in a relationship may do to make things worse for themselves. Record the answers.

Ask if anyone can think of new things the people could do to make things better. Again record the answers.

Have to hand a list of professional help; some examples are at the end of this module. Suggest that aggression, nagging, bullying, threatening are not helpful ways to resolve problems for either partner. Clearly time out, assertiveness skills or professional intervention to help manage various issues and stages in relationships will be useful and necessary. Discussion with others about avoiding situations and behaviours which lead on to bullying or to abusing another are needed.

The next session looks at communication skills, these may help in difficult situations. Acknowledgement of changes in relationships or of the end of a relationship may also help. Understanding the warning signs, reading a partner and knowing personal boundaries help as do knowing what are reasonable expectations of another.

Session Six: Communication

A key area where relationships may go wrong is because of poor communication. Those in close relationships may:

- not set aside time to talk about and consider things which are important to themselves as individuals and as a couple
- may prioritise doing things or talking about easy things rather than making time for serious conversations
- may not want to hear truths or things they perceive to be hurtful to them
- may fall into habitual responses, ways of thinking and talking which may act as buffer to communication while seeming like good communication
- frame events, issues or situations in certain ways which leads the communicator to 'blame' the hearer
- may get into the habit of always blaming the other rather than finding more assertive ways of communicating concerns

Communication is about what is said and prioritised to be said, the way it is said, what is heard and how it is acted upon.

By the close of these activities on communication the learners should have developed greater awareness of the importance of communication in maintaining relationships and in effectively instituting relationships. They should also have acquired some further communication skills.

Brainstorm (20 min)

Ask the group to brainstorm:

> **Why is it important for couples/people in close relationships to communicate well?**

> **What happens if they don't?**

Talk through these two exercises fairly quickly then move into the three role-plays outlined on RWP10.

Role-plays (40 min)

Give a situation to a pair/three and ask them to work up the situation into a role-play.
Ask for them to be performed. While the characters are still in role ask them:

- how does it feel to be in this situation?
- how did it come about?
- what would you like to have done differently?
- what could you have done differently?

At the close of all the role-plays ask the learners what learning points there are in terms of good/bad communication and record these.

Lecturette: Getting communication right (30 min)

Use the following points to structure talk about good communications. To ensure the learners understand what is meant ask them for examples of good and proper communication.

1. Be assertive – not aggressive or complaining. Decide what it is you want to say. Write down the key points.

   Work through your list of points, try not to get distracted or allow an argument to develop. Put your points as positive statements. I would like, It seems to me that we could improve on ... Don't just blame the other person.

2. Make statements 'I' statements, not 'you' statements – take responsibility for what you want – what you have done. No-one made you do anything.

3. Pick your moment. Don't try to have important conversations in the heat of the moment, when tired, when there are interruptions or when the other person is not interested.

4. Check that the other person understands. Ask what they think you mean.

5. Treat the discussion in a positive way. See it as a way to solve problems and seek solutions.

6. Find out what the other person thinks/feels. Don't assume just because they used to feel/think something they still do or that just because you think/feel something that they ought to too.

7. Be prepared to hear things you do not like if you ask for the truth. If you are threatening, hysterical, abusive, angry ... when you don't like what you hear you'll encourage lying.

8. Communication is about sharing ideas and thoughts. It is about negotiation and compromise. It is not about bullying someone, changing what has been agreed into something else or refusing to give in. It is not about blackmailing or wearing someone down into agreement.

9. Create time to talk about important matters before they become issues.

10. Respect the fact that your partner has a voice and opinions and should be consulted over important or large issues. Be prepared to change direction or modify your opinions.

11. Make time to talk over day-to-day matters.

12. Reminding a partner continually of shortfalls, how what they did caused... that things were better in the past..that it was better with someone else in the past ... that they were better in the past...will not help communication or to make changes. It will make someone defensive and not listen. The hearer will only hear nagging, complaints and 'put downs'.

13. Knowing when to stop. A lengthy or circular argument which goes nowhere, tires out those involved, does not lead them to a solution and may just make them more defensive. Call a halt – decide the discussion is going nowhere and should be stopped.

14. Don't overload your listener. Make a key point and stick to it. Don't bring in lots of different things. Don't use an opportunity to talk about going on holiday as the chance to air every grudge you can think of.

15. Summarise what you have decided. At the end of any discussion agree what you have discussed and decided. This will mean that you don't go off in different directions.

The notes which you make with the group and the examples they offer will make a useful handout if copied for them.

Putting it into practice (20 min)

Use RWP11. The learners should work in pairs/threes and decide how to manage the five situations so the communications are positive ones.

Review some of the suggestions.

Do you listen or just think you do? (30 min)

Ask for some volunteers to tell you what good listening means. Record the ideas. Offer some points about good listening. Go through some of the ideas listed below, ask the learners for examples when they tried them or failed to try them.

1. Check you understand by repeating what you think is being said "So, I think what you mean ... are saying ... what you want is ..."

    Get agreement that what you have heard is what has been said and is right.

2. Ask questions if you can't follow what is being said. Ask for it to be repeated in another way if you do not understand.

3. Make an effort to concentrate – don't jump to conclusions, try to finish off the sentence or guess what answer someone wants.

4. If you are finding it hard to listen ask for a break. If you are too tired, stressed or preoccupied to take in any information then say so.

5. Try to hear what is being said. Try to see the situation from someone else's point of view even if you are hearing things you do not want to hear. When you may not like what you hear you should distance yourself from yourself, put yourself to one side and make an effort to check what you are being told, that you have understood the problem and understood what the other person thinks and feels. The consequences of not listening properly include:
    *   escalating conflict by appearing to not care and indeed by not caring
    *   failing to hear something important, e.g. early warning signs that something is wrong in a relationship
    *   not hearing a request to put something right
    *   appearing to be careless about someone else and their feelings
    *   your partner won't bother to tell you things next time and may seek out someone else
    *   if you cannot be bothered to listen then why should someone be bothered to listen to you? This may lead to a relationship of limited communication and increasing problems.

6. Wait until you are asked before leaping in with your opinions and answers.

7. Listen and thinking about what is being said is said in a positive way to help some problems or make a situation better not as a way to attack.

A group made handout will be useful to the learners.

Review (15 min)

Ask the group to list out a few ideas in small groups:
*   ways to listen well
*   ways to show you are listening well

Review these lists in a whole group. Some of the work on showing listening will have been covered in the earlier modules on Non-Verbal Communication and Communication Skills.

Acting on what you know

🍎 *Trainer's notes*

The outcome of communication should be taking some action to make changes, to deal with the issue explored or to try to modify behaviours a partner finds difficult.

Brainstorm (15 min)

Ask the group to think about the kinds of problems which couples may have and may discuss and the types of actions which they could take.

Problem	Solution/Action

Taking action may be trying to set aside some time each day/week to talk, or it may be seeking the help of relationship experts, or counsellors expert in dealing with e.g. bereaved parents or those expert in substance abuse problems etc. Action will only work if both partners commit to taking it, to allowing for mistakes and to check on progress.

There are some scenarios for which the learners can try to work out an action plan in RWP12.

Small group planning (20 min)

Review (10 min)

Check on the suggestions which each small group makes. How much agreement is there? What other steps could be added to their plans.

Session summary (20 min)

As good communication is such a key to starting and to maintaining healthy relationships, set the group a final task to summarise important points from the session and ones they would like to remember to act on in their own lives. Ask the learners to think of three or four key points and the reasons why these are important. They should note these. Then ask each learner to offer one in a closing round. The learners should try to cover as many different points as possible.

Session Seven: Close of module

Closing review of module (20 min)

Allocate a different section of the module to each small group and ask them to present their key learning points from their allocated session. They should have ten minutes to prepare and three to present. Check those listening do not want to add any ideas. Check understanding by asking why something has been particularly key or meaningful.

Checking back (10 min)

Refer back to the earlier brainstorm flipcharts about what makes relationships work well or badly and definitions of a close relationship. Ask the learners what they would now add to any of these brainstorms.

Expectations and responsibilities (20 min)

Review with the learners the earlier brainstorms recorded on flipchart paper of expectations and responsibilities. Again, from the sessions they have experienced, from discussion and role-play would they add to their ideas about responsibilities in a relationship or revise their ideas on expectations of others?

What key learning has there been?

Emphasise the importance:

- of realism
- of communication eg. taking the initiative and opening discussion, asking, good listening skills
- planning action and checking on progress
- seeing things from another's point of view
- acknowledging change is natural
- acknowledging each partner has a right to growth and that there may be growing apart

Alone (15 min)

Ask the learners to consider RWP13 and take time to think about their own goals. These do not have to be shared. Some may like to seek out the trainer for referrals.

Wind down (10 min)

Complete the session with a cooling down game and thank the group for its hard work.

Further sources of help and guidance

Learners may find it useful to be directed to the following organisations:

RELATE – National Office Herbert Gray College, Little Church Street, Rugby CV21 3AP, tel. 01788 573241 or look in yellow pages. Provision of Counselling Service for couples. People seen in couples or on their own.

Samaritans – telephone number in Yellow Pages. Provide non-judgemental counselling and know of many sources of help which they can suggest.

Women's Aid Federation England, Box 391, Bristol BS99 7WS – tel. 0117 944 4411. A network of locally-based groups providing temporary refuge for women who have been abused physically or emotionally. For women and children.

Welsh Women's Aid, 38-48 Crwys Road, Cardiff, CF2 4NN, tel. 01222 390 874

Scottish Women's Aid – 12 Torpichen Street, Edinburgh EH3 8JQ, tel. 0131 321 0401

Northern Ireland Women's Aid – 143a University Street, Belfast BT7 1HP. National Helpline, tel. 01232 249 041 (for emergencies: open 10am-4pm and 7pm-10pm weekdays).

Parent Network – tel. 0171 735 1214, has addresses of local groups which teach parenting skills in a structured 12 hour programme.

Parentline OPUS – tel. 01702 554 782, an organisation for parents under stress to help them to help themselves not abuse children. Head Office has lists of local groups to help parents in distress.

SANDS – Stillbirth and Natural Death Society – tel. 0171 436 5881. Network of Counsellors and befrienders to help parents of children dead at birth or shortly after.

CRY-SIS – tel. 0171 404 5011. An organisation to help parents under pressure because their young children cry a lot.

Men's Centre – tel. 0171 267 8713. Organisation helping men violent to women.

Citizen's Advice Bureaux – see local yellow pages. An organisation providing help to deal with a range of problems. A good starting point. Some CABs have specialist debt centres.

AA and NA – see local address book. These organisations can help both the substance abuser and partners of such.

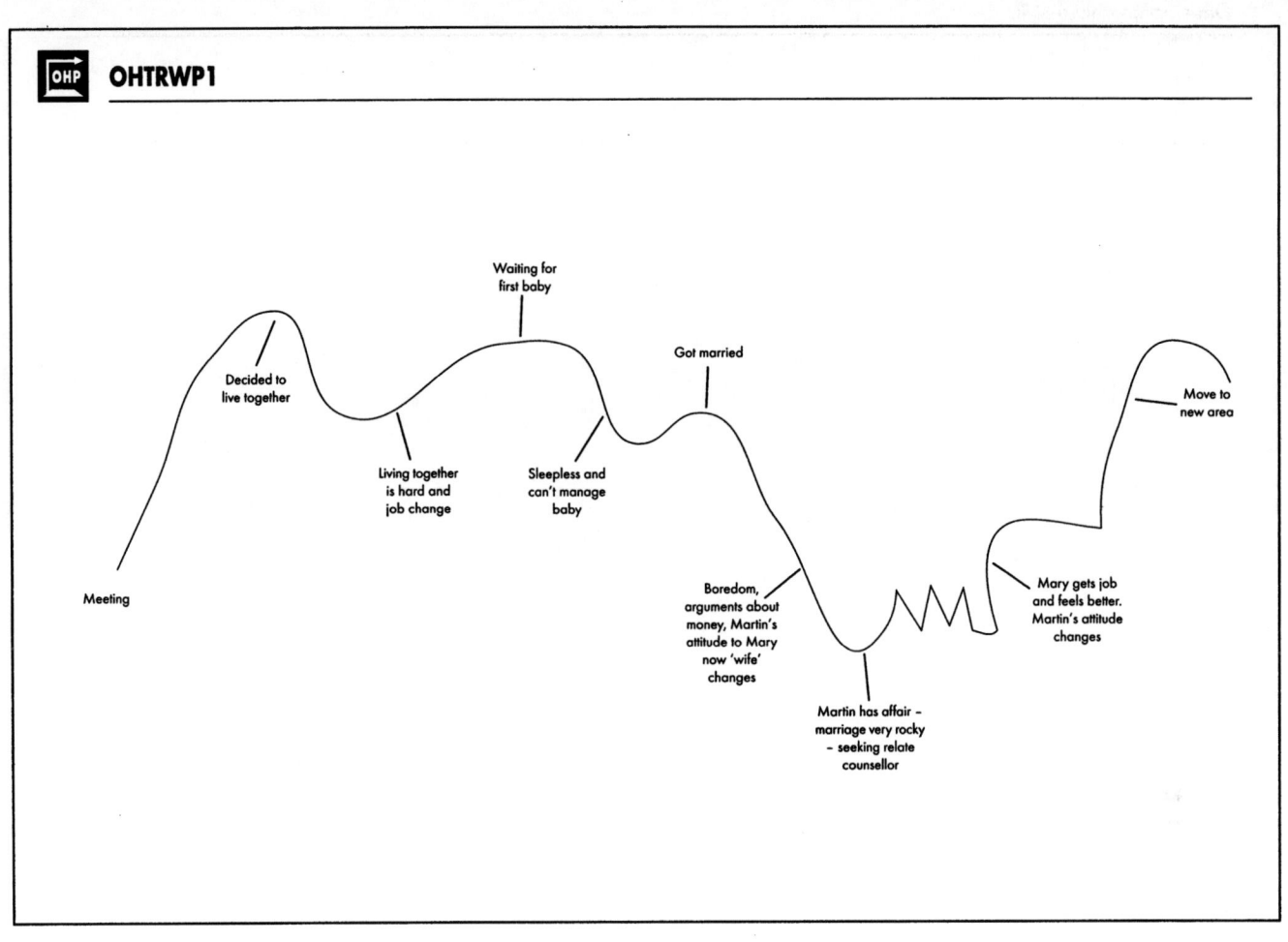

Meeting

Decided to
live together

Living together
is hard and
job change

Waiting for
first baby

Sleepless and
can't manage
baby

Got married

Boredom,
arguments about
money, Martin's
attitude to Mary
now 'wife'
changes

Martin has affair –
marriage very rocky
– seeking relate
counsellor

Mary gets job
and feels better.
Martin's attitude
changes

Move to
new area

RWP1: What does a close relationship mean to me?

✓ ☹ (No), or ☺ (Yes) by each statement and add some more of your own

	☹	☺																														
1. Having someone to share problems with																																
2. Someone to cook for me																																
3. Having a family																																
4. Sexual relationship																																
5. Belonging to someone																																
6. Affection																																
7. Someone who values me																																
8. Someone to do things for me																																
9. Not having to look for people to go out with																																
10. Someone to look after me financially																																
11.																																
12. Someone to talk to																																
13. Being accepted by someone else																																
14.																																
15. Someone to do things for																																
16. Other people knowing I am in a relationship																																
17. Social life at home, no need to make friends																																
18.																																
19. A really close friend																																
20. Someone to support me emotionally																																
21. Feeling more whole with someone else																																
22.																																
23. Someone to do things with																																
24. Not having to live alone/in a shared house																																
25. Feeling secure																																
26. Having someone to do things for																																
27. Having children																																
28. Being in love																																
29. Not being different - everyone else has someone																																
30. Belonging to someone's family																																

Add any other things which are important to you

RWP2

Look at the ✓ and ✗ on your list and decide what it tells you about what relationships mean to you

Look at the things you have ✓ and ✗ and think about how these match a current or recent relationship

---

RWP3

Using the spider chart follow and fill in as many ideas as you can

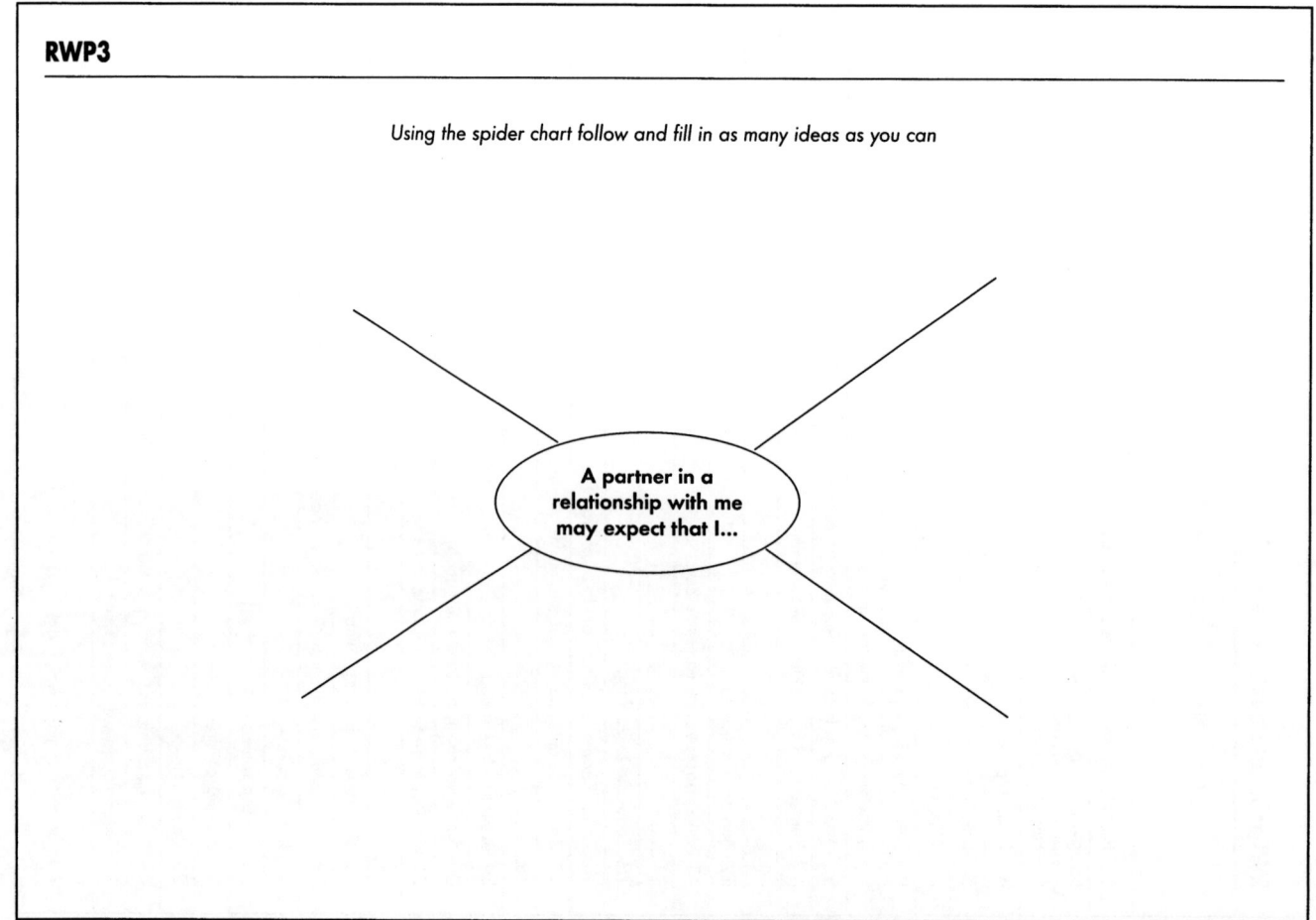

A partner in a relationship with me may expect that I...

RWP5: I would rate myself as good at relationships

1 – very poor and 10 – very good

1   2   3   4   5   6   7   8   9   10

"Good at" relationships means to me that:

The things I think I do well are:

The things I could do better are:

RWP4: Starting out

Read these statements

✓ T (rue), or F (alse) as they apply to you

	True	False
I have started a relationship because I felt lonely		
I have started a relationship because I was bored		
I feel empty sometimes and a relationship stops this		
Being in a relationship makes me feel safe		
I don't like to be the only person not in a relationship		
I drifted into it, I didn't really think about it		
By my age I feel I should be settled		
I felt bad about saying "no" to someone who asks me out		
Most of my mates are going steady with someone - I want to be		
I don't like my own company		
It started with sex.		
She/he was really good looking and I wanted to be seen out with him/her		
My friends encouraged me		
I hadn't been out with anyone for a while and was lonely		
He/she asked me - so I went		

Look at the statements you have ticked as True - as reasons for your starting a relationship. How positive are these as reasons?

What other reasons have you had for starting relationships?

RWP7: Situations – what next?

1. John and Zoe

   John and Zoe have been married for four years. They have known each other from school. Zoe used to go to work but stopped when Ben was born three years ago. Zoe finds being at home dull and feels restless. John is having problems at work and has been getting increasingly short-tempered. They have not spoken since they had a big row two nights ago.

   What happens next?
   What could be done to put the situation right?

2. Dave and Jenny

   Dave stops at the pub every night for a few drinks with his mates. Sometimes he gets in after nine. Most nights he doesn't see his two kids before they go to bed. He has stopped being the man he was before he married Jenny. She looks at him and wonders what she saw in him. He used to not expect that just because he was the man that she would do all the housework as well as her job. They used to share. Now with two children, the house, her job and his expectations she wonders how much longer she can go on.

   What's wrong here?
   What do you think will happen?

3. Shaz and Bob

   Shaz and Bob have been going out for 11 months. Shaz is keen to move in with Bob. He's not sure but does not want her to leave him. She's beautiful, fun to be with and his mates are really jealous of him. Bob thinks he's too young and not ready to live with someone. His mates think he's daft - there are lots of advantages in having your girl living with you. Shaz has been getting depressed and tetchy because he won't decide. Bob doesn't like this side of her.

   What might happen and why?
   What are the consequences?

RWP6: Keeping a good relationship healthy

1. Now and again take stock of your relationship, your partner's goals, lifestyle and values and your own. Check if there are differences. Talk about this.

2. Make time for each other to talk about problems, issues or important things as well as what happened during the day. Practice communication skills:
   - Hear what is being said
   - Make time to listen carefully
   - Check that you understand what is being said

3. If you are bothered about something - bring it up, don't just let it drift.

4. Make time for each other to do something new or special. Some marriage guidance and relationship counsellors talk about "dating your partner". Not taking them for granted, doing something special and doing something new together.

5. Don't assume. Check your partner's thoughts and feelings on anything which may change a relationship. For example, moving, change of job, change of working hours and having children.

6. Check how your partner is feeling - don't assume because nothing is said that everything is alright. He/she may not be brave enough to talk about it.

7. Recognise that changes in relationships do happen. Couples get older, change their interests, things happen which cannot be controlled or affect how one or other feels. For example, the birth of a child, death of a parent, problems in employment or with being unemployed.

8. If you cannot deal with issues or problems on your own seek help.

RWP8: Me and my relationship

*Read the statements and decide which apply to you in a close relationship
1-poor, 5-good*

✓ the number which applies

	1	2	3	4	5
I think about the other person					
I can put myself second sometimes					
I know when something's important and stop and listen					
I am interested in his/her views					
I try to see things from his/her point of view					
I make time to listen					
I suggest going out or doing something special					
I try to raise issues which are important					
I try to remember things which are important to him/her					

Look at your scores, 1– poor and 5 – good, and decide where your strengths lie. Use the checklist to help. ✓ which apply.

Raising issues and communicating well ......

Thinking about someone else ......

Making time available ......

Being considerate ......

Not bearing resentments ......

Other – add your own thoughts

Look at the list below and your scores and ✓ the areas of weakness.

Being thoughtless ......

Not making time ......

Seeing it from someone's point of view ......

Not taking time ......

Being resentful ......

Other – add your own thoughts

RWP8 – continued

I would like to improve on:

Goal One:

Goal Two:

Goal Three:

I shall try to do this by:

Action One:

Action Two:

Action Three:

RWP10

Read through the situation you have been given. Each one is a stressful situation with one in a couple shouting at the other. Work out what's going on with the couple you are role-playing and why.

Lucy: "How can you not be pleased I'm pregnant. You knew I always I wanted children. I thought you wanted a son - you're so good with your sister's kids."

How did this situation come about?

What are Lucy and Damen going to do now?

How would you advise them in the future?

Rick: "What do you mean he always listens to you? You've been married to me for seven years! How can he know you better? That's just some excuse for an affair."

What has happened and why?

What's going to happen next?

How would you advise Rick and Annie to carry on?

Julie: "I'm sick of you always being in the pub with your mates. Why are you avoiding me? It's never been the same with us since ..."

What's the situation?

What has happened and why?

What's going to happen next?

RWP9: Endings

1. Sarah and Sean have two children - 3 and 9. The firstborn Steven was by another man and this had always caused difficulties. Sarah had decided to leave. She was fed up that Sean was now suggesting after all these years that she was seeing Steven's father. She was fed up with his jealousy, threats and abusive comments. She knew leaving would be difficult.

2. They'd grown apart. There was nothing to say. In the pub they would stare at the walls, other people, anything rather than face each other. But how would it end and who would do it?

3. She'd suspected he was having an affair, and this morning she saw them arm in arm. When she told her mum all she could say was she was surprised it had taken her so long to find out and anyway this wasn't the first one.

RWP12: Problems

What would you suggest to these couples?

1. The baby had been suffering from various illnesses from birth. It only ever seemed to be his mother who looked after him. She was getting more tired and depressed and this made her increasingly short-tempered. She and Max argued most of the time they saw each other. He was thinking about leaving.

2. Despite the debt counsellor's advice they couldn't manage to get themselves back on track. Al was in and out of work – always cash in hand and casual work so Corina never really knew what he had earned. The bailiffs had taken back the stuff on HP.

3. His mum had dementia. It had been confirmed. She was getting harder to cope with. He couldn't manage just going in at lunch-times and after work. His mum had never got on with Carole and he didn't know how to persuade Carole that his mum should live with them.

RWP11: Managing communications

1. You have been offered a new job fifty miles from your current one. Do you just tell your partner you're going to take it?

2. You'd rather go out and talk to your best best friend than share what's been going on for you with your partner. What do you think the outcomes of this will be?

3. If we hadn't moved from the flat into this house. If you hadn't made me give up my part-time job. You know I never wanted to be at work full-time. How does this make the listener feel?

4. You're fed up with your partner not paying attention to what you want. Think of three ways to express this.

5. Think of three nagging statements to make about how your partner spends money. Think of three positive ways to bring up your complaints about how your partner spends money.

RWP13: Thinking about my close relationships

The most important things to me about close relationships are:

The things I would like to work on are:

The things I don't want from a close relationship or about a close relationship are:

Developing and maintaining friendships

 The module is divided into five sessions:

1. Introducing friendships (1 hour 45 min)
2. Looking at friends and friendships (2 hours 40 min)
3. Starting friendships (3 hours 25 min)
4. Maintaining friendships (4 hours 40 min)
5. Summing up (40 min)

The module may take 13 hours and 10 minutes to work through.

 The module uses:

- role-play
- self-assessment
- hot seating
- discussions
- brainstorming

 Trainer's notes

This module focuses the learners' attention on the importance of developing friendships and maintaining them in their own lives. The module encourages the learners to:

- consider what qualities they seek in friends
- consider what friends can expect of them and what they may expect of friends
- consider the importance of friendships in developing personal support networks
- consider the value of friendship in the lives of their children and partners
- reflect on how friendships change with time
- develop skills to manage and maintain friendships

Why consider friendship?

For many adults friendships may get little attention. They may be more preoccupied with having partners or developing family relationships. Some may have friends but not really consider friendships as relationships which may need to be maintained and supported or addressed when they tire or go sour. Others may have not developed friendships.

Friends and friendships are important in providing extra support, affection, other views and a sense of well-being in everyday life. Friends may help when there are problems, they can provide support when close relationships are struggling, they may offer practical support or advice. Friends seek help and affection and encourage a sense of belonging and sharing in life.

Session One: Introducing friendship

 Trainer's notes

This session asks the learners to consider friendship; its benefits, the obligations it brings and the role it plays in their lives.

Why have friends? (30 min)

Open the session with a brainstorm:

> ## Why have friends?

This will focus on the advantages of friends and friendships. Later exercises will look at obligations.

Brainstorm:

> ## Who can be friends?

The list may throw up some surprises – parents, partners, people they may not have thought of as friends.

> ## The disadvantages of having friends

Disadvantages may well shade into issues such as having responsibilities towards friends or needing to share or to provide support.

Continuum (20 min)

Run a continuum with friends are extremely important at one end and friends are not important at the other. Ask the learners to place themselves on the continuum. Explore the reasons why the learners have adopted the places they have. Particularly those at either end of the continuum and towards the middle. Mark the positions and then allow learners to move if they wish. Record changes and explore reasons for movement.

Retain this. The same continuum will be run later in the module to explore any changes in opinion.

Qualities in friends (20 min)

Divide the group into two. One set is to look at:

1. Qualities I look for in friends and expectations I have of friends

The other set should brainstorm:

2. Qualities and expectation friends have of me

Ask the two groups to keep a list of their ideas and to prioritise their five main ideas.

Review (10 min)

Share the two types of list. How much similarity was there? What does this tell the learners about what people look for in their friends and friends in them?

Self-assessment (10 min)

Ask the learners to think about the qualities they have listed and then to think about themselves as friends to others. They should think about three friends and complete F1. Check on progress.

Review (15 min)

What things did the group members think they do well?
What would they like to improve on?
What were the strategies for improvement?

Session Two: Looking at friends and friendships

 Trainer's notes

This session considers in more detail the role friends play, the differences between real friendships and fantasy friendships. The role and importance of friendships in the lives of others.

Brainstorm and discussion (30 min)

1. Ask the group to brainstorm all the friendships they can think of between characters in television programmes or films.

2. Then work through some of these examples:
   - why are the people friends?
   - what holds them together?
   - how attractive is the friendship to the viewers and why?
   - how realistic does the friendship seem – why or why not?

3. Are there TV/film characters the learners would like as their friends and why?

Discussion (20 min)

Ask the learners to consider the differences between TV friendships and real life friendships. Work out a list to contrast all the elements of the two types of friendships.

TV Friendships	Real Friendships

Explore what may make a TV/film friendship easier to manage than a real one.

Individual reflection (5 min)

Ask the learners to consider whether they prefer to
   - have just a few close friends
   - a number of close friends
   - a mix of a few close friends and several more distant friends
   - a number of friends but no one too close

The learners should think about why they prefer one option to another.

Discussion (20 min)

Ask the learners to discuss why certain people have become important in their lives. Points to consider may be:

- do we select different friends to meet differing needs? Who? How? What needs? Why do we do this?
- how do we replace those we value when they go?
- do they sometimes pick people to be friends because there is no-one else available and not because they particularly value them?

Trainers need to encourage an examination of why people have or need friends and why these needs may vary in different circumstances. For example what friends do they have in the workplace and why? What friends do they have in their street, club, or pub? What are the differences within these friendships?

Brainstorm (30 min)

1. Brainstorm: The differences between a friendship and what might be a close relationship. Are there differences or no difference?

2. Brainstorm: Can partners be friends?
   Discuss after the brainstorm: What happens when a relationship is/becomes sexual? How does the friendship develop? What could get lost from the friendship once it is a partnership? What could be added?

What is the importance of friends other people's lives? (20 min)

Ask the learners to think of others in their lives, partner, children, friends and family members. They should think about the sorts of friends these people have and what the friendships may give them. Use F2 for this.

Discussion (20 min)

Using F2 ask the learners to explore the range of types and reasons for friendship which others have around them.

Many of the reasons should be the same as their own reasons for having friends – support, affection, emotional security, help with problems, someone to talk to, a way to deal with feelings and isolation.

Explore – has anything surprised them about their discoveries?

Ask them to consider carefully how much they support and help others' friendships and to what extent they may damage or undermine them. The learners should use F3.

Brainstorm (15 min)

Brainstorm:

> ### Why may people upset others' friendships?

Once the group has offered a number of suggestions look at the reasons and some strategies to prevent upset in the future.

Summarise (10 min)

Review the main points of the session. The nature of real friendship and its value. The importance of friendships to others as well as to themselves. Their own roles in supporting or damaging others' friendships.

Session Three: Starting friendships – getting on with other people

Getting to know someone (50 min)

This activity encourages open questioning, active listening, the giving of information and importantly looking for the positives and interesting qualities in other people.

Ask the group to work with another person who they do not know well. Trainers must encourage this and not allow learners to settle with the person they have worked with or seem to enjoy a friendship with.

The pairs must sit close together, back to back, and out of the hearing of other pairs. Within the pairs each person is to ask questions and learn about the other (they may need to take notes) and then present a positive description of his/her partner to the rest of the group.

Questions learners may wish to consider about their partner are:

- what do other people say about you?
- what type of sense of humour have you got?
- what things are you good at?
- what interests do you have?
- do you have a particular ambition?
- why do other people like you?
- what is your favourite food, colour, sport, film and so forth?

When this activity is complete, each partner then presents a positive account of the other to the group.

Discussion (15 min)

Check with the group what it felt like to be listened to?
Whether they were surprised about what they found out?
How often they make an effort to find out about another person?
What the rewards may be from finding out about someone in this way?

This activity has taken place in a controlled way. The pairs had little choice in who they could work with. The following activities focus on why we chose certain people to be friends and what we may expect from them.

WHAT ATTRACTS YOU TO OTHERS?

Brainstorm (30 min)

Brainstorm with the whole group what it is they believe attracts people to one another. Encourage the learners to consider different combinations of gender, age and cultures within friendships. Does this alter what people may look for in friendships? e.g.

- males and males
- females and females
- female and male
- male and female
- younger and older people

If possible record what the group have to say about what males may seek in males and each of the other categories on separate sheets of the flip chart. When the brainstorming exercise has ended, place each of the sheets next to one another to allow a contrast and comparison.

Develop discussion about the differences and similarities between the attractions of each of the relationships.

In pairs: discussion (15 min)

How do people approach each other or go about starting a friendship? The learners may like to tell each other stories about occasions they have begun friendships.

Discussion (15 min)

Share some of the ideas from the pairs. Check how often friendships just happen and people just drift into relationships and how often they are more deliberate.

Check whether the learners chose someone for a friend and worked at the friendship.

Meeting people: making friends (10 min)

Brainstorm where people may meet possible future friends. Ask for the types of places the learners met their friends.

At the close of the brainstorm find out from the learners a few examples of:

- how long the friendships lasted
- how deep the friendship is
- on what it is based

Being fair (30 min)

How often do people jump to conclusions about others? Or not give anyone the chance to show the best of themselves?

Brainstorm examples, occasions and times when the learners did not give someone an opportunity or were dismissive. Check how many in the group have done this, what the consequences were and whether they wished they had done something else.

List as a group the reasons for making these decisions, e.g.

- prejudice about race, class or area someone comes from
- not giving someone of the opposite sex the chance or someone younger/older
- dismissing someone with a disability or disfigurement

Remind the learners of the opening exercise to this session.

Role-plays (30 min)

Ask the learners to work in pairs or threes to work up a short sketch in which one person does not give someone a chance, is dismissive, or is prejudiced and so fails to see the best in someone.

Ask for one or two sketches to be played.

While still in character hot seat the learners. Ask them to describe how they were treated:

- how did it feel to be treated that way?
- how did it make you feel about yourself?
- what did you want to say?
- what do you feel you have to offer as friend?

Of the person doing the rejecting:

- how do you feel about what you have done?
- now you have heard what's been said how would you defend what you have done?
- what do you think you could have lost by your actions?

Open the discussion to the group and invite comments on the role-plays and what has been said.

Game (10 min)
Bring the group back together with a game.

Session Four: Maintaining friendships

 ### Trainer's notes
This session considers equity in friendships how there can be sharing, discussion, trust, support and giving. It considers some of the communication skills needed to support friendships and recognises the changes which take place over the life of friendships.

Game (10 min)
Open the session with a game to get the group moving – Fruitbowl, English Bulldog or Throwing the Ball.

Warm up (15 min)
Brainstorm:

> **Why do friendships not stay the same?**

Reasons for a change may include:

- getting a partner
- moving
- not spending time
- other worries, e.g. money
- drifting apart
- gave up football team, etc.

Developing and keeping friendships (40 min)

Ask the learners to think about three friendships and to consider how they have changed over time. They can draw each one as a line. This should be done on A1 sized paper and will be needed for several activities in this session.

Work as example:

Friendship with Sean

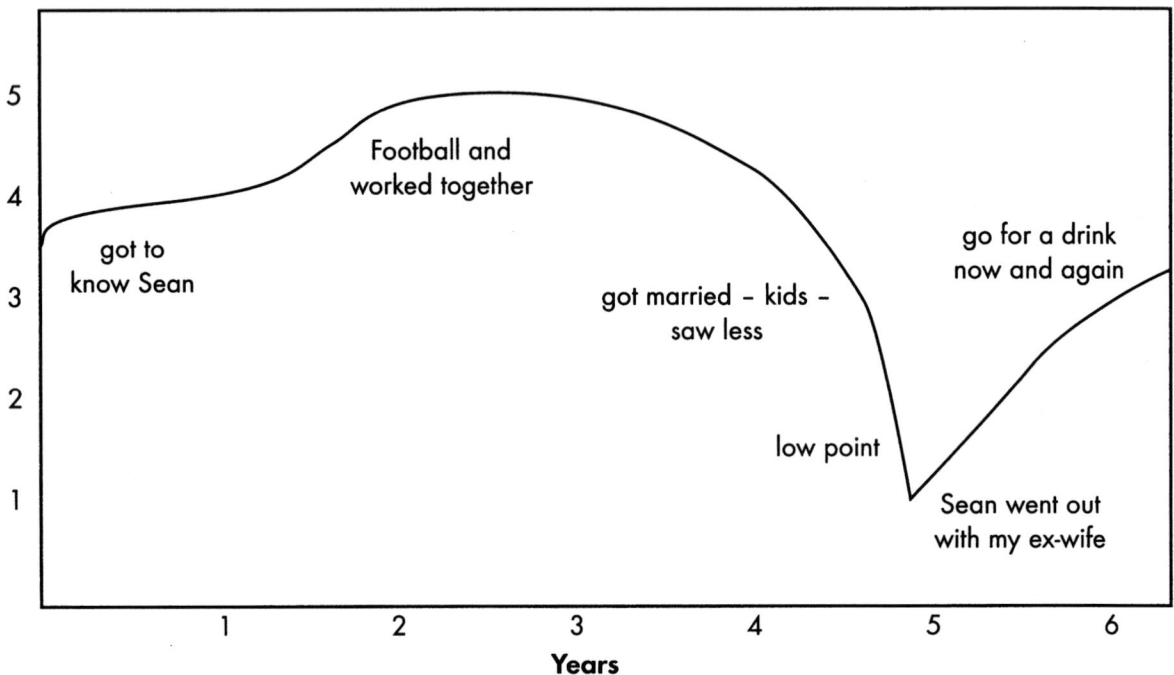

The learners should rate the closeness 1-5 and put on a timescale. They should think about reasons behind the highs and the lows.

Review (30 min)

1. Ask the group members to review some of the reasons for the highs, lows and plateaux.

2. Ask them to look again at their lines and to mark anything which they wish they had or think they could do something about.

3. Share with the group the area which they could have done something about or would like to do something about.

The list may include:

- not made any time for friends
- drifted and didn't stop this
- moved and didn't bother to call/write
- rowed and didn't make it up
- couldn't be bothered
- he/she moved and I didn't make an effort
- I got absorbed with wife and kids
- he/she did a spell inside and I left it
- he needed help and I didn't give any

Your values (15 min)

Whether relationships fall apart or drift or whether something is done to save them will depend on both people. It will mean that the relationship has to have a value, that it has to offer something to the individuals and that they have to place a value on long-term friendships.

Ask the learners to complete F4.

Review (10 min)

What has the group found out about the ways friends are valued?

Role-plays (40 min)

Give out the various situations on F5 and ask the learners to work up a role-play. Ask for some to be performed. While the learners are in character question and encourage the audience to question around such issues as:

- how do you feel about the situation?
- what you would you like to happen next?
- is this what you want?
- how could the friendship be saved?

Brainstorm (15 min)

What is needed to keep friendships healthy and strong?

- time
- good communication
- trust
- common interest

- honesty
- sharing
- taking an interest

Getting communication right (15 min)

Ask the group to list in threes what issues may be hard to discuss with friends or about a friendship and why.

Hard Areas	Reasons

Review (10 min)

Review the group's ideas.

What happens when people don't tackle issues?

Brainstorm (10 min)

Brainstorm:

> **What is needed for good communication between friends?**

The list should include the range of skills such as:

- being able to say what you think/feel
- listening skills
- making time
- questioning, challenging
- being able to tell the truth

Self assessment and plan (10 min)

In light of the brainstorm and the activities so far, ask the learners to use F6 about themselves as friends.

Changing relationships (30 min)

Ask the learners to look again at their friendship life lines.

How many have experienced changes in the type of friendship?
What were the changes?
Did they like or dislike the change?
What were the reasons for the change?

Explore with the learners the fact that changes are natural. That people do grow apart, have new interests and that people grow and change.

Introduce the idea that friendships, like all relationships, can stop making you happy, can become difficult and indeed can become too difficult to sort out. The learners may need to take stock of friendships to decide if they are still valuable, what they want to give to the friendship and whether they want to continue with the friendship.

Friendships, like close relationships can be finished. Like close relationships this can cause grief and upset. The people involved may mourn the loss of a friend. Sometimes friendships just slip by and their passing is not noticed.

Encourage the learners to see this as normal. Encourage them to think about whether they want to keep the relationship and whether to finish it, to take some control. Conversations about terminating friendships can be added to the list of issues which are difficult to have.

Story telling (20 min)

The learners can share stories of changed or finished friendships either as a group or in small groups. They should think about why the friendship changed. What learning points are there? Record these.

Closing game (10 min)

Complete this session with a lively and upbeat game to balance any upsets from discussions about lost friends.

Session Five: Summing up

Review (20 min)

Ask the learners to work in small groups to consider the key ideas of the module and then to present what they have found important to the group.

As trainer add other ideas which the learners may have forgotten.

This session should cover:

- realistic expectations
- sharing
- friendships develop and change
- the importance of keeping an eye on the friendship and working at it
- the value of friendship to others
- communication skills

Continuum 10 min)

Re-run the initial continuum. Plot the learners positions against their earlier ones and consider whether there have been any changes and why this was so.

Final game (10 min)

Bring the group together with a calming game. Thank the learners for their contributions.

F1: Thinking about my friends

Friend's Name:		
Things I do well	Things I don't do well	
I would like to improve: I'll do this by:		

Friend's Name:		
Things I do well	Things I don't do well	
I would like to improve: I'll do this by:		

Friend's Name:		
Things I do well	Things I don't do well	
I would like to improve: I'll do this by:		

F2: The friends of others I know

Person I know	They're friends with	I think their friendship gives them

Looking at your friendship lines and thinking about your friendships so far. Then ✓ any statements which apply to you

I know that my friends will be there for me	
I like meeting new people	
I can always be relied on even if I don't see people for a while	
I'm not bothered about having friendships which go on for a long time	
It's important to me to know a few people very well	
I don't really like people to get to know me	
It doesn't bother me if I lose friends	
I don't have deep friendships	
I value making an effort to keep friendships going	
I have friends from childhood	
I spend time trying to sort out my friendships if they are going wrong	
I know that my friends think they can count on me	
If a friend's in a huff I let them get on with it	
I try to stay in touch with people by phone and letters	
I prefer to change quite often the people I know	
I let months drift by without phoning/calling round on some people	

F3

Being honest I think I help or hinder the friendships of people I know because:

Name of person	Help/Hinder and Reason

The changes I want to make are:

F5: Friendships

1. I would rate friendship as important to me as:

   1   2   3   4   5   6   7   8   9   10

   (1 = low and 10 = high)

2. I would like to develop my friendship with:

   I will do this by:

3. Overall, I would like to improve my friendship skills by:

4. In general I think to maintain my friendships I should:

Relationships with people in the workplace

The module is divided into six sessions which in total could take 11 hours to complete.

1. Introducing workplace relationships (2 hours 20 min)

2. Teamworking (1 hour 45 min)

3. Working with others (1 hour 40 min)

4. Working with those in authority (2 hours)

5. The workplace (1 hour 45 min)

6. Summary and closure (1 hour 30 min)

The module uses:

- role-play

- team games/activities

- self-assessments

- discussions

- brainstorms

 ## Trainer's notes

This module encourages the learners to:

- consider the types of communication skills used in the workplace

- be more aware of the differences between workplace, home and social relationships

- think about what they should expect in a workplace and of workplace relationships

- think more about what may be expected of them in the workplace and in workplace relationships

Race and equality issues **will** arise during this module. The trainer should be prepared for this and have worked out a strategy for dealing with these issues.

Session One: Relationships in the workplace

Trainer's notes

It will be important to find out how much experience and the range of experience the learners have of the workplace. It may be helpful to be ready to counter any learners' concerns about undertaking this module by encouraging them to think about the workplace in its broadest terms. Defining the workplace as a training course; a period of work experience or work shadowing etc.

Opening activities (40 min)

1. Ask the learners as a group to list the range of places where they have worked. Note these. Find out what type and amount of experience they have of the workplace.

2. Brainstorm with the group the following:

> **What can go wrong with relationships in the workplace?**

3. In a second colour add in the consequences of things going wrong thereby extending the spider diagram.

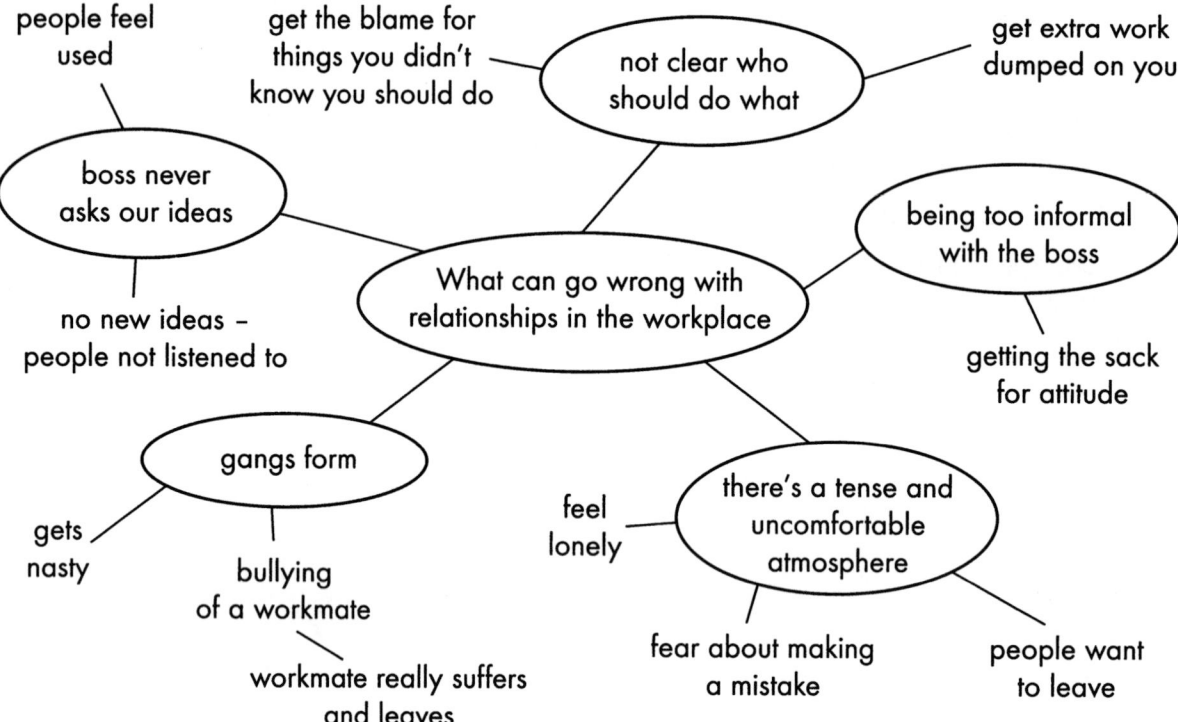

4. To reinforce the activity ask the learners why it is important to think about relationships in the workplace and in groups to list their top five reasons.

5. Collect these ideas together through a group feedback session, ticking any which occur frequently.

What's the difference? (20 min)

Ask the learners to move into small groups. Ask them to work on sheets of A1 paper. They should

1. firstly brainstorm the differences between:

| **Relationships at home or with friends** | **Relationships with people at work** |

2. then order their brainstorms into a list of twenty differences about relationships in the workplace. One member of the group should be ready to present the group's ideas during a feedback session.

Feedback (20 min)

Manage this so it is not repetitive. Ask for any new ideas to add to the list and an explanation if this is necessary. Ask which ideas already on the list should be ticked.

The learners are likely to cover:

- type of language you use – more formal in the workplace
- fewer opportunities for saying things, e.g. to the boss so thinking carefully about what is to be said
- not taking things for granted
- checking understanding

- having to get on with people you don't necessarily like
- having to get on with people you don't know
- not always having the opportunity to get to know people
- being in a relationship where people have power over you – to tell you what to do, to fire your, to dock pay, to offer training, to promote you, to give you more/less work
- having power over others – to give them more/less work, to dock pay, to recommend sacking
- having to think about how you present yourself – e.g. clothing, being punctual
- managing pressure and not getting stressed
- managing/covering up feelings

Group discussion (15 min)

Discuss with the learners the key things needed to make workplace relationships go well. Ideas might include:

- good communication skills
- having the right attitude
- knowing boundaries and limits
- knowing what happens in a workplace and particular workplace rules

Brainstorm the key things which can make workplace relationships go badly.

Role-plays (45 min)

Give out the different situations on WR1 and ask the groups/pairs to prepare their role-play.

The pairs/small groups will need to think about the situation

- from both points of view
- the implications of particular actions
- what may be a likely cause of action
- how they would learn from this experience for the future

After 15 minutes preparation, ask for volunteers to role-play their situation.

While still in character ask them:

- to describe the situation as they see it
- why they think the situation has reached this point
- what could have been done to prevent the situation getting to this point
- what might be done now
- who might help
- what they would say to their workplace colleagues

Run as many role-plays as there is time, group interest and willingness for.

Thank the actors.

Recap (10 min)

Return to the list of key features of workplace relationships and ask the group to add any further ideas.

Thank the group for their work on this session.

Session Two: Working in teams

 Trainer's notes

Many of the learners will work in teams or have contact with many others at a similar level. This session focuses on teamworking, the next on workplace relationships more generally.

- its advantages
- why it is important to get it right
- why it may go wrong

The brainstorms (20 min)

> **What are the advantages of working in a team?**

Responses may include:

- sharing work
- it is not so lonely
- sharing ideas – better ideas
- helping each other out

> **What are the disadvantages of working in a team?**

Responses may include:

- not getting credit for own ideas/work
- having to do everything as a team
- going as slow as the slowest
- being dependent on other people

What makes a team? Small groups (15 min)

Encourage the learners to share some stories of activities which they have undertaken as a team. From these stories ask them to think of five things which makes a team work well.

Share these ideas as a whole group.

Their suggestions may include:

- a small group works better than a larger one
- clear ideas and goals
- something everyone wants to achieve
- putting personal differences aside
- being able to depend on others
- trusting team-mates

Working as a team (40 min)

Divide the group into teams of up to five and then set them a task. If possible mix the teams so they do not know each other so well.

1. The group will present a seven minute talk, perhaps with illustrations or examples on health and safety in the workplace.
   - where will they get the information?
   - who will get it?
   - who will do the presentation?
   - who has prior knowledge?
   - how will they be ready to do the presentation?
   - what timetable will they follow?

   The group which chooses this task/is given this task should present how they will go about it for the immediate feedback, but should know they will be called upon to do the presentation for Session Five: The Workplace

2. The same brief as team 1, a 7 minute talk later in the course. Their topic – bullying in the workplace.

   This team has the same issues to tackle.
   - who has prior knowledge?
   - where might they get information?
   - how will they present the information? – as a role-play? as a quiz, as a talk?
   - who will do what task?
   - how will they be ready for the deadline?

Group review (15 min)

Discuss with the teams what worked well and why and what worked less well and why. Do not endorse attacks on people, although behaviours, e.g. trying to dominate, not listening, may be criticised.

Self-assessment (15 min)

The learners should complete WR2 on their own. It will act as a reminder about the key features of good and bad teamworking and will help them to plan some personal learning points.

Session Three: Working with others

 ### Trainer's notes

Some workplaces do not function as working teams. Workers however still need to get on with one another, establish good working relationships and effective communications.

As a group (15 min)

Explore the differences between working as a team and working with others in the workplace. List some of the differences following a brainstorm.

Small group discussions (20 min)

In small groups ask the learners to work out:
1. what the atmosphere is like in a place where people work well together
2. what it would be like in a place where people do not work well together
3. what helps people to get on
4. what might prevent people getting on well together

The differences in working experience will show itself in the depth and sophistication of the learners' descriptions. Encourage the learners to draw on their experiences.

Group feedback (15 min)

Discuss each of these four points and ask the learners to illustrate any of their suggestions from their own experience.

Brainstorm (30 min)

Divide the group into two and set one the task of brainstorming:

1. What they would look for in workmates able to get on well in the workplace?

Set the other the task of brainstorming:

2. What would workmates look for in you as a good workmate able to get on with others?

Ask each group to provide some feedback. Check on the extent to which each list overlaps. What does this tell the learners?

Self-assessment (20 min)

Ask the learners to complete WR3 and to note some action points. Check on progress. These sheets will be considered at the close of the module.

Session Four: Working with those in authority

 Trainer's notes

This session alerts learners to the importance of managing relationships with those in authority. While it is important to behave appropriately; for example in language, dress, style of address, it is also important to not just give in, to accept being bullied or to accept dangerous health and safety practices. Given the power and the potential for abuse of power in the relationship it is important that the learners feel comfortable with this relationship and confident to get help.

Opening brainstorm (10 min)

Ask the learners to brainstorm who has authority in the workplace and why, and why it matters.

Defining what works well and what works badly (20 min)

1. Ask for any learners to volunteer examples of getting on well with authority figures in the workplace. List the key features on the flipchart and check with the group if they can think of any others.

   They may include:
   - dressing smartly
   - addressing the manager properly
   - being punctual for a meeting
   - using formal language
   - being polite
   - having reasons for what you say/ask for

2. Ask for any volunteers to describe situations when an encounter went wrong with someone in authority. Again list the key features. Ask the group to add more suggestions. They may include:
   - being late
   - not following the firm's rules

- being rude
- not making an effort in appearance or language
- not showing an interest in the firm or the job

In small groups (20 min)

Ask the learners to pretend to be employers and to decide on the top five qualities they would like to see in employees. List these and then list ways an employee could demonstrate or evidence that quality. This will encourage the learners to think of some strategies for dealing with any shortfalls they have.

Group review (15 min)

Ask the small groups to compare lists. Check for consensus about any of the qualities.

Role-plays (45 min)

Give out a situation (WR4), one to each pair/three. These situations all concern an issue on which an employee wants to challenge or question someone in authority. The learners should think about how best to ask for or say what they want, to try to gain the outcome they want. The pairs/threes might find it useful to use (WR5) as an aid.

Ask for two sets of volunteers to role-play their situation. Ask the learners in role to:

- describe the situation as they saw it
- describe how they felt
- describe what they wanted and how well they would rate their attempts to gain it
- describe how they felt they appeared to the other person

Encourage the role-players to continue to talk to one another in role. Were any surprised by what they have heard the 'opposite side' say?

Group review (20 min)

As a group, decide what has been learned from the exercise. It may include:

- preparing what to say
- listening carefully
- asking clearly
- discovering all sides have feelings and are human
- realising people may seem rude or arrogant because they are not confident

Future relationships (10 min)

Ask the learners to spend some minutes thinking about the ways they currently conduct themselves with those in authority and how they might improve on this.

Ask for a list of 3 or 4 possible actions. This will be needed for the final session.

Session Five: The workplace

 Trainer's notes

This session offers:

1. some pointers for the learners towards expectations in the workplace. The learners will need to find out about particular expectations and policies in their work or training place and will need to be familiar with them

2. some pitfalls which can occur in the workplace

Group discussion (25 min)

Ask the learners to brainstorm what makes up the workplace. Use as many themes as possible:

- people
- policies
- a place
- the thing made/service offered

Try to build up a picture of a lot of different work places

Ask the learners to think about what is common to all types of workplaces. The list might include:

- roles
- policies – equal opportunities
- having certain responsibilities, e.g. having to turn up, completing a job
- having rights e.g. to safety, to breaks, to heat/light/ventilation, to pay
- duty of care to others

Small groupwork (15 min)

Split the group into three.

- Ask one group to brainstorm rights of employees
- Ask one group to brainstorm the expectations of employees
- Ask one group to brainstorm what makes it a good workplace

Group review (15 min)

Share the findings of each group:

- How much overlap was there?
- How much do individual learners know about workplaces?
- In what areas are there information gaps?

Some shortfalls in information may be met by information leaflets, for example from ACAS, Health and Safety Executive.

It is important that the learners have a sense of the importance of the way workplaces are structured and the ways in which relationships in the workplace are formalised. It is important that learners know there is legislation to protect them and the reasons for such legislation.

The learners should be aware that they also have responsibilities in the workplace, for example, for abiding by health and safety rules, for following equal opportunities and for acknowledging that people should have dignity in the workplace.

Presentations (30 min)

The two teams given their tasks in Session Two now have their opportunity to present on:

- Health and Safety in the workplace
- Bullying in the workplace

There should be time after each presentation for discussion.

Closing the session (20 min)

Ask each learner for something they have found out and something they would either like to know more about or would like to change in the way they behave in the workplace.

Keep these lists. They will be needed for the final session.

Session Six: Summary

Group review (1 hour)

Split the group into small groups and ask for volunteers to take one of each of the five main areas of the module, i.e.

- teamworking
- working with others
- relationships with those in authority
- the workplace
- relationships at work

Ask each group to think through the main ideas which were discussed in their area. They may want to do a brainstorm to revise it. Then ask the groups to decide on five key points and to have a reason for selecting each of these points.

Each group should be prepared to present back for five minutes and take questions on their selected area.

Other activity break/game (10 min)

Individual work on action plans (15 min)

Ask the learners to review their checklists and action points in light of the points they have heard and further ideas they have had. Use WR6. Check on individual progress.

Closure (15 min)

Ask if there are any final comments, observations, questions or concerns. Thank all the learners for their hard work.

Close with a group game.

For further information contact:

Health and Safety Executive Information Centre, Broad Lane, Sheffield, S3 7HQ

HSE Books, PO Box 1999, Sudbury, Suffolk CO10 6FS

Royal Society for Prevention of Accidents, Cannon House, The Priory, Queensway, Birmingham B4 6BS

Trades Union Congress, Congress House, Great Russell Street, London WC1B 3LQ

Confederation of British Industry, Centre Point, 103 New Oxford Street, London WC1A 1DA

Commission for Racial Equality, Elliot House, 10-12 Allington Street, London SW1E 5EH

Equal Opportunities Commission, Overseas House, Quay Street, Manchester M3 3HN

WR2: Me and teams

Read through the statements below and ✓ which applies to you

	Applies to me
I like sharing ideas and talking things through	
Working in a team makes me feel secure	
I prefer to be on my own	
Being a team means having a laugh	
I prefer to be anonymous	
The others in the team are often too slow for me	
Teams are good – you cover for one another	
I prefer working on my own	
I see team-mates out of work	
I hate it that others get the praise for my hard work	

Re-read the statements you have ✓

What do they say about you?

Are there any areas you would like to change – Yes/No? Which?

How would you do this?

WR1: What happens next?

Mark has been regularly late over the past couple of months. His team-mates have covered for him. They suspect he is drinking, to cope with his marriage break-up. Mark has to see his boss Judith. Judith is not well respected in a company of nearly all men.

Bobbie is younger than most of the workers. Bobbie has had experience of up-to-date technology and knows all the latest ideas. Bobbie keeps telling everyone so. Bobbie's a pain for the rest of the workgroup. What's going to happen? How could things be put right?

Four of you work as a team. The work is shared fairly evenly. Each of you has special skills and strengths. Two of you do meet for a drink, the other two don't ever join in. It's been noticed that materials have been going missing from the workplace. Yesterday some money went from the cash box. It can only be one of the four of you. How are you going to sort this out?

WR3: Working with others

✔ the statements which you think best describe you when working with other people

	Tick
Even if the job's boring the people make it okay	
Can't be bothered to say hello	
Workmates are often a good bunch	
It's us against the managers	
I like working in a group	
I would miss the people if I left work	
I think those who work hard are mugs	
I can't get on with workmates	
I don't join in the conversations with people at work	
I think people would agree I pull my weight	
There's always someone to talk to	
I try to be reliable for workmates	
I think most of them are stupid	
I get others to do my job for me	
You can have a laugh	
I think my workmates would say they could depend on me	
They don't work as hard or fast as me	
I skive as much as I can	
I wouldn't mix with them out of work	
You cover one another's backs	
I don't want to get on with people at work	

WR3 – continued

Look back at the statements you have ticked. How do you think someone else seeing the ✔ would describe you?

Share your comments about yourself with someone else in the group. Do they agree with you?

Thinking about getting on with others in the workplace, what might you like to change?

How would you make those changes?

WR5: Managing important meetings

Meeting with someone in authority can go wrong because:

- you are not clear what you want to ask for
- you are muddled in what you want to say
- you make yourself sound rude or arrogant
- you undersell yourself or the seriousness of your concerns
- you get side-tracked onto unimportant other things
- you agree to things you don't want to because it's the boss
- you come across as silly because you're shy
- you get fobbed off with promises because you are intimidated
- you get too aggressive and are not taken seriously

So:

- plan clearly what you want to say. Pick one or two big issues, if necessary ask for another appointment to tackle something else
- don't moan or blame other people
- be clear about your issues, have reasons for what you are saying
- have some suggestions to make as solutions to problems or ways to move forward
- know how to be assertive but not hostile
- know what you will compromise over and what you do not want to

When you meet:

- be assertive
- listen carefully
- repeat back the main ideas so you are clear you agree
- check you understand the reasons for decisions which have been made
- ask for time to think about matters if you need it
- ask for something in writing if it helps

WR4: Sorting it out

Three weeks ago your firm was taken over by a larger one. You were all told that it would mean better salaries and better working conditions. But there have been several changes to the production line which don't seem to be safe and certainly don't mean a good product going to the customer. After a meeting with your workmates two of you are voted as the ones to see the managers.

How does the interview go?

Tina's been in charge of a small team during a period of sick-leave. She's been taking on more responsibility because staff have been laid off and jobs have been passed down the line. Tina's spoken to her Union rep. and wants to ask for a pay-rise and a proper position in the firm.

How does she manage the meeting – what is she told?

As the group leader you have had Sanjay coming to you several times for the past few weeks complaining of racist comments and being picked on. Your firm does have statements about equal opportunities and no bullying but that seems to be all they are – just statements – just words.

What are you going to do?

WR6: Action plan

Looking back over the checklists and statements you have completed, pick three areas you would like to target

1.

2.

3.

Decide:

Why you want to make these changes	How you are going to make these changes

Dealing with authority

 The module is divided into 4 sessions:

1. Understanding the difference between authority and power (2 hours 20 min)

2. Personal authority and using it (2 hours and 10 min)

3. Bureaucracy and official authority (3 hours 35 min)

4. Dealing with authority (2 hours 15 min)

The module takes approximately 10 hours 20 minutes to complete.

 This module links with those on:

• relationships in the workplace

• developing assertiveness

• developing communication skills

• communities and relationships

 The module uses the learning styles of:

• small and whole group discussion

• role play

• brainstorming

• games

 Trainer's notes

Why consider dealing with authority?

Everyone comes into contact with individuals or groups which have authority during their daily lives. It is important that people have an understanding of the functions, purposes and the necessity of authority and the responsibilities which it imposes on those who have it. Such awareness is important for many people may otherwise come inappropriately into conflict with authority. Understanding the different types of authority and its supporting structures may increase individuals' chances to successfully negotiate their way through bureaucracy and decision making processes without conflict.

This module encourages the learners to:

• see the roles of authority in daily life, for example in maintaining social order and justice

• to explore the differences between power and authority

• to understand the differences between making decisions or taking action which has been based on fear and intimidation and those based upon a knowledge that something has to be done

• appreciate that they have authority for example in relationships with fellow workers, authority over their children or family members and as citizens

Although the learners will be defining power and authority some working definitions are useful. Power may be defined as an interest in controlling people, behaviours or access to resources. Power may be used to bolster self-esteem or status of those who have it and to undermine those who do not. Power is needed when decisions or actions are taken which disregard the wishes of others.

Authority, may be given or may be personal authority. A person or body with authority may require things to be done or may make demands on others. However the person or agency has a right to make such demands. In response to authority rather than power, others will mostly agree that they should accept and comply with demands made of them.

The learners will explore the ways in which power and authority can be communicated and ways to differentiate between the two. The learners will consider ways to respond appropriately to authority and the reasons that people and bodies have authority.

This module encourages learners to:

- develop an understanding of the differences between personal authority and authority which comes with a job or position of power
- recognise the differences between power and authority
- consider the uses and responsibilities of authority
- develop an awareness of the need to develop their own authority within a variety of personal and official situations

Session One: Understanding the difference between authority and power

 Trainer's notes

This session asks the learners to consider and to define the differences between authority and power. They will be asked to think about verbal, non-verbal and other indicators of power and authority.

Much of this module will involve physical activity so the learners must feel comfortable in using the space and moving about the room. The opening activities encourage this.

Warm up: marking out the territory (10 min)

Ask the group to move the chairs to the sides of the room and return to the centre. Tell the group that they will walk around the room at various speeds and in the directions which they will be told. Call out – fast, slow, slower, faster, clockwise, anticlockwise etc.

After a few minutes, call the group back into the centre. Explain to the group that on the command "Go!" they are to touch each wall in the room and return to the centre as fast as possible. Repeat this three times.

Ask the group to get into pairs. One to be A the other B. Tell them they will do the same exercise but this time B is to follow A to all the walls then try to return to the centre before A. Repeat this twice and then have A follow B.

If the learners ask why this is being done then use the following as discussion points:

- In these activities has power or authority been exercised?
- Who has had power or authority and why?

Territorial walks: using authority and power (25 min)

In this activity the learners assume the identities of people with differing professional and social roles and walk around the room as if they are those people with their power or their authority. The learners will need to think carefully how they are to demonstrate power and authority.

Try a practice walk. Ask the learners to move as if they are soldiers at time of war, then to move about as prisoners of war.

Ask them to freeze in mid-movement. Discuss how they are showing who has power or authority and who does not have authority or power? They should consider body language, use of space, the ways they hold themselves, how they look at each other etc. Divide the group in two, half are to be prisoners of war, the other half soldiers. Ask them to move and again freeze them mid-movement and ask them how they are showing their differences in status.

Try the exercises with other pairs of oppositional roles e.g.

- bank manager – someone in serious debt and needing help
- owner of a firm – a worker about to be made redundant
- millionaire – someone homeless
- gang leader – person being bullied

The trainer must encourage the learners to assume the roles and think whether it is power or authority these people possess.

Group review (20 min)

- Ask the learners to list how they were able to show the differences between those with authority and power and those without authority and power.
- Ask the learners to think who had power and who had authority. Was it possible to have one without the other?
- How might power appear as different to authority?

List the ideas. These will be needed later.

Brainstorming (30 min)

Move the group on to brainstorm:

> **What is power?**

> **What is authority?**

Brainstorm:

> **Who has authority?**

> **Who has power?**

During the brainstorms ask them to consider how people gain authority or power. Consider such questions as:

- What does money give people?
- How much power or authority comes from professional status?
- Can some people have personal power? Who?
- Can some people have personal authority? Who?

In small groups (15 min)

In small groups ask the learners to list the differences between power and authority. Is one is better than the other and why.

This should spark some debate as the learners will base their decisions on the contexts in which they have experienced authority, on personal experiences of poor use of authority or power etc.

Ask the learners to feedback their ideas and list these.
Ask them to consider are there any benefits in people having authority and who are these benefits for?

Continuum (10 min)

 ### *Trainer's notes*

This activity uses three continuum exercises. Prepare a flip chart with three lines on which to record the initial of the learners in the places they choose to stand. Do not stop to discuss the learners' positions.

Continuum One:
Ask the group to form a continuum on the need for some people in society to have authority. One end a great need, the other end no need at all.

Continuum Two:
Ask the group to form a continuum on do they have personal authority. One end lots of personal authority, the other end no personal authority at all.

Continuum Three:
Ask the group to form a continuum on personal power. One end lots of personal power, the other none at all.

Note people's initials on the appropriate line on the flipchart.

Discussion on the continuums (30 min)

Ask the learners to look at where they placed themselves on the three lines. Ask for volunteers to explain why they adopted those positions. Ensure those who adopted extreme position offer their reasons.

The discussion will cover complex areas and will help the learners to define and explore the issues. Keep a note of key ideas on the flipchart and ensure that there is some comment of what is meant by:

- personal authority
- personal power
- authority in society

Ask the learners if following the discussions any would like to change their original positions. Ask for reasons and mark the changes with another colour on the lines on the flipchart.

Brainstorming (30 min)

Return to the brainstorms on authority and power and review what has been suggested. encourage the learners to consider additional issues and to make further suggestions. Of authority explore areas such as:

- authority in the home and within the family

- authority as knowledge
- authority in the community
- authority at work
- whether authority is given or is natural?

Of power, consider questions such as:

- Is power threatening if so why?
- What is the relationship between power and humiliation?
- Is power more dangerous than authority?
- Do some people have natural power? How do people get power?
- Is there a difference between the people who have power and those who have authority? What is it?

Conclude this session by recapping on the definitions of authority and power and the differences between them.

Thank the learners for tackling difficult issues.

Session Two: Understanding personal authority

 Trainer's notes

This session makes use of one long activity which asks learners to adopt a role and to explore the authority within that role, its limitations and its responsibilities.

The car park game

The moves (20 min)

Clear the chairs and draw an imaginary rectangle on the floor. No learner can go out of the rectangle. Ask all learners to line up on one side.

The learners will all be given a role (AUTH1). In this role they will be asked questions. If they can answer "yes" to any of the questions they can take one step forwards towards the other side of the Car Park. The questions are printed on AUTH2.

At the end of the Car Park exercise, the group should be fairly well distributed across the room. Keep the group in their positions across the room and ask the individual learner who has moved the furthest to declare the person s/he was portraying. Ask the rest of the group why that 'role' was able to say "yes" to so many decisions.

Now ask the group to turn around and face the direction they started and to face any learner who is still either close to or on the point of the original starting line. It is likely that the 5 year old child is still very close to the original line.

Ask the rest of the group to guess what role or person could have so little authority. Briefly discuss whether it is fair or why that role has very little authority.

Making statements (20 min)

Ask the group to collect their chairs and to return to their positions on the 'car park'. The learners will need to sit in such a way as to be able to see most if not all of the rest of the group.

Beginning at the top end of the room – where the positions indicate most authority ask each member of the group to make a statement about their 'role'. The statement should include:

- for whom the role has responsibility or authority
- what type of decisions can that role make?
- what are the limits of their authority?
- what are the burdens and responsibility of the role?

They should keep clear the distinction between authority and power.

Discussion (20 min)

After the statements discuss the following questions:

- Are people in the right positions?
- Why should the five year old be where he/she is?
- What sort of authority do parents have and why?
- Does the unemployed single working male have more personal authority that the working mother of three children? If so why? If not why not? Is it fair?
- What is charismatic authority and how is it used?
- What is personal authority? Is it separate from the authority of a role?
- Why do people have personal authority and how do they get it?

Distinguish between power and authority. Still in role ask the learners to consider what happens if something goes wrong? Who do they turn to and for what? What are the limitations of personal authority?

In pairs (30 min)

Ask the learners to work in pairs. They may have similar levels of authority or may have very different ones. The object of this exercise is for the learners, still in role, to describe to one another what it feels like to have;

- their level of authority
- their responsibilities
- their rights to make/not make decisions
- the types of problems they may face and how they have the authority to deal with them
- who may have authority over them
- what care needs to be taken when exercising authority
- their lifestyle

Explore these questions and write them on the flipchart so the pairs know what they should be discussing. At the close of the time allowed each pair should be able to describe how the other in the pair experiences his/her authority.

Ask for some volunteers to describe how their partner experiences their authority.

Drawing together the threads (30 min)

1. Review what the learners have gained from the car park experience.
   How many felt uncomfortable in their role?
   How many would have preferred someone else's role and why?
   How important is it to have personal authority?

2. Brainstorm

> **Who does personal authority mean?**

3. Brainstorm

> **Where do I gain my authority?**

4. Summarise the key points.

Closing game (10 min)

Conclude the session with an energetic game such as English Bulldog or Fruit Bowl.

Session Three: Bureaucracy and authority

 Trainer's notes

This session alerts the learners to the need for rules and for roles in society which have authority delegated to them. The session uses a long role-play.

Introductory rounds (10 min)

Ask the learners to sit in a circle and to introduce themselves with a name, a position of authority and a statement about what that position can do.
Trainers may wish to begin this exercise to set the style. The game might begin with statements such as:

- I am Sanjay. I am a dentist and I have the authority to write a prescription

- I am Susan. I am in the police force. I have the authority to control crowds

- I am Mike. I am a lollipop patrol. I have the authority to stop traffic to allow children to cross the road

If learners are struggling to think of something encourage them to think about everyday authority – doctor, bus drivers, lawyers, benefits workers and so-forth. Ask each learner to make two contributions, one in each round.

Brainstorm (20 min)

Recall some of the positions that the group managed to think of and then brainstorm with the group:

- a list of all the positions of official authority

- which of all of those positions are the ten most important

- briefly discuss with the group the importance of these ten positions

Consider the role that the ten positions of authority play in everyday life. What might be the consequence if those positions did not exist and how would decisions be taken?

As a group, discuss the role of authority in everyday life.

Our land our rules

Preparation (40 min)

This exercise is a lengthy and a complex one. It offers much interesting material for the learners to consider both in preparing for and actually undertaking the exercise. The preparation and the full final role-plays should be videoed for best usage of the material. This may mean some shyness and some silliness, it may also mean that there is a need for a few repeats of the video so people can overcome feelings at seeing themselves in role.

There will need to be some breaks between

   i) preparation and the full role-play
   ii) the completion of the exercise, initial discussion and the watching of the video

Divide the group in two. One group is The Council, the other are The Visitors.

Explain that The Council are part of a group of survivors in a world which has suffered much warfare and then disease. They live in an ideal place and they want to keep it as a well functioning society. The Visitors are people who might like to settle, but would certainly like to see the Land to see if they could live there.

Give them AUTH3 and AUTH4 as appropriate.

Read through the sheets with the learners, check they understand what they need to do.

The Council needs to decide how it wants to run its country and The Visitors need to think of reasons why The Council will let them in.

Both groups will need to pay attention to the three stages of the problem.

1. What are the rules – who do we want?
    Why do we want to go to the Land and why should the Council let us in?

2. Why should they be let in as visitors? The Council will only accept a few.

3. A month later why should one of them remain and who should it be?

The two groups need to rehearse separately and to decide upon a strategy. The Council needs to work together, it may need to elect a spokesman. This group will need to reach consensus about its rules, how the Land functions and who should be admitted to the Land. There may be someone who takes authority and leads the group. The process of group formation and management, the ways in which leaders come forward and are accepted or not should form part of the process of debriefing.

The Visitors may work as a group, they may have a common deputation with the individuals speaking or the group may act as isolated individuals each one in competition with the other. Again the way the group functions will be important material for the debriefing.

The trainer will need to note group roles, who takes authority, how authority may be tied to assumed roles or to taking personal authority.

These preparatory stages could be videoed for the learners to analyse.

The groups will need several warnings that they are running out of preparation time.

Whole group role-play (25 min)

Then run the whole group role-play. This needs to be videoed so the learners can analyse what happens.

Initial discussion before showing the video (15 min)

How did the learners find the exercise?

How had it added to their thinking about authority?

What had they discovered about rules and rule-making?

What had they discovered about authority in relation to their own authority and the roles they and others assumed?

Video and second discussion (50 min)

Was what they saw on the video the same as they had remembered it?

Were the same people the ones they thought had authority?

How did the Visitors feel having to make their case?

Who wanted to break the rules and why?

Who wanted certain rules and why?

How was the rule-making decided and how was agreement reached?

What feelings were there amongst the Visitors?

Were they united or in competition?

Who felt they managed to   a) explain the rules well
                             b) argue their case well

What did it feel like for the rule makers who were in a significant position of authority?

How did it feel to turn people away?

Did anyone feel uncomfortable with the role of turning Visitors away?

Check if there are any outstanding issues.

Thank everyone for their work. Ask the group to applaud each other.

Authority and rule-making (20 min)

Move the group to thinking about rule-making, rule compliance, authority and denial of rules and authority more generally in society.

Explore with the group

> **Why have rules?**

Ask the group to then brainstorm:

> **Where do rules come from?**

Continuum (15 min)

Ask the learners to form a continuum on their views on rule acceptance. One end frequently breaks rules, the other end abides by rules.

Ask the learners to volunteer why they have adopted these positions. Allow for any learners to change.

Mark their positions on a flipchart line and compare these with the first continuum exercise.

Have any people changed their views on rules and authority?
In which direction and why?

Close (10 min)

Close the session by reviewing the key points about bureaucratic authority, rule making and rule compliance.

Dealing with authority

 Trainer's notes

This session focuses the learners' attention on the importance of managing themselves in relation to authority figures. It reminds them that there are procedures, forms and processes and ways to speak with people in authority.

Opening activity (20 min)

Ask the learners to work in pairs and to exchange stories about encounters with officials. They should each think of two occasions when things went well and two when things went wrong. Between them the pairs will have eight stories and should make two lists:

i) things not to do when dealing with authority

ii) things to do when dealing with authority

Group brainstorm (20 min)

Ask for feedback from the pairs in the form of two brainstorms:

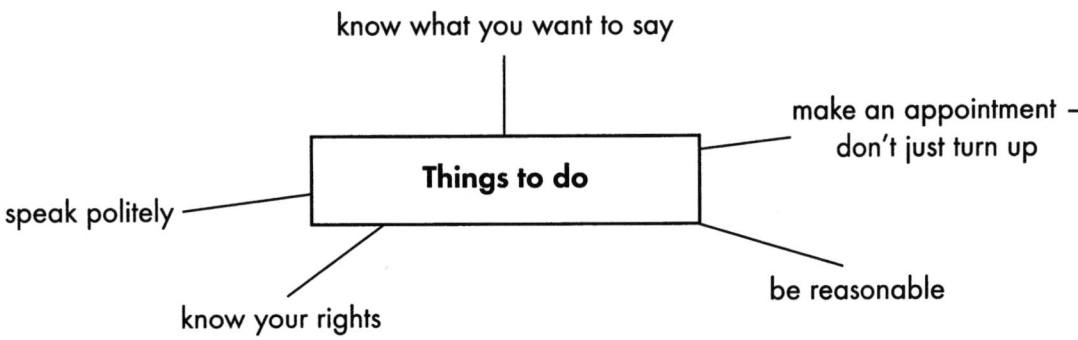

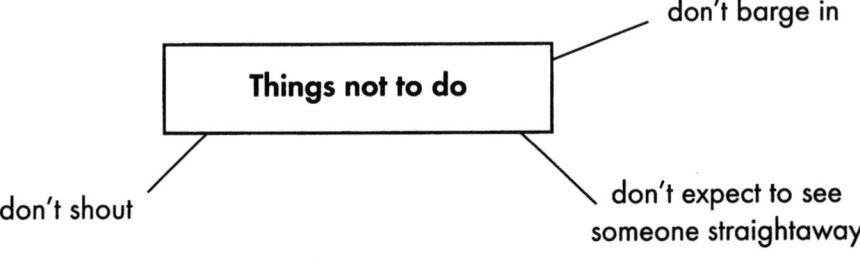

Encourage the group to add to either list and any of your own ideas. Ask the group if they can prioritise five key things to do and five not to do. Mark these.

Role-plays (45 min)

Give the learners one situation from AUTH5. Ask them to work in pairs or threes on their problem and to be ready to perform it.

Run two or three role-plays. After each, keep the characters in role and ask them questions such as:

Of the person wanting to change a decision:
- what were you feeling?
- what did you want to achieve?
- how did you feel the authorities were treating you?
- how did you see the person dealing with your case? did he/she understand?
- how do you think you presented yourself? how were you seen?

Of the person/people in authority:
- why did you make the decision you did?
- how did the applicant appear to you?
- what impressions did he/she make?
- could you see his/her point of view?
- what helped you or stopped you seeing their view of the situation?
- what could have made you help him/her?

Reaching successful outcomes (15 min)

Ask the audience to select one of the role-plays and to direct the characters to reach a another outcome. The characters should do as the audience suggests and see if they are able to reach a more positive outcome. (If no role-plays went wrong then the audience could comment on ways in which the characters could have handled themselves better.)

Trainer summary (10 min)

Summarise the learning from brainstorms and role-plays. The learners should have made a number of gains in thinking about ways in which they should behave to get what they would like in a situation.

Brainstorm (10 min)

Ask the learners to brainstorm sources which may be able to support them when they have to tackle difficult situations. The trainer will need to have some suggestions both of help and of possible areas of problems. This final brainstorm should be upbeat and should challenge any prejudices that 'the authorities' are never there to help.

Conclusion (15 min)

Thank the learners for their work. Ask each one to offer something they have found out about better understanding or better managing their relationships with authority or better managing their own authority.

AUTH2: Questions for the car park game

Read these instructions to the group.

In the role that you have just been given, if you should or can answer "yes" to any of these questions take a step forward. If the answer is "no", stay still.

Can you tell someone what time to be home?

Can you ask someone to stop doing something?

Are you responsible for making sure another person is fed?

Are you responsible for the safety of anyone else?

Can you stop someone from doing something silly or naughty?

Do you have some knowledge that others may need?

Can you make a choice about what you eat?

Do you have a choice about what you can spend and how much you can spend?

Can you make a choice about what you can do with your time?

Can you make a set of rules for people to obey?

Can you get up or go to bed when you choose?

Can you make a choice about which sports or leisure activity you wish to do?

Do you decide what to watch on TV most of the time?

Can you choose your own clothes or decide what you are going to wear at any time?

Can you make an official complaint?

Can you refuse to do something that is against your will?

AUTH1: Roles for the car park game

Photocopy this sheet and cut out the roles. Trainers may prefer to write out some other more typical roles appropriate to their particular group.

19 year old college student

10 year old with 5 year old sister

unemployed male, single, 30 years old

mother of three children, has a job, is always tired, has very little money

father of two difficult boys both on probation, father also has a record

5 year old child, with a four year old friend

husband separated from wife and children, living with someone else and her children

a next door neighbour to very noisy children and untidy family. No children, retired from work.

a close friend of someone needing help

young teenager, 14, hates school, likes going out, does not like mother's cooking

AUTH4: Our land, our rules

THE VISITORS

Your Situation

You have heard that there is the Land. It is very safe, there is plenty of food and you have decided you are going to see if you can visit the Land.

You have heard that there are strict rules for entry set up by The Council of this new Land and that you have to ask The Council whether or not you can visit or stay in the Land.

As a group of visitors you have got to think how you want to get into the Land. You must explain to The Council who you are and why you want to visit and try to persuade them to let you in.

The Visitors

Pick one of these roles and decide how you will persuade The Council.

- You are a very healthy young mother of two young children also both very healthy. You believe the rest of your family are already in the Land. You have never travelled very far and you have never worked. You must think carefully to persuade The Council to let you in to live in the Land.

- You are a retired school teacher. You are reasonably healthy. You have some money to invest in the Land You want to get in to retire. Think of a good argument to make The Council want you to live in the Land.

- You are a 20 year old bricklayer, you smoke and drink and have had many sexual partners. Your friends think you are a good laugh. You only want to visit to have a holiday and have a good time. Ask The Council for a visitor's pass.

- You are a young doctor but you suffer with very bad hay fever and you are diabetic. You want to live in this new land to work as a doctor and settle down to have a family. Ask The Council about their hospitals and other health systems and ask them to allow you in.

- You are a family man. You have worked all your life as a technician. You are very good at your job. You are not sure what has happened to your family and you are searching everywhere to look for them. Persuade The Council that you must enter their Land to look for your family and if they are there you will want to stay and work hard for them.

- You have been in the army and the police force, you rose to the rank of sergeant in both jobs. You are ill sometimes and you admit it is because you drink too much and can lose your temper and get into a fight. You do not want The Council to find this out because you want to get into the Land to live. Try to persuade The Council to let you in.

- You are a famous football player. You want to get your wife and family into the land but you want to inspect it first. You want to know if it is has clean hospitals, good schools, good sports' facilities and whether it has got a good police force. Convince The Council that you are worthy of a visitor's pass.

- You are a young female hairdresser. You have always had lots of friends, been invited to all the parties and have had a steady boyfriend. You think it is time for a change. Ask The Council to let you in to visit, tell them that you can do lots of other things but if you like the Land you would like to stay to be a nurse.

The Problems

The first problem will to be persuade The Council to let you visit

The second problem will be for those who wish to stay and live to argue their case.

AUTH3: Our land, our rules

THE COUNCIL

The Situation

You are some of the survivors from a war which has caused a lot of disease and starvation. You call yourselves The Council.

The Land you are have claimed has food, water and good soil. It does not have any diseases or people carrying any diseases.

The Council have decided to keep the Land clean and safe for you, your families and for the other people who live there.

The Council are worried about people who might try to visit the Land or try to come to live.

The people The Council believes it does not want to let into the Land include:

people who have had lots of sexual partners, travelled to lots of different places or have had many jobs during their lives. This is because you think they may be weak or may have got the disease that has killed so many people.

Your Job

As The Council, you must now decide the following rules:

- The Land can support 1,000 people to live on it, then it is full. You already have 400. How many visitors will you let in during one month?

- Who are you going to let visit the region? Think of age, sex, whether they are married, what workers the Land needs and anything else that will help the Land. Also think of people you do not want in the Land.

- What level of health will you expect from visitors and how can you find out if they are ill?

- Who can visit the doctors and the hospitals? Are they free services or will The Council charge?

- What houses have you got and what sort of houses will you let visitors stay in? Will you have a visitors' estate?

- Will you have schools? Who will go to school? Will school be compulsory?

- Will the Land have a police force? How will The Council keep order?

- How will you recognise visitors from locals and how will you keep track of them?

- What other rules and regulations do you need to have?

Problem One

A group of visitors are going to ask permission to enter the Land. When you meet the visitors, think of questions to ask.

Only accept some of the group of visitors into the Land. Set a time limit of one month for their stay and tell them of the rules you want them to obey.

Problem Two

One month later tell the visitors to come to a meeting with The Council.

The Council will allow one of the visitors to stay. The others must leave immediately.

Tell the visitors who is to stay and give reasons why.

AUTH5: Situations

HIV CASE

Your child got HIV during a blood transfusion two years ago. The child is often ill. The school he/she goes to have suggested you remove him/her from the school. They say it is because he/she is often ill and would receive better lessons at home. You know it is because other parents have complained and that they do not want your child at the same school as theirs. You have been called to a meting with the Head of the school. Argue the case to keep your child at the school.

HOSPITAL WAITING LIST

You have been told that you need an operation fairly urgently. The doctor at the hospital asked you about your lifestyle, habits etc. You have received a letter from the doctor and it tells you there is an 8 month waiting list and that you will not even get onto the waiting list until you have given up smoking and start exercising. You go straight to the hospital to argue your case.

COUNCIL HOUSE

You and your partner have one child and a baby on the way. You live with your parents and it is already over crowded. You want to apply for your own council house. You are invited to meet them. Convince them that you need a house more than other couples.

SCHOOL APPLICATION

You want your child to go to a school down the road because it is a good school and close to home. Your application has been rejected. The school they have given your child has a very bad reputation. You have asked to see the Head of the school you want your child to attend to persuade the authorities to let your child go there. What will you say?

Section Four: End notes

This section is intended to help the trainer to better deliver the modules in this manual and to more effectively manage the various groups of learners with whom he or she will work. It is essential to remember that in working with the learners on social skills that the learning sessions should not only be opportunities to discuss and examine social interactions, the skills which underpin them and the ways in which existing skills may be developed but also be occasions when social skills are used and developed. As a social skills trainer there is a burden to ensure that there is effective modelling of good social skills, that there are many opportunities for developing and consolidating such skills and that the learners experience some personal success in using their skills within these sessions.

All the modules involve the trainer managing a significant number of practical exercises. These include: discussions; role plays; hot seating; using self-assessment check-lists and working on action planning activities with learners. The modules require the trainer to be socially effective and an adept group manager. The trainer will need to challenge learners who demonstrate for example, poor listening, aggressive rather than assertive behaviours, those who do not take turns or who try to undermine others.

The learning opportunities should provide the learners both with the opportunity for developing a greater awareness about the behaviours for and approaches for effective interpersonal relationships and they should give the learner the opportunity to test out such skills. The learning opportunities will draw attention to developing good listening skills, to the messages which certain non-verbal communications are offering and to the ways in which learners may not be encouraging each other but closing down talk.

It is essential that the power of the learning cycle is harnessed throughout delivery of the modules.

The learning cycle

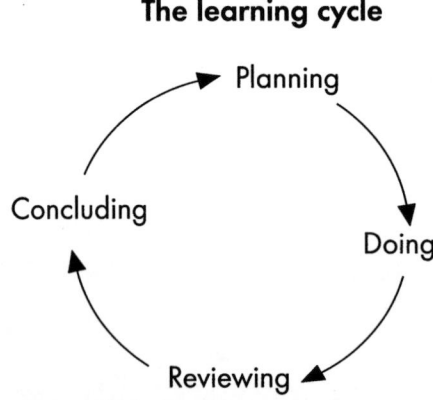

This section considers the following:

- trainer's techniques and strategies
- valuing the learners and their role
- evaluation and self-assessment

More information can be found in *Becoming an Effective Trainer*, Russell House Publishing 1998. The following pages offer some pointers but should not be considered an exhaustive discussion of these issues.

1. Trainer's techniques and strategies

There is some information in each module to assist the trainer. These notes try to bring some of the general principles together.

Use of space

Many of the sessions make use of role-play, encourage small group work or require that the learners move about the room. All activities require a high level of discussion, participation and parity between the learners. It is essential that all learners can see one another that there is no sense of any ranking according to status in the way the room is laid out. The space should be set up as a circular arrangement of chairs, everyone having the same type of chair and everyone being able to see each other. Any furniture should be light enough to move easily to allow for a re-arrangement of the learning space. There are a few occasions when the learners are working on collage activities or on A1 sheets then there may be a need for tables. The rest of the writing activities can be undertaken on a clipboard. The least furniture in the room the more space for role-play, for games and movement and for small groups to have some privacy for their discussions.

The learners should be encouraged to use the available space to move about and to enact. Many of the exercises will encourage them to think about non-verbal aspects of communications, ways of walking using personal space, sitting and standing. To engage with this free space will be necessary.

Brainstorming

This is used to introduce and explore topics. There are no right or wrong answers in a brainstorm. Brainstorming generates ideas, those fanciful and practical. It is a way to encourage lateral thinking, creative thinking and to encourage a broad consideration of issues. There need to be groundrules for the activity. Brainstorming is about exploration, the flow of ideas and comments and it is about everyone participating. There should be no personal attacks about what is said, no personal comments nor criticisms. Brainstorming is about generating a host of starting points for later exploration.

All suggestions should be written up clearly and in the speaker's own words. It is important that the person writing the suggestions does not translate the ideas into his or her own language. The trainer will have to decide when to tackle any outcomes from the brainstorming which contravene group groundrules or equality of opportunities issues.

Once the brainstorm has run its course the ideas can be used to stimulate role plays, as starting points for problem solving and as a stimulus to explore any patterns or themes in the ideas.

Group discussion

Discussions need managing to be successful. Effective discussion does not spontaneously happen. All group members need skills to manage their participation in discussions and to understand that discussion is an opportunity to explore ideas and perhaps to reach a consensus. Discussion should not become an opportunity for personal comment or criticism.

As a trainer it is important to manage discussion activities. This should however not be confused with controlling the content of the discussion.

Discussions can become:

- unfocused leading away from the topic and onto individual participants' concerns. This can drain energy from the group, generate frustration amongst learners who feel they gain nothing from the discussion.

- an opportunity to attack a fellow course participant
- a chance for one or two to monopolise the session
- a time when the trainer dominates the session offering often unsolicited views
- a time when the trainer tries to give a short lecture
- a way of filling time and giving the sense that much has been done

Group discussions have many benefits:

- they bring the group together to share ideas
- they give everyone a broader range of insights into an issue
- they give the trainer and group members a clear sense of people's starting points or entrenched ideas which can be challenged or confirmed as appropriate
- they break up a learning day or session
- they bring the group back together after individual or pair work
- they can be a structured chance to report back on other learning activities to the whole group
- they are a chance to explore understandings of material being worked with
- they can re-focus the group
- successful discussions can re-energise the group and offer it new leads for further thought and work
- they encourage participation
- they can be used to draw out those who are silent

Managing the discussion

Some actions need to be taken to ensure success. These include the following:

1. Clear groundrules about lengths and frequency of individual contributions
2. There should be opportunities for all to participate
3. There should be no personal attacks nor undermining of others
4. Equality of opportunities and other group rules should be observed
5. Objectives of the discussion should be clarified at the outset
6. The objectives should be re-visited if the discussion drifts
7. A trainer or other group member should summarise the key points part way through the discussion and set out questions or areas to be covered to keep the discussion on course for the remainder of the time allocated
8. The trainer should not be afraid to guide the discussion
9. People should have some time for reflection and making other notes
10. The outcomes of the discussion should be used, for example, notes for personal plans, as a starting point for another activity, as in group agreement about an issue

Role-play

This activity offers much to the learner through immediate and significant engagement in the issue. Role-play needs thoughtful preparation, this needs to be clearly explained to the participants along with any groundrules, and the activity needs on-going management.

Role-plays take problems or situations as their focus. They offer learners the opportunity to explore the issues and to gain insights into how others perceive the same problem. Role-plays can give people the chance to experience a new or unfamiliar situation and help them to prepare to face it; e.g. an interview, a court appearance or a review. They allow people to try out different behaviours or espouse opinions which are not their own and see how it feels to model such ideas or opinions. They offer the learner the chance to be on the receiving end of their own behaviours or attitudes. It allows them to feel what it is like to be a victim, to behave considerately to others, or to act out the anger they feel towards someone.

To set up the role-play the trainer needs to establish some parameters with the group. These may include:

- experiencing the feelings can then form the basis for analysis and review (see below Hot Seating)
- the extent and nature, if any, of physical contact
- the possible role or use of shouting, swearing or offensive language
- firmly establishing the understanding that the role-play is a fiction and that the participants are in role. It needs stressing that when in character the learners are not really those people
- the exercise will be challenging and may open up a number of memories and issues and that these should be talked through with the trainer or other appropriate person
- that anyone experiencing upset must say so

The trainer needs to prepare for the role-play: to have the physical space cleared for the action, to provide a few props if these are necessary, to outline the situation on which the role-play is centred and to outline the brief roles for each player. The trainer needs to impose time limits and rules for proper behaviour.

The trainer needs to decide how much time will be available for preparation of the role-play or whether people are to react to a given situation in their role straightaway. The trainer needs to decide what all the learners do if, for example, one role-play is to be enacted:

- What will happen to the rest of the group members while the role-play is being rehearsed?
- What should the rest of the group do while the role-play is taking place?

The trainer needs to decide how to manage the debriefing. The trainer must debrief the learners.

De-roling
In every instance it is important for those who have been in role to come out of role. They may do this by:

- commenting on what it felt like to play the part
- commenting on how and why there are differences between the real self and the role-play self maybe commenting on the ways their real self would have managed the situation
- being applauded for taking the part

The continuum
A visual way to show one's position on an issue. The group members are asked to place themselves on an imaginary and graduated line in a position which represents the view, opinion or feeling which they hold.

Within the group room draw an imaginary line across it. One end represents one extreme of an opinion or state, and the other end the opposite extreme or state. The group members are asked to place themselves on the line where they think that their point of view or set of feelings are best represented. They should do this without taking much notice of anyone else in the room and to react to the statement fairly spontaneously.

The result may be an even scattering along the line or a bunching of people at certain points on the line. It is a way of asking people to declare their starting points and to think about why they opt to place themselves at that point. It is interesting for the group to see where people place themselves and to discuss the reasons for this. The exercise can help define understandings about issues. Group members should be able to move their position if after discussion they feel they have changed their minds. Running a continuum before and at the close of working on an issue will also help learners explore why they have changed or not changed their minds.

There should be no comment on why people have adopted certain positions or whether they are right to do so.

Ranking exercises

A way for people to confront issues and raise awareness of their own priorities is that of undertaking ranking exercises. Group members are asked to confront a particular issue or aspect of themselves and to mark their responses on a graduated line on paper or to place themselves on an imaginary line, by giving a number from one to ten or by selecting pre-printed statements on cards. The pre-printed cards may then need further ranking into priority order.

Learners are then asked to consider patterns or themes which may emerge from their ranking activities.

Talks by the trainer

These are infrequently used. They are a necessary route for conveying information and ideas with which the learners may not yet have had contact. Trainer's input adds new material to discussions. Such inputs should not be occasions for talking at the learners. This is damaging to the group dynamic, may remind learners of past experiences and may provide an opportunity for the learners to absent their minds from the session.

Any trainer input should have clear signposting so the listener knows what is happening, should be punctuated by opportunities for asking questions and for the trainer to check the learners have understood. There should be opportunities for the trainer to ask for examples from the learners to illustrate the key points. Any trainer inputs need:

- a clear structure
- a clear purpose and defined outcomes
- to be supported with simple phrases or key words on handouts or OHTs
- review and repetition to ensure consolidation of information and that the ideas can be linked

Hearing a lecture is a fairly passive experience unless the listener can make notes on handouts or can perhaps complete the gaps in pre-made notes. This task gives an additional reason to listen and to seek out information.

Material from a trainer input should be used quickly after hearing so that learners are forced to revisit it, use and internalise it.

Collage work

Learners can work alone or in small groups to make representations of feelings, relationships, issues or ideas through original drawing or collage work. The opportunity to work visually provides an interesting and other way to stimulate thinking, ideas and feelings. It may raise buried ideas to consciousness. Collage work is an ideal way to work to explore images and non-verbal communications. Time should be allowed for learners to view each others work and to discuss content.

Self-assessment checklists

There are a number of checklists in the modules. These are intended to encourage the learner to think about him or herself, about current levels of skills, areas on which he or she would like to work further and to undertake some review of patterns of responses. Checklists can be helpful in encouraging learners to look at ways in which they see themselves and the world around them, the types of assumptions they make, ways in which they often behave and reasons which might lie behind their assumptions and behaviours. There are no right or wrong answers. The checklists are just that, they are not any sort of scientific or psychological exercise. They are just a short-hand way to open areas for review.

Check-lists should be a prompt to self-reflection. They are *only* of value if something is done with the findings. This may be mean using the findings in discussion with other group members, or reviewing findings to highlight areas on which the learner and trainer could usefully build an individual learning plan.

Checklists are not a way to silence a group. They should certainly not be used as a means of making anyone feel they are without skills or positive qualities; they are a rather crude indicator that change may be useful in some areas. Care should be taken in using the check-lists. Can the learner read what is there? Is the check-list understood? What help may be needed to manage the check-list? What may be the necessary referrals to make to the learner following the exposure of some issues from the check-list?

There is a danger that checklists given to the learner to complete in an unsuspected and unsupported way will mean:

- little is understood

- the checklist is completed perfunctorily and little is gained from it

- the learner has a false sense of current levels of achievement not having any sense of standards nor appreciation of what is asked

The trainer should:

- explain the purpose of the checklist activity

- explain what its content covers, perhaps picking one or two questions and asking the group to explain what they mean

- be on hand to help, to review and to question as the learners undertake the task of completing the checklists

- know why the activity is being undertaken and to have clear intentions about how the information or/and raised self-awareness will be used next

Games

These serve many functions. They work to:

- create a change in activity or focus of attention

- re-energise or to calm a group

- encourage a focus on a particular skill

- encourage working with a partner

- encourage concentration on something else

- provide fun

- involve everyone in a common activity

Fruit bowl

The aim is to get the group moving around the room and to concentrate on something else, have some fun, focus on being in the training room and on those around them.

Only have enough chairs for each member of the group to sit on. Take away your chair. Then, stand in the middle of the group and name each member one of three fruits e.g. orange, pear and plum. Give yourself a fruit name too. Explain that when you call the name of a fruit, those named must move to another chair, the one without a chair stands in the middle and calls out a fruit name. To begin the game you should use your fruit name. This will get you onto a chair and a learner into the centre.

Name game

The group sits in a circle. The first person names themselves. The person to his or her right has to say the previous name and his or her own. The next person to the right has to give the two preceding names plus their own. And so on. The group is likely to bond around this common task. It encourages concentration and the knowledge of group members' names.

Throwing the ball

Everyone needs to be in a circle with easy eye contact. All names need to be known to each group member. An object needs to be used as a 'ball'. Someone has the 'ball' and throws it while calling out a name and making eye contact with that person. The ball however is not thrown to that person but to someone else in the group. It encourages concentration and the knowledge of group members' names.

African rain forest

The leader makes a noise such as rubbing hands together, gentle clapping like rain, hissing, tapping feet and finally clapping hands on thighs louder and louder then quieter etc. The sounds have to travel around the circle until everyone is making the sound, then the leader changes the sound until all sounds have been made. The game encourages concentration.

Counting to ten

The group members stand in a circle. They may look at each other or not as they choose. Everyone needs to be quiet and then it should be explained that:

- as a group the learners, including the trainer, will count to ten

- each person should speak at least once (if there are less than 10 in the group)

- the learners have to concentrate on who has spoken, who is preparing to speak and try to sense when it is appropriate for them to speak.

If two or more people speak at the same time, then the group must begin again at one.

Bumper cars

The group splits into pairs. One of each pair is blindfolded. The blindfolded person is the car. The other person, the driver. The driver has to be the eyes for both of them and instruct the car what to do. It is important not to crash into others.

- Hand on the left shoulder   –   go left
- Hand on the right shoulder   –   go right
- No hands   –   stop
- Hand on centre of back   –   go straight ahead
- Hand on neck   –   reverse
- Faster   –   harder pressure
- Slow down   –   softer pressure

This encourages working with others, concentration and trust.

Liar

One person enters the middle of the circle and performs an action e.g. brushing their teeth. They are asked what they are doing but have to describe a different activity e.g. I am changing a car tyre. The person who asked what was being done then enters the ring and then has to mime changing the tyre and when asked what they are doing they say, for example, digging the garden. The person who asked the questions then enters the circle and so on.

Boxing match

In pairs, one person takes the lead and boxes the other. The other has to dodge the blows reacting to the imaginary blows. The roles are reversed – both cannot concentrate on fighting at the same time. Concentrator, observing the other person and controlled movement. Obviously the aim would not be to hit anyone.

Observation

In pairs the two face each other and have one minute to try to memorise everything about the person. Both shut their eyes. In turn, one describes the other in as much detail as possible.

Who's the leader?

A person leaves the room.

The rest of the group decides on a leader. The group gets in a circle so all can see each other. The leader starts an action and all have to copy it. The learners should try not to give the game away by letting the person who is allowed back in the room know who is the leader. The members of the circle need to concentrate on changing their actions to follow the leader. They need to be causal in the way they look at the leader.

The person guessing can have an agreed number of guesses to say who is the group leader.

Cops and robbers

The groups are given an identity as a cop or a robber. No-one knows anyone else's identity. The whole group is stranded e.g. on a broken down plane/train. Each suspects the other of belonging to the wrong group.

The learners have to work out who is on their side and who is not. They can ask questions, tell stories, tell lies, but they need to identify themselves to those on their side and not to the opposite side. The group has fifteen minutes to unravel who is who.

The learners need to list out who is who; those who get it right win, those who don't lose.

English bulldog

A game of tag. The learners are ranged along one wall and have to cross to the other side without being caught by the bulldog. The catcher will need a scarf or something to indicate who he/she is. Inevitably one will be and that person is then the bulldog who has to catch another learner and so on.

Shaking the demon

Not a game, but a way to release tensions. The learners all stand in their own space. They should tense their muscles and then begin to shake their arms, legs and loosen their shoulders, roll their heads and if they wish jump or hop about. Physical tensions should be released.

These are tools to provoke learning. The trainer needs to confidently manage such tools to better help the learners to explore and to express their ideas. These are tools to stimulate, to encourage thought and as necessary to help move the group along.

In addition the trainer will need to be able to manage situations in the training room; for example, conflicts between learners, a learner threatening to get into conflict with the trainer or even the trainer generating conflict situations. The trainer will need to establish groundrules with the group before starting so that there are agreed and commonly accepted behaviours which can be referred back to if needed by the trainer or other group members.

2. Valuing the learners and their role

The activities in all of these modules require the learners to take stock of themselves, to explore issues in interpersonal relationships and to consider their own current levels of social skills. There are challenging areas with which to confront the learner. They are areas in which everyone could find areas of weakness and areas to improve. The challenge to the learners should be acknowledged.

Throughout the sessions learners should have been thanked for their input, hard work or for trying something which was for them a new type of learning activity. The learners need to be aware of the learning cycle and how what they do in the sessions fits into their life. The learners will have been completing and discussing their learning and action plans and again these discussions with the trainer should have generated positive feedback from the trainer about effort, attention, aspirations and good work, as appropriate. Where feedback may centre on areas for improvement this should be given. Learners need to know how they are performing and will value honest comment rather than no comment or falsity.

Where there is any form of assessment taking place is something the learners need to know. They will need to know what the assessment criteria are and how assessment is being undertaken. Much about the way these personal development modules are structured does not lend itself to formal assessment. The assessment should be the learners' own of their progress or of the areas they have yet to develop.

Trainers' assessments may best be suited to focusing on learner inputs into sessions, punctuality, to the willingness to try out new things or engage with ideas.

3. Evaluation and self-assessment

Learners' evaluations and trainers' self assessments differ from the learners' assessments of their own progress and their action plans. They focus on the content of the learning activities and on the ways in which they are shaped and delivered. Encouraging the learners to offer evaluations of the learning activities has several functions. It encourages the learners to think of themselves as learners with opinions and as learners who are taken seriously. Evaluation will help the learners to think about the ways in which they learn things and to consider again the sorts of activities which they have undertaken and their impact. It again gives them the opportunity to consider what may not have been clear and what they need to review.

The learners' evaluations will assist the trainer in thinking how best to deliver these learning activities on subsequent occasions.

Learners' evaluations

The process of the trainer's self-assessment is discussed at some length in *Becoming an Effective Trainer*, but like the activities which the learners undertake to consider their own strengths and weaknesses so self-assessment assists the trainer in developing his or her training skills.

It is imperative to understand how the learning activities have been received by the learners for the only purpose in running any learning activity is for the sake of the learner's development. Evaluation should cover some of the following.

1. At the outset of the learning activity:

- How has the first session has been received and perceived by the learner?
- Is it meeting learner identified needs?
- Are the learning styles appropriate?
- Is the pace of the session right and is it pitched appropriately?
- Are learners uncomfortable with the style or content? How can this be better managed?

2. How are the learners experiencing the learning programme once it is underway:

- Is the content and style accessible?
- Is the learning programme meeting needs?
- Are the activities too difficult or insufficiently demanding?
- What is its value?
- How much is not useful and why?
- Does anything appear muddled or confused to the learner and what?
- How can session based learning be supported in real life?

3. At the close of the programme discover:

- What do the learners consider they have learned?
- What has been of value?
- What would they like more of or less of within the programme and why? – this may apply to content or to types of learning activity

Some examples of evaluation forms are included on pages 248-249.

Evaluation may be undertaken on paper, during a group brainstorm, orally, or one to one. Evaluation should not be confused with individual learner's progress reviews. The focus of evaluation should be on the programme, its integrity, the types of training and learning styles and materials used. Evaluation should not be thought of by either trainer or learner as likely to lead to punitive action. It should be part of the learning experience for learner and trainer. Encouraging the learner to reflect upon the learning experience, the types of materials, the activities and how they may be experienced by others helps to make the learning activity a more conscious and serious one.

It is important for the trainer to be confronted with suggestions for change, improvements and with the thoughts, experiences and perceptions of the learners. It encourages the trainer to appreciate the importance of the learner, their critical judgements and to understand the learning role more. The learner, in offering feedback through an evaluation and seeing it accepted and probably used, will gain practical experience of the value and role of feedback.

Trainer self-assessment

To be an effective trainer, to gain from the training role and be effective in discharging it requires that the trainer becomes reflective. This means taking note of what happens and analysing why something has happened. The trainer may want to reflect on a single session, reflect on the course of a programme or select a particular theme. For example:

- why the group dynamic develops as it does
- the trainer's own role in encouraging or squashing learning
- how the trainer's attention is shared among the learners and with what effect
- why a particular or critical incident evolved as it did
- how he/she has developed a particular training skill

Self-assessment can be undertaken by: keeping an after-session log; completing a checklist about key aspects of the session; or by undertaking a trainer's SWOT and planning then reviewing progress.

Further information on the training role, the learner and learning process and on tools to provide learning can be found in *Becoming an Effective Trainer*.

Learner's activity sheet: learners' views 2

Name of course: ....

1. When I came to this course, I had hoped to achieve:

2. I wanted to achieve this because:

3. Now that I have taken the course, I feel that I have gained/achieved:

4. Now that I have taken the course, I feel that I have not gained/achieved:

5. One or two things I plan to use from this course is/are:

    i.

    ii.

6. My suggestions for the improvement of the course are:

    i.

    ii.

Name .... Date ....

Learner's activity sheet: learners' views 1

Title of session/workshop ....

1. The three most important things for me which we covered today were:

    i.

    ii.

    iii.

2. A key idea I gained from today was:

3. I am still unsure about:

4. I would like to find out more about:

5. From this session I would like to make use of:

Name .... Date ....

Learner's activity sheet: learners' views 3

Title of programme: ....

How many sessions have you been to?

What have you enjoyed most so far?

- Why is this so?

What have you enjoyed least so far?

- Why is this so?

What do you think will be of greatest long-term use to you?

- Why is this so?

What would you like to find out more about?

Name .... Date ....